History and Memory in the Abbasid Caliphate

The Early and Medieval Islamic World

Published in collaboration with the Society for the Medieval Mediterranean

Society for the
Medieval Mediterranean

As recent scholarship resoundingly attests, the medieval Mediterranean and Middle East bore witness to a prolonged period of flourishing intellectual and cultural diversity. Seeking to contribute to this ever-more nuanced and contextual picture, *The Early and Medieval Islamic World* book series promotes innovative research on the period 500–1500 AD with the Islamic world, as it ebbed and flowed from Marrakesh to Palermo and Cairo to Kabul, as the central pivot. Thematic focus within this remit is broad, from the cultural and social to the political and economic, with preference given to studies of societies and cultures from a socio-historical perspective. It will foster a community of unique voices on the medieval Islamic world, shining light into its lesser-studied corners.

Series editor

Professor Roy Mottahedeh, Harvard University

Advisors

Professor Amira Bennison, University of Cambridge
Professor Farhad Daftary, Institute of Ismaili Studies
Professor Simon Doubleday, Hofstra University
Professor Frank Griffel, Yale University
Professor Remke Kruk, Leiden University
Professor Beatrice Manz, Tufts University
Dr Bernard O'Kane, American University in Cairo
Professor Andrew Peacock, University of St Andrews
Dr Yossef Rapoport, Queen Mary University of London

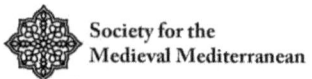

New and forthcoming titles

Cross Veneration in the Medieval Islamic World: Christian Identity and Practice under Muslim Rule, Charles Tieszen (Fuller Theological Seminary/ Simpson University)

Power and Knowledge in Medieval Islam: Shi'i and Sunni Encounters in Baghdad, Tariq al-Jamil (Swathmore College)

The Eastern Frontier: Limits of Empire in Late Antique and Early Medieval Central Asia, Robert Haug (University of Cincinnati)

Writing History in the Medieval Islamic World: The Value of Chronicles as Archives, Fozia Bora (University of Leeds)

Narrating Muslim Sicily: War and Peace in the Medieval Mediterranean World, William Granara (Harvard University)

Gender and Succession in Medieval Islam: Bilateral Descent and the Legacy of Fatima, Alyssa Gabbay (The University of North Carolina at Greensboro)

Music and Musicians in the Medieval Islamicate World: A Social History, Lisa Nielson (Case Western Reserve University, Cleveland, USA)

Roma in the Medieval Islamic World: The History of a People, Kristina Richardson (City University, New York)

History and Memory in the Abbasid Caliphate: Writing the Past in Medieval Arabic Literature, Letizia Osti (University of Milan)

History and Memory in the Abbasid Caliphate

Writing the Past in Medieval Arabic Literature

Letizia Osti

I.B.TAURIS
LONDON • NEW YORK • OXFORD • NEW DELHI • SYDNEY

I.B. TAURIS
Bloomsbury Publishing Plc
50 Bedford Square, London, WC1B 3DP, UK
1385 Broadway, New York, NY 10018, USA
29 Earlsfort Terrace, Dublin 2, Ireland

BLOOMSBURY, I.B. TAURIS and the I.B. Tauris logo are trademarks of Bloomsbury Publishing Plc

First published in Great Britain 2022
This paperback edition published 2025

Series design by www.paulsmithdesign.com
Cover image: Kitab fi al-shatranj wa-mansubatihi wa-mulahih [15v] (39/276), British Library: Oriental Manuscripts, Add MS 7515, Qatar Digital Library

A catalogue record for this book is available from the British Library.

A catalog record for this book is available from the Library of Congress.

ISBN: HB: 978-1-7883-9232-2
PB: 978-0-7556-4781-1
ePDF: 978-0-7556-3503-0
eBook: 978-1-8386-0056-3

Series: Early and Medieval Islamic World

Typeset by RefineCatch Limited, Bungay, Suffolk

a Dina e Piero

Contents

Acknowledgements		xi
Transliteration and Translation		xii
	Introduction	1
1	Life and Afterlife	9
	‘Biography’	9
	Using biography	12
	Where: the pervasiveness of al-Ṣūlī	15
	What’s in a profile?	19
	The power of stories	25
	Person or persona?	37
2	In his own Words	39
	Terminological traps	39
	Motivations, intended readers and time	42
	Al-Ṣūlī’s voice	45
	‘Der blosse Lebenslauf’ and beyond	50
	Rights and wrongs	51
	Person, persona and an arc	53
3	In his own Time	55
	The classroom	58
	The court years	65
	The legacy of notebooks	74
	Networks and texts	80
4	In his own Books	83
	Career path	86
	The well-organized mind	90
	The well-organized life	94
	A well-organized time	95

5 Insight and Hindsight 99
The clueless observer 100
Persuasion 109
Access 117
The vain memorialist 123

Conclusion 125
Notes 129
Bibliography 163
Index 179

Acknowledgements

This book was such an embarrassingly long time in the making that I will not even attempt to write an exhaustive list of friends, colleagues and institutions to whom I owe thanks: it would be too long to print. I will limit myself to those who have been subjected to an unfair amount of information on this volume's topic and have patiently listened and commented on it.

Whatever intellectual discipline I have, I owe it to Julia Bray, whose guidance and friendship I am honoured to have, and who is the model of the scholar I hope to become. Hugh Kennedy, with his contagious curiosity and enthusiasm, has encouraged and helped me in more ways than I can describe. He has the magic power of translating my incoherent ramblings into a sensible argument. My fellow Muqtadir partisans, Maaike van Berkel and Nadia M. El Cheikh, have shown me the joy of real collaboration. As we have often said, friends usually fall out when they write a book together; we, on the contrary, became friends through this book. The same can be said for Judy Ahola and James Weaver. I seem to be unable to write anything without citing Hilary Kilpatrick's work. Antonella Ghersetti has taught me a lot of what I know about *adab*, and many other things. Through Sarah Savant, and through my colleagues in Milan – really too many to name – I have discovered new ways of reading and interrogating sources with tools I would never have found on my own. I would also like to thank my family, and especially my parents, to whom this book is dedicated.

All errors are, of course, my own.

Transliteration and Translation

I follow the transliteration system used by the *Encyclopaedia of Islam, THREE.* Familiar geographical names such as Iraq, Mecca and Baghdad are given in their common English spelling. Dates are given according to both the Islamic (*hijrī*) and the Common Era calendars. Translations from the Arabic are mine unless otherwise stated.

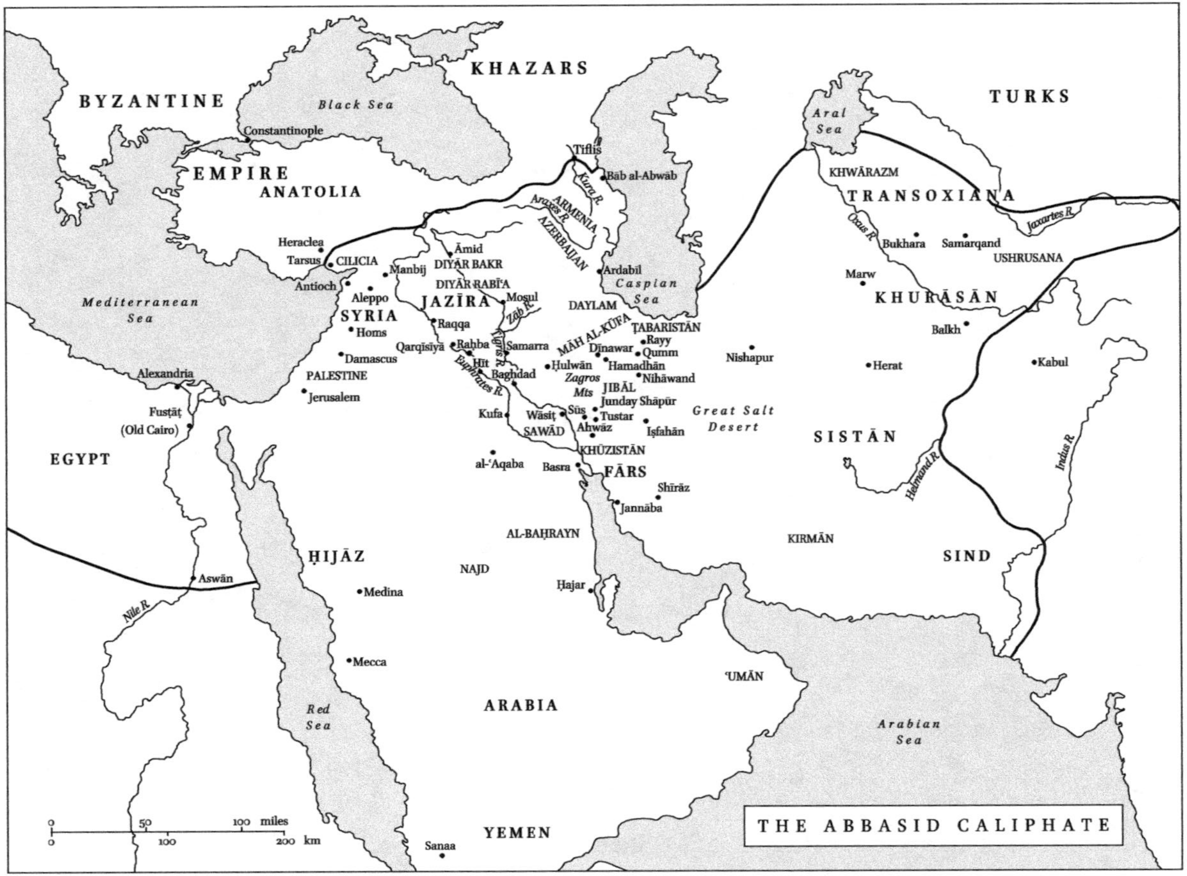

THE ABBASID CALIPHATE

Introduction

The reader might object to our including al-Ṣūlī amongst the greatest authors, but he is indeed one of them because he was innovative, and a unique figure amongst the men of those days: while there were, even in his own time, greater scholars than he in ḥadīth, and better in adab, what matters is that he was someone who united all these elements in the culture of that time, enjoyed such a standing in the caliphal palaces, and did not squander the useful lessons that came his way, but instead he wrote them down and passed them on to later generations, that they may benefit from them.[1]

Muḥammad Kurd ʿAlī

In 1950, the great Syrian intellectual Muḥammad Kurd ʿAlī collected the profiles of fifty-one 'treasures of the ancestors', from Ibn al-Muqaffaʿ (d. 139/756) to Ibn Khaldūn (d. 808/1406).[2] He seems to have expected his thirteenth choice, Abū Bakr al-Ṣūlī (d. 335/947), to be controversial: a boon companion of the Abbasid caliphs, who dabbled in several disciplines and whose work, while vast, was preserved in a piecemeal fashion and only partly used by later sources, is hardly as impressive a figure as the other names in this list. Still, Kurd ʿAlī is not overly apologetic: Abū Bakr al-Ṣūlī deserves attention as a representative of various scholarly disciplines and facets of élite culture, because of the unique way he combined these aspects within himself, and as an interpreter of the past for posterity.

The last part of this statement may seem banal: there is little doubt that we see the first centuries of Islam through an Abbasid filter – especially twenty-first century scholarship has given much thought to the question.[3] On the other hand, we are still processing the first part of Kurd ʿAlī's remark: the prison of modern, mostly European interpretive categories makes it difficult to approach a figure like al-Ṣūlī, who is either casually labelled a polymath, or pigeonholed into one discipline at the expense of others.[4] This book is an attempt to approach the question from the opposite direction: by exploiting, rather than downplaying, al-Ṣūlī's versatility, it looks at material *by* and *on* this single – if complex – individual, and uses it to discuss specific issues in Arabic literature and historiography.

The very expression 'Arabic literature *and* historiography' is key here: while al-Ṣūlī's important contribution to, for instance, poetic criticism and administrative literature is universally acknowledged and studied, his role as an historian is more controversial and, as this volume will hopefully illustrate, is often approached with inadequate analytical tools. It is a typical problem for the study of third-fourth/ninth-tenth century Iraq: scholarship on history and scholarship on literature have no choice but to work on the same textual sources, but they interrogate the material in vastly different ways and, rather than sharing results, they often coexist as non-communicating vessels. While this may have its merits, in the case of al-Ṣūlī it seems a waste, especially in the parts of his work where he is both author and eyewitness. An obvious example is al-Ṣūlī's use of his own poetry in the historical narrative: while it is a standard practice, up to al-Ṣūlī's time, to include verses in *akhbār*, these verses are not usually – or possibly not ever – the author's own. The poetry which al-Ṣūlī chooses to include in his historical work, then, is unique and deserves consideration, regardless of its perceived artistic value and of modern literary sensibilities, not only as a stylistic quirk but also as a specific historiographical tool. To disregard it would lead to missing potentially important elements for the reconstruction of the past and of its memory.

Nevertheless, attention to al-Ṣūlī's life and work has almost always been fragmented along the perceived genres of his production. As far as I am aware, the only survey of his life and body of work as a whole is a Master Thesis by Aḥmad Jamāl al-ʿUmarī, first published in 1973, and in a later edition in 1984.[5] Most studies have been devoted to al-Ṣūlī's scholarship on poetry: his recensions of 'modernist' poets (*muḥdathūn*) have been published or taken into account in modern editions, and the principles of his literary criticism are part of the canon.[6]

In particular, the *Akhbār Abī Tammām* and its introductory epistle, which were edited and published already in the 1930s, have been the object of renewed scholarly interest in the twenty-first century, especially after Beatrice Gruendler's new edition and English translation.[7] Gruendler and others have studied the principles of al-Ṣūlī's literary criticism but also his narrative techniques. In this latter investigation, they have confined themselves to what they describe as 'literary *akhbār*' on poets – i.e. not part of the caliphal chronicles – and have not looked at accounts where al-Ṣūlī is an intradiegetic narrator. By and large, these studies ignore one another.[8]

Al-Ṣūlī's largest and most complex work, the *Kitāb al-Awrāq*, has had an equally complex reception. To my knowledge, all parts of *Awrāq* known to be extant are available in print, but they were retrieved from separate manuscripts at different times. In the mid-1930s, James Heyworth-Dunne published three volumes, on the poets of the caliphal family, the modern poets, and the caliphates of al-Rāḍī and al-Muttaqī respectively.[9] This latter part was translated into French by Marius Canard one decade later. More recently, Anas B. Khalidov has edited and translated into Russian the annals of the caliphates of al-Wāthiq to al-Muhtadī (227–56/842–70). Both translations are equipped with lengthy critical introductions.[10] Finally, the turn of the century saw the edition of the last extant fragment, covering the caliphate of al-Muqtadir up to the year 318/931.[11] The section on al-Rāḍī and al-Muttaqī has received the most modern attention and has been used alongside Miskawayh's (d. 421/1030) *Tajārib al-umam* as a source for the history of the mid-fourth/tenth century. On the other hand, the section on al-Muqtadir, which is the main source for the much better known *Ṣila* by ʿArīb (d. *c.* 370/980), has largely gone unnoticed.[12] In short, while modern scholarship on medieval Arabic poetry and chancery often relies on al-Ṣūlī's work, his chronicles are rarely cited in modern historiography.[13]

In contrast, most of the material used in this volume belongs to the annalistic sections of the *Awrāq*, and especially to the chronicles of al-Ṣūlī's lifetime, where he produces his own evidence as eyewitness. This is the point where al-Ṣūlī's life and his work intersect, and where, as Kurd ʿAlī put it, he formulates lessons from the past for future generations. This intersection is the starting point for investigating al-Ṣūlī not only as an author, but also as an individual and member of a specific cultural environment, as seen by contemporary and later scholars.

It should be made clear from the start that this is not a life-and-times study. There are, however, qualifications. Indeed, biography and authorship have made up an uncomfortable pair for the past several decades. Formalists spoke of the 'temptation of the biographical in literary criticism', i.e. what was seen as the unprofessional and unscholarly investigation into the gossip of biography and biographical interpretation.[14] While this debate has caused some soul searching in the field of medieval Arabic studies and has known alternate fortunes in literary studies in general,[15] it seems particularly significant when related to classical Arabic writing, not only as a by-product of longstanding artisanal practices of our discipline connected to the sheer quantity and complexity of the source material, but also because the material seems to require it. Premodern Arabic culture has *in itself* a biographical obsession – to be precise, a prosopographical obsession, which strives to organize and classify different categories of famous and lesser-known individuals, most of whom were authors. It is also worth noting that this attention to biography is by no means limited to prominent personalities: in comparison to its European counterpart, medieval Arabic culture places an enormous importance on the lives of relatively unknown individuals – compiling vast collections of biographical profiles is, after all, *totum arabum*. This is why, before delving into al-Ṣūlī's work, this volume begins with an investigation of his *Nachleben*.

Chapter One looks at biographical information on al-Ṣūlī in contemporary and later sources, illustrating how each author chooses from a common pool of material to produce a – sometimes significantly – different portrait. The chapter traces the development of al-Ṣūlī's reputation after his death and gives an overview of the resulting persona. The analysis of this specific case contributes to recent debates on the role and significance of life writing, both within the canon of classical Arabic literature and as a source for historical information.

Given the general abundance of biographical material in premodern Arabic literature, the investigation of Chapter One may be conducted fruitfully on countless Abbasid personalities. Chapter Two, on the other hand, begins to explore areas which are unavailable for most of al-Ṣūlī's contemporaries. It casts a second glance at the life of al-Ṣūlī, this time using narratives in the first person found in his works. This results in a self-portrait of sorts which can be contrasted with the image resulting from Chapter One. Al-Ṣūlī's sense of self-worth and of his role in the world emerges clearly from these accounts, as do his principles and preoccupations. Through this analysis, the chapter discusses the concept (or lack thereof) of autobiography in premodern Arabic literature, in particular exploring Hilary Kilpatrick's idea of a 'fragmented autobiography'.

Chapter Three uses both al-Ṣūlī's work and that of his biographers to explore his social network. It looks at his relationships with colleagues, pupils, and employers, within and outside the caliphal court.[16] This investigation sets al-Ṣūlī's professional and intellectual personality against the background of his social circle, thus facilitating our evaluation of his role, as well as unpacking the practical aspects of the intellectual environment where al-Ṣūlī operated. The chapter relies on narrative accounts as well as taking into consideration the individuals regularly cited by him, or by other sources in connection to him, testing concepts such as Shawkat Toorawa's 'proximity' and 'resemblance', and tools of modern social network analysis as employed by, for instance, Monique Bernards.

Chapter Four surveys al-Ṣūlī's written production. It cross-references the bibliography provided by Ibn al-Nadīm's *Kitāb al-Fihrist* with remarks by al-Ṣūlī and discusses how his work in different disciplines is evaluated and used by later authors and by modern scholars, focusing especially on how the large amounts of poetry, often his own, present in much of al-Ṣūlī's *akhbār*, is alternatively considered a strength or a weakness of his work as chronicler, connecting the question to the wider one of the Arabic prosimetrum and in particular the role of poetry within historical narratives. The resulting scholarly portrayal of al-Ṣūlī calls for a reconsideration of how modern ideas of genres and disciplines may – or may not – be fruitfully applied to pre-modern Arabic writings. The focus is instead on one quality for which al-Ṣūlī is praised: his ability to organize objects, both physical and intellectual, in the proper order. The chapter examines remarks by al-Ṣūlī on the subject as well as illustrating his principles in action: his library on the one hand, and the internal organization of his books (tables of contents, macro-structure, chapters and subchapters) on the other. This results in an argument linking the emergence of book culture, of which al-Ṣūlī is an exemplary representative, with a new impulse towards organization, seen holistically as one global phenomenon including material and immaterial elements: classification of knowledge, arrangement of archives, systematization of disciplines, etc. The complex intersecting organizational principles of the *Kitāb al-Awrāq* raises a final question: what are the markers of al-Ṣūlī's individual style, and do they convey a mature view on his time? Does this view go beyond that of a narrow-minded courtier?

Chapter Five focuses in on the question of al-Ṣūlī's value – or lack thereof – as an historian. It looks at how his account of specific events and periods compares with that of other authors, thus bringing into focus his distinctive voice and vision. The chapter explores the different ways in which al-Ṣūlī intervenes in the narrative flow by inserting himself in the events he relates, not only as an eyewitness but also as a co-protagonist who is able to influence the very course of events by interacting with others. Is al-Ṣūlī's style of intervention as effective as he implies it to be, and how does its strong performative aspect affect the value of his scholarship? Finally, the chapter looks at how al-Ṣūlī evaluates the events he describes, and how he identifies and organizes causal links between them. In particular, it addresses the commonly held view that his narrow perspective, while rich in details, does not allow him to recognize and make sense of crucial turning points in the history of the caliphate. Here it is argued that two levels of writing coexist in the *Awrāq*, one personal (biographical) and one general (historiographical). The former, far from being a hindrance to his understanding, imprints on the *Awrāq* the mark of its author and, at the same time, illustrates the rigorous principles along which he makes sense of the past, uses it to interpret the present and, in turn, shapes its memory.

Memory is of course another keyword. For the purposes of this investigation, my point of reference is the interplay between communicative memory – one type of collective memory as conceptualized by Halbwachs – and cultural memory. When Jan Assmann, in 1995, highlighted the difference between communicative and cultural memory, he set time as the discriminating factor: the temporal horizon of communicative memory is one century at most and 'offers no fixed point which would bind it to the ever expanding past in the passing of time'.[17] Cultural memory, on the contrary, transcends the everyday and has fixed points, i.e. fateful events of the past which function as 'figures of memory'.[18] In Assmann's – and Halbwachs's – frame of reference, these different types coincide with distinct practices and interpretive methods. In particular, communicative memory is tied to orality as an independent form of reproduction of the past. Even from the few examples discussed in this volume, it will be clear that such a distinction does not fully apply here. For one thing, it is well known that the relation between writing and orality in Arabic-Islamic culture has moved along different tracks from those of Western European culture.[19] On the other hand, Assmann also talked of the 'transition' from 'the area of everyday communication' to 'the area of objectivized culture', arguing that, even after such transition, *mémoire* does not simply morph into *histoire*. Rather, objectivized culture has the structure of memory because it allows a group to reproduce its identity. The material discussed in this volume will hopefully illustrate how, in the *Awrāq*, the typical objects of communicative memory as described by Assmann – 'a joke, a memory, a bit of gossip, or an experience' – are integrated into the wider narrative and related to the more distant past for evaluation and assessment.

Timeline of al-Ṣūlī's life

Caliphate	**al-Ṣūlī**
Al-Muʿtamid (r. 256–279/870–892)	• Born in Baghdad. • Part of adolescence/youth in Basra.
Al-Muʿtaḍid (r. 279–289/892–902)	• At court. • Access to the caliph.
Al-Muktafī (r. 289–295/902–908)	• At court. • Chess player. • Access to the caliph's table. • With caliph on his deathbed.
Al-Muqtadir (r. 295–320/908–932)	• At court. • Irregular access to the caliph. • Tutor and companion of the caliph's sons.
Al-Qāhir (r. 320–322/932–934)	• Presumably at court.
Al-Rāḍī (r. 322–329/934–940)	• At court. • Regular role at the caliph's table. • Follows the caliph in expedition to Mosul.
Al-Muttaqī (r. 329–333/940–944)	• Leaves court. • Moves around (Baghdad, Wāsiṭ, Basra). • Briefly works for different generals.
Al-Mustakfī (r. 333–334/944–946)	• Moves to Basra. • Teaches.
Al-Muṭīʿ (r. 334–363/946–974)	• Dies in Basra in mysterious circumstances.

1

Life and Afterlife

> *A very long account is given of the grammarian al-Kisāʾī, which proves, though the Ḫaṭīb is quite unconscious of it, that he was a mixture of a charlatan and a man of learning, conceited, and never sure of his knowledge.*[1]
>
> Fritz Krenkow

More than a century after this statement, it is clear that the naivety which Krenkow imputes to al-Khaṭīb al-Baghdādī as a biographer is, in fact, his own: scholarship in the twentieth century has amply demonstrated that the *khabar*, the basic building block of classical Arabic narrative, is a powerful tool in the hands of an able compiler, a device to convey, with little apparent authorial intervention, specific interpretations of events, concepts, and opinions.[2] This can be observed when *akhbār* are organized into chronicles, but it is equally true of *akhbār* which are clustered around a theme or used to illustrate traits of character and poignant moments in an individual's life. Within this framework, this chapter looks at information on al-Ṣūlī in contemporary and later sources, illustrating how each author chooses from a common pool of material to produce a – sometimes significantly – different portrait. The investigation provides an opportunity to reflect on how classical Arabic culture records itself for posterity through the lives of its protagonists.

'Biography'

The starting point is as obvious as it is difficult to put into words: there is no scholarly agreement as to how to define and contextualize a number of texts which intuitively belong together because they concern themselves with the lives of homogenous groups of people. There is no doubt that Arabic culture has paid, in comparison with other contemporary cultures, particular attention to the lives of individuals not only in their singularity, but *as groups and as networks*, and that it has recorded information not only on prominent figures but also on less obvious strata of society. This type of information has never ceased being a research tool for classical and modern researchers alike. However, it does not follow that it is possible to cluster everything under one name: as Wadād al-Qāḍī stresses in her seminal 1995 study, 'biographical dictionary' does not immediately translate any Arabic expression.[3] Two more recent surveys illustrate this point: although the corpora they refer to largely coincide, their terminology differs; Claude Gilliot uses 'prosopography in Islam,' while Wadād al-Qāḍī, returning on the subject in 2006, explicitly rejects this term, maintaining 'biographical dictionaries'.[4] Indeed, Gilliot's article appears in a special issue of the journal *Medieval Prosopography*, devoted to Arab-Islamic medieval culture, which contains all of the following: studies on medieval Arabic sources which may be thought of as prosopographies; prosopographical studies based on different types of pre-modern Arabic sources (such as, for instance, poetry and epigraphy); and prosopographical studies based on pre-modern Arabic sources which may be thought of as prosopographies.[5] This reflects an as-yet-unresolved ambiguity: by calling certain sources 'prosopographies', or 'biographical dictionaries' for that matter, we run at least two risks: first, we are tempted to disregard those features which do not belong to our modern concepts of these terms; second, we are forced into creating a somewhat artificial genre and decide which sources belong in it and which do not.[6] Al-Qaḍī, for instance, does not consider Ibn al-Nadīm's *Kitāb al-Fihrist* a biographical dictionary and lists it among the 'quasi-biographical books' which 'cannot be considered biographical dictionaries since biographies are not a determining factor in their construction'.[7] This is an extremely fine line: Ibn al-Nadīm aims to provide a catalogue of all extant books *together with information on their authors and compilers*;[8] by the same token, it could be posited that the main aim of al-Khaṭīb in the *Ta'rīkh Baghdād* is to record *ḥadīth* circulating in Baghdad ordered by transmitter, or to write an history of Baghdad where a geographical and historical description is followed by a list of people who inhabited the city. In other words, edges are fuzzy.

Still, the need to establish the boundaries of a genre is valid. It stems from a fundamental question which is the object of scholarly discussion since the early twentieth century: whether the emergence of *ṭabaqāt* works originates in an interest in genealogy innate in a tribal society, or whether it was primarily motivated by the need to evaluate religious scholarship. A researcher's stand on this issue has often determined the corpus she selects for investigation.[9] The debate continues in the twenty-first century; for example, Michael Cooperson argues that biography 'originated among *akhbārīs*, not *ḥadīth*-scholars proper, who in the early third/ninth century had barely come into existence as writers of books'.[10] Al-Qāḍī counters that it was created by 'scholars' as an alternative, competing way of recording the history of the Muslim community to the *akhbārīs*' chronicles.

It seems less time-consuming to follow Hilary Kilpatrick and Stefan Leder in acknowledging that there are many ways of arranging information about the past, one of which is to organize it around the lives of individuals so as to provide personal profiles, which in turn may be grouped together along different criteria.[11] This approach dispenses with the need to justify an all-encompassing genre, and to rationalize the use of *akhbār* found in different types of compilation to reconstruct someone's life. Cooperson, for instance, does discuss the origin and evolution of a biographical genre; however, in his case studies, where he examines the biographies of four individuals connected with the notion of 'inheritance from the Prophet', he draws from a large variety of sources, by no means restricted to what al-Qāḍī discusses as biographical dictionaries. After all, general surveys of Arabic historiography, rather than looking at a unified biographical genre, have consistently identified three separate groups connected with successive periods: genealogies and *ṭabaqāt* at the time of the Muslim conquests, 'local histories' (such as al-Khaṭīb's *Taʾrīkh Baghdād*) around the fifth/eleventh century, and universal compilations such as Ibn Khallikān's *Wafayāt al-aʿyān* a couple of centuries later.[12]

The question of origins remains important, as it investigates the basic nature of early Arabic-Islamic society, but again, it may be distracting: while highlighting common features and tracing an evolution, it disregards, on a general level, intertextuality, and on a specific one, the power of *akhbār* and compilation. In short, the idea of biographical dictionary as a distinct type of work gets in the way of a genuine understanding of life-writing as an evolving practice. And indeed, in practice these elements are almost always considered when using biographical material.

Using biography

Notwithstanding the disagreements described above, it is unanimously understood that collecting material on the lives of individuals, both in the form of data (times, places, book titles, affiliations) and in narrative form, is one of premodern Arabic culture's main historical endeavours.[13] The type and arrangement of the information provided, as well as the prevalence of biographical profiles within single works, depend on the author's specific aims. Gilliot, al-Qāḍī and those who preceded them have the merit of having identified and discussed macro- and micro-structure of this arrangement and helped make its use less naïve. Thus, over the past century, the casual extrapolation of information on specific individuals or events has been supplemented, if not supplanted, by more deliberate queries:

1 Prosopographical studies based on snippets of anagraphical data usually found at the beginning or end of individual profiles (dates, genealogies, place names, professions, religious and scholarly affiliations, etc).[14]
2 Structural analyses of context, aims, macro- and microstructure of one or more works.[15]
3 Literary surveys of the portrayal of specific individuals across more than one source.[16]

Besides reconfirming the importance of biographical collections as a record of specific groups in society, these enquiries have highlighted the powerful tools at the disposal of the author to convey ideological meaning. In particular, as the same pool of material may be used by an able compiler to different effects, it is not possible to approach these sources without the tools of literary analysis, nor is it advisable to consult them in isolation. In short, scholarship in the last fifty years has made it clear that the subject cannot be tackled elliptically: the study of biography-writing in its various forms must involve both close and distant reading, and take into account intertextuality as a foundational and necessary element.[17] For the specific purposes of the present chapter, this means that examining al-Ṣūlī's profiles in different sources helps us not only to establish the basic facts of his life, but also to place him in the intellectual history of the period and its understanding in later times.

Such a comparison is made easier by an element that tends to be taken for granted: biographical profiles may be grouped around different principles – geography, discipline, even first name – and arranged in different ways – alphabetically, by year, by generation – but their essential micro-structure is constant. As such, it may be examined as a frame which can be filled with predictable slots containing different types of information, which in turn may be equipped with corroborative or illustrative fillings such as narratives, poetry, or both.[18] The typical framework is as follows:

1 Full name, including *nisbas*[19] indicating scholarly, religious or professional affiliation; remarks on lineage.
2 Presentation, summarizing evaluation.
3 Date, place and circumstances of birth, places of residence.
4 Scholarly/professional relations (teachers, students, employers, etc.).
5 Character, physical traits.
6 Date, place and circumstances of death, place of burial.
7 Sample (and evaluation) of poetry.
8 List (and description/evaluation) of books.

Such a framework may be applied to the biography of individuals in any walk of life. Hilary Kilpatrick, for instance, describes poets' profile in the *Kitāb al-Aghānī* as follows:

> In the first place, the poet appears as a member of society, attached to a tribal and family group, sometimes with a fixed residence or exercising a profession, or involved in political or politico-religious movements. In the second, he is an individual, with distinct character traits and sometimes eccentricities, which may influence his literary career or be reflected in his poetry. Thirdly, he belongs to the literary community and interacts with fellow poets, musicians and patrons. And fourthly, he is the maker of poems whose salient characteristics can be defined and related to those of others in the tradition.[20]

There are, of course, many possible variations: the date of death may sometimes be mentioned in slot 3; any slot except 1 and 2 may be missing completely or be in a different position; the author/compiler may be more or less forthcoming in stating his opinion; and they may or may not add a summarizing sentence to introduce a narrative. Naturally, the more illustrative material selected for a certain slot, the more important such slot; and finally, the way in which the material is arranged may guide the reader to a specific assessment of such material – even a modern reader, as Krenkow's comment above demonstrates. Here is, for example, Yāqūt's profile of al-Ṣūlī. Numbers in square brackets refer to the list of types of elements above:

> **[1]** Muḥammad b. Yaḥyā b. ʿAbdallāh b. al-ʿAbbās b. Muḥammad b. Ṣūl, the *kātib*[21] known as al-Ṣūlī. His grandfather, Ibn Ṣūl al-Turkī, was one of the early supporters (*duʿāt*) of the Abbasids. **[3]** Abū Bakr was born in Baghdad and received his education there. **[4]** He studied with Thaʿlab, al-Mubarrad and Abū Dāwūd al-Sjistānī. The *kātib* and historian Abū ʿAbdallāh al-Marzubānī and others studied with him. **[2]** [al-Ṣūlī] was an historian, an *adīb* and a *kātib*. **[4]** He was a well-established boon companion (*nadīm*) of the caliphs, having served al-Muktafī, then al-Rāḍī, then al-Muqtadir.[22] **[2]** He was also unequalled in his times in the game of chess, to the point that it was said that he was the one who invented it; but it is not so, as chess was invented by the Indian Ṣiṣṣa for Shihrām, king of al-Fars. It was related that al-Rāḍī bi-llāh went out for a stroll and came to a pleasant and blooming garden. He said to the people who were present: 'Have you ever seen a view more beautiful than this?' Everybody praised what was there and described its beauty. Al-Rāḍī said: 'The way al-Ṣūlī plays chess is more beautiful than this, and than anything you have described.'
>
> **[5]** Abū Bakr al-Ṣūlī had a library which he had devoted to the different books he had collected. He had organized them very well in it. He would say to his friends: 'All the books in this library have been checked and corrected by a teacher'.[23] When he wanted to consult one of these books, he would say: 'Boy, bring me such-and-such book.' Abū Saʿīd al-ʿUqaylī [d. 322/934] heard him say this one day, so he recited (*ramal*):
>
> What a *shaykh* is al-Ṣūlī indeed
> librarywise he's the best there is!
> If we ask him a question,
> seeking from him the explanation
> He says 'Quick, boys, bring
> of science the *Such-and-such* ream!'

[**8**] Among al-Ṣūlī's books are: *The Life and Times (akhbār) of the Poet Ibn Harma*; *The Life and Times of Abū Tammām*; *The Life and Times of Abū ʿAmr b. al-ʿAlāʾ*; *The Life and Times of Isḥāq al-Mawṣilī*; *The Life and Times of the Poet al-Sayyid al-Ḥimyarī*; *History of the Qarāmiṭa*; *Guidelines for Scribes (adab al-kuttāb)*; *Types of Poetry (al-anwāʾ)*; *Kitāb al-ʿIbāda*; *Kitāb al-Ghurar*; *Book of the Leave (al-waraqa)*; *Book of Viziers*; and others.[24]
[**6**] He left Baghdad because he had become poor and went to live in Basra, where he died in 335/947.[25]

In this profile, most of the slots listed above are filled, and two of them are equipped with narratives. The first of these illustrates al-Ṣūlī's profession as a courtier and his skill at chess, the second one expands on his bibliophilia and includes poetry.

Before looking into the contents of this and other profiles of al-Ṣūlī, it is worth reflecting on what surrounds them, for three reasons: first, the types of works where a subject's profile is found tell us which social and professional groups the subject belongs to; second, the material each biographer selects tells us the latter's focus; third, the arrangement of such material conveys the biographer's evaluation and as a consequence, on a macrolevel, the subject's reputation in their afterlife. We shall now investigate these points – where, what and how – in al-Ṣūlī's profiles.

Where: the pervasiveness of al-Ṣūlī

In works written between his death and the eleventh/seventeenth century, I could identify nineteen biographical profiles of varying lengths for al-Ṣūlī. These are, in rough chronological order:

1 Al-Marzubānī's (d. 384/994) *Muʿjam al-shuʿarāʾ*[26]
2 Al-Marzubānī's *al-Muqtabas* (in Yaghmūrī's digest)[27]
3 Ibn al-Nadīm's (d. 380/990) *Kitāb al-Fihrist*[28]
4 Al-Khaṭīb al-Baghdādī's (d. 463/1071) *Taʾrīkh Baghdād*[29]
5 Al-Samʿānī's (d. 562/1166) *al-Ansāb*[30]
6 Ibn al-Anbārī's (d. 577/1181) *Nuzhat al-alibbāʾ*[31]
7 Ibn al-Jawzī's (d. 597/1201) *al-Muntaẓam fī l-taʾrīkh*[32]

8 Yāqūt's (d. 626/1229) *Irshād al-arīb*[33]
9 Ibn al-Athīr's (d. 630/1233), *al-Kāmil fī l-taʾrīkh*[34]
10 Ibn al-Athīr's *al-Lubāb fī tahdhīb al-ansāb*[35]
11 Ibn Khallikān's (d. 681/1282) *Wafayāt al-aʿyān*[36]
12 Abū l-Fidāʾ's (d. 732/1331) *al-Mukhtaṣar fī akhbār al-bashshar*[37]
13 Al-Dhahabī's (d. 748/1348) *Tadhkirat al-ḥuffāẓ*[38]
14 Al-Dhahabī's *Taʾrīkh al-islām*[39]
15 Al-Ṣafadī's (d. 764/1363) *al-Wāfī bi-l-wafayāt*[40]
16 Al-Yāfiʿī's (d. 768/1367) *Mirʾāt al-jinān*[41]
17 Ibn Kathīr's (d. 774/1373) *al-Bidāya wa-l-nihāya*[42]
18 Ibn Taghrībirdī's (d. 874/1470) *al-Nujūm al-zāhira*[43]
19 Ibn al-ʿImād's (d. 1089/1679) *Shadharāt al-dhahab*[44]

Whether this number of profiles is high or not is difficult to establish: leaving aside the fact that the corpus of medieval Arabic sources is far from finalized and that more references may always appear, having one's anagraphical data recorded does not imply being part of a very restricted canon. To be sure, al-Ṣūlī's anagraphical data is often equipped with narratives, which indicate that events in his life have some interest for later generations, but this, too, is far from rare. What points to al-Ṣūlī's importance is, rather, that he is pervasive: firstly, he is given a profile in works with different focuses; and secondly, within those same works he is cited outside his own profile as a source for prose and poetry, as well as appearing as a secondary character in other people's stories. For instance, despite his relative short entry, he is the sixth person of his generation most cited in Yāqūt's *Irshād al-arīb*, together with five professional grammarians and one of his own most prominent students. In *Taʾrīkh Baghdād*, where, as shall be seen, his portrayal as a religious scholar is hardly flattering, he is given a long, detailed profile, is cited extensively as a teacher and student, is part of *isnād*s for historical narratives and, most importantly, is an eyewitness for many others. In the *Fihrist*, out of the roughly 800 individuals active in Baghdad between 279/892 and 334/946, he is amongst the 120 who appear in more than one chapter – in fact, besides being cited as source and as an important editor of poetry, he has two separate profiles. A more systematic review will reveal more: most of the later works in the list above are what historians of historiography would call universal compilations, where biographical profiles of notable individuals are ordered either alphabetically by name or chronologically by death, appended to the chronicle of each year; two are interested in the origin of the 'al-Ṣūlī' *nisba*. On the contrary, most of the earlier sources have more specific criteria. In some cases, these are implicit in the title of the work or its contents. In others, we have an introduction describing the author's rationale and reviewing previous similar works. Based on this evidence, we can identify the different groups to which al-Ṣūlī is connected.

Firstly, al-Ṣūlī is an author. In the introduction to his *Kitāb al-Fihrist*, Ibn al-Nadīm defines his subject as any book on any topic, available in Arabic either in the original or in translation, together with 'biographical information on their compilers (*muṣannifīhā*) and arranged biographies of their composers (*muʾallifīhā*)'.[45] Within this broad category, Ibn al-Nadīm places al-Ṣūlī in the third section of the third chapter: he is found amongst the '*udabāʾ*, table-companions (*al-nudamāʾ wa-l-julasāʾ*), men of letters, singers, slap-takers, buffoons, and comedians',[46] first with a main profile, and further down in a subsection on 'the chess players who wrote books on the game of chess'. As has been argued elsewhere, the third chapter of the *Fihrist* does not organize authors around a set of related disciplines; rather, it organizes disciplines around a group of professionals who all share the place of their main activity: the court.[47] As for poetry, while the *Fihrist* does highlight al-Ṣūlī's activity as an editor and critic, it does not list him amongst the poets, nor does it quote any of his own production. On the other hand, most profiles in other sources do contain some lines by al-Ṣūlī, and his student al-Marzubānī includes him in his *Muʿjam al-shuʿarāʾ* as a poet in his own right.

Whether al-Ṣūlī may be described as a traditionist is debatable: although most biographers mention his religious studies, these are rarely highlighted. To be sure, al-Ṣūlī is given a long profile in al-Khaṭīb's collection on Baghdadi religious scholars and deserves a brief mention in al-Dhahabī's *Tadhkirat al-ḥuffāẓ*. However, al-Khaṭīb's introduction provides context: *Taʾrīkh Baghdād*, he says, includes

> [. . .] caliphs, great men, judges, jurists, traditionists, Qurʾān readers, ascetics, pious men, men of letters and poets from Baghdad, by birth or by residence; the Baghdadis who left and died in another land; those who were in nearby areas; those who were not Baghdadis but went there.

On the other hand, al-Khaṭīb continues, he does not include traditionists who passed through Baghdad without transmitting any *ḥadīth*, except for 'a few people who are highly regarded by scholars'.[48] In short, *Taʾrīkh Baghdād* includes all traditionists who have ever transmitted *ḥadīth* in Baghdad, very few important ones who have not, and all other categories of prominent people who were active in the city at some point in their life. Al-Ṣūlī's inclusion in *Taʾrīkh Baghdād* certainly places him amongst the notable Baghdadis, but it does not necessarily qualify him as a religious scholar.

The most recurrent category to which al-Ṣūlī is associated is that of *udabāʾ*: beside belonging to the *Fihrist*'s sub-chapter containing that name, his profile is found in three collections devoted to that group: those by al-Marzubānī, Ibn al-Anbārī, and Yāqūt. The pre-modern meaning of *adab* contains a multitude of aspects, and the same is true for its derivate *adīb*. Biographers help us identify an *adīb*'s characteristics: while Ibn al-Nadīm connects an *adīb* with the court, Ibn al-Anbārī and Yāqūt draw a different line. The former mentions those who were notable in the craft of *adab* (*ahl hadhihi l-ṣināʿa al-aʿyān*),[49] but his focus is very clearly on grammar, a discipline whose practitioners deserve a whole separate chapter in the *Fihrist*.[50] Yāqūt's much larger book has a correspondently larger scope, including disciplines listed by Ibn al-Nadīm but adding others that appear in the *Fihrist* in separate chapters. In fact, it seems to contain the practitioners of all disciplines described in the first three chapters of the *Fihrist*:

> I have collected in this book the information I have on the *akhbār* of grammarians, philologists, genealogists, famous Qurʾān readers, historians (*wa-l-akhbāriyyīn wa-l-muʾarrikhīn*), well-known *warrāq*s, famous bureaucrats and writers of collected epistles, good calligraphers, and all those who compiled a work of *adab* or composed something in its style.[51]

Beside appearing first in Yāqūt's list, grammarians do not appear to have prominence. However, Yāqūt's review of previous scholarship lists biographical collections on grammarians almost exclusively.[52] The only discipline which remains separate is poetry: while most *udabāʾ* are proficient in both prose and poetry, continues Yāqūt, he has put together a separate collection for those who were chiefly poets, 'whose poetry was arranged into a *dīwān*, whose name and story became famous because of that and who did not become known for their transmission and composition of books, or for *ādāb* and *adab* compositions'. The present collection includes 'those who were known as authors, who were famous as compilers, who transmitted other people's work reliably, whose knowledge was broad but who wrote little poetry and much prose [. . .]. I am satisfied that there is no repetition, except for a few individuals for whom it was necessary because they mastered both arts'.[53] This biographical collection on poets has not come down to us, therefore, we cannot be sure whether al-Ṣūlī had a profile there: it is not mentioned in his profile here, as is done in other cases.[54]

At this point, we have a general idea of the scholarly and professional fields with which al-Ṣūlī's identity is associated: a prominent courtier, author, and *adīb*; less surely, a poet, and even less surely, a religious scholar; in these disciplines, he is a pervasive source. Our next step will be to investigate how biographers describe and evaluate al-Ṣūlī's skill in the initial part of their profiles.

What's in a profile?

Is a compiler an author? One of the most common criticisms levelled at premodern Arabic writers consists of dismissing their accuracy in quoting their sources as mechanical, thoughtless repetition devoid of any authorial choice. Still, even this assessment – by now mostly outdated, at least with literary historians – must acknowledge that the initial part of biographical profiles records the author's perspective, as it is the place where he condenses what he considers the essential information on an individual: name, qualifications, presentation and a summarizing evaluation. Some of the shorter profiles consist entirely of either of these elements and append no corroborative testimony in the form of *akhbār* or poetry.

First impressions: the versatility of al-Ṣūlī

The very name at the beginning of a profile may contain a clue, as it may be equipped with *nisba*s, nouns, or adjectives, attached directly to the subject's full name, which qualify his *ism*, *nasab* and *shuhra*. Where sources append such qualifications to al-Ṣūlī's name, they are not homogenous, as can be seen in the table below:

Source		Presentation
Al-Samʿānī	*Abū Bakr al-Ṣūlī al-nadīm*	the boon companion
Yāqūt	*Muḥammad b. Yaḥyā b. ʿAbdallāh b. al-ʿAbbās b. Muḥammad b. Ṣūl al-kātib al-maʿrūf bi-l-Ṣūlī*	the *kātib* known as al-Ṣūlī
Ibn Khallikān	*Abū Bakr Muḥammad b. Yaḥyā b. ʿAbdallāh b. al-ʿAbbās b. Muḥammad b. Ṣūl Tikīn al-kātib al-maʿrūf bi-l-Ṣūlī al-shiṭranjī*	the *kātib* known as al-Ṣūlī the chess player
Al-Dhahabī, *Tadhkira*	*al-ʿallāma Abū Bakr Muḥammad b. Yaḥyā al-Ṣūlī ṣāḥib al-kutub*	the scholar . . . author of books
Al-Ṣafadī	*Muḥammad b. Yaḥyā b. ʿAbdallāh b. al-ʿAbbās b. Muḥammad b. Ṣūl Abū Bakr al-Ṣūlī al-baghdādī*	the Baghdadi
Al-Yafiʿī	*al-ʿallāma al-akhbārī al-adīb ṣāḥib al-taṣānīf Muḥammad b. Yaḥyā al-Baghdādī al-Ṣūlī al-shiṭranjī*	the Baghdadi scholar, historian, *adīb* and author . . . the chess player
Ibn Taghrībirdī	*al-ʿallāma Abū Bakr Muḥammad b. Yaḥyā b. ʿAbdallāh b. al-ʿAbbās b. Muḥammad b. Ṣūl Tikīn al-Ṣūlī al-imām al-muftann al-maʿrūf bi-l-Ṣūlī al-shiṭranjī al-kātib*	the scholar . . . the versatile *imām* known as al-Ṣūlī the chess-player and *kātib*
Ibn al-ʿImād	*Abū Bakr Muḥammad b. Yaḥyā al-baghdādī al-adīb al-akhbārī al-ʿallāma ṣāḥib al-taṣānīf*	the Baghdadi *adīb*, historian and scholar, author of books

It is immediately apparent that later sources append more qualifications to al-Ṣūlī's name; intuitively, this is understandable: sources more distant in time and less specialized will have shorter profiles and will therefore need to summarize points which earlier authors have made with a sentence and/or illustrated with a narrative. However, this is not always correct; sometimes a qualification in the name announces the author's particular focus in the profile, and sometimes a noun disappears from the name to reappear later in the profile. For now, it is worth noting that two qualifications, *nadīm* and *kātib*, are not present in later sources; and three others, *al-shiṭranjī*, *al-ʿallāma* and *al-imām*, appear later. *Imām* is used by only one source, and there is no mention of poetry.

Whatever the reason for these changing qualifications, one thing is certain: al-Ṣūlī is versatile at least in the activities connected with the court environment such as these are circumscribed in the third chapter of the *Fihrist*.

Essentials: the skills of al-Ṣūlī

I call 'presentation' one or more short segments of text, not accompanied by a *khabar*, following the subject's name and summarizing his main claims to fame and their value and status. These segments are edited depending on the material the biographer has at his disposal, as well as his focus, approach, and personal assessment.

For instance, Ibn al-Nadīm's profile begins thus: *Abū Bakr Muḥammad b. Yaḥyā b. al-ʿAbbās al-Ṣūlī, min al-udabāʾ al-ẓurafāʾ wa-l-jammāʿīn lil-kutub.* 'A refined *adīb* and a collector of books' is especially illustrative of how powerful the first words of a profile are in defining their subject: while *adīb* is in the very title of this section of the *Fihrist*, *ẓarīf* carries a more precise qualification. In general, the word designates, as Montgomery put it, an individual in whom certain features of the *adīb* are particularly strong.[55] The existence of a book such as al-Washshāʾ's (d. 325/936) *Kitāb al-Muwashshā*, which is specifically devoted to the norms of behaviour for a *ẓarīf*, implies that there is a group adhering to those norms.[56] Such a group has been sparsely investigated by modern scholars, mainly on the basis of the *Muwashshā*, but it has been difficult to distinguish the use of the word as a specific definition from its use as a general term of praise.[57] Here, however, the former seems more likely. In fact, only al-Ṣūlī and six other individuals are described as *ẓurafāʾ* in the *Fihrist*: two are presented, like al-Ṣūlī, as refined *udabāʾ*; one as a refined *kātib*;

a fourth one as a refined *adīb* and *kātib*; a fifth one as a refined jester (*aḥad al-ẓurafāʾ al-mutaṭāyibīn*).[58]

Finally, that Ibn al-Nadīm should be interested in al-Ṣūlī's bibliophilia is hardly surprising, and it is all the more remarkable because he reserves this description for just eleven individuals in the whole book.[59] As shall be seen in Chapter Three, for other biographers this qualification may become a slur on al-Ṣūlī's reputation.

Al-Ṣūlī's earliest biographer, al-Marzubānī, gives a personal presentation: 'Abū Bakr Muḥammad b. Yaḥyā b. al-ʿAbbās b. Muḥammad b. Ṣūl Abū Bakr, our master (*shaykhunā*), the Almighty have mercy on him'. As for the rest, most later sources give a version similar to that of al-Khaṭīb al Baghdādī: 'one of the [best] scholars in the literary arts, knowledgeable in the chronicles of the rulers, the account of the caliphs, the glorious deeds of the nobles and the classes of poets' (*aḥad al-ʿulamāʾ bi-funūn al-ādāb, ḥasan al-maʿrifa bi-akhbār al-mulūk wa-ayyām al-khulafāʾ wa-maʾāthir al-ashrāf wa-ṭabaqāt al-shuʿarāʾ*). In short, al-Ṣūlī's crystallized standard presentation is as an *adīb* and historian. There are expansions to this presentation, and they concern three main points: al-Ṣūlī's lineage, his work at court, and his scholarly activity, all of which we shall now look at.

Al-Ṣūlī is an unusual *nisba*, and most biographers make at least a passing reference to a noble lineage in Jurjān, either in the presentation or within the name; in the *Muqtabas*, for instance, al-Marzubānī says 'Abū Bakr Muḥammad b. Yaḥyā b. ʿAbdallāh b. al-ʿAbbās b. Muḥammad b. Ṣūl, the ruler of Jurjān'. Many other biographers quote the *Muʿjam al-shuʿarāʾ*:

> He had noble ancestry, as his forefather was Ṣūl, whose people ruled Jurjān;[60] then his descendants after him were leading bureaucrats (*kuttāb*) and held government offices.

Beyond this reference to other bureaucrats in al-Ṣūlī's family, none of the presentations mention his great-uncle, the poet and *kātib* Ibrāhīm b. al-ʿAbbās al-Ṣūlī (d. 243/857). The only source going into more detail is al-Samʿānī's work on *nisbas*, where it is explained that Ṣūl, the first to have converted to Islam, was killed in the battle of ʿAqr in 102/720.[61]

Al-Ṣūlī's activity at court is also described fairly consistently: all sources say that he was a boon companion of the caliphs, many name these caliphs, and two of the earlier sources, al-Marzubānī and Ibn al-Nadīm, specify that he was particularly attached to al-Rāḍī (r. 322–9/934–40). Some attribute scholarly value to this post, adding that he collected the poetry and the accounts of the caliphs.

The most varied topic is the assessment of al-Ṣūlī's scholarly and character qualities. In particular, the four earliest biographers, who are clearly familiar with al-Ṣūlī's work, highlight different points. In both his profiles, al-Marzubānī mentions al-Ṣūlī's mnemonic skills, his vast authority for transmission and his competence as a writer of books. Ibn al-Nadīm selects different skills: 'he was one of the best of his time at chess, and a man of value' (*ḥasan al-murūʾa*). The latter is, like that of *ẓarf*, a specific trait of character. There is no single meaning for the word *murūʾa*,[62] and its general sense of virtue can be attached to moral qualities as well as to good manners and wealth. The term had evolved since pre-Islamic and early Islamic times and the values attached to it certainly changed, but we do not know how. However, if we take Ibn al-Nadīm's definition of al-Ṣūlī as a *ẓarīf* as an indication of belonging to a precise group, we may go a step further and look at the definition of *murūʾa* found in the *Muwashshā*. According to al-Washshāʾ, *murūʾa* is an essential requisite of the *ẓarīf*, and four chapters of the book (10–13) are devoted to its description. A man with *murūʾa* is 'gentle and diffident, speaks sincerely and avoids calumny, has a beautiful character, forgives when it is expected of him, gives generously and keeps promises'.[63] If Ibn al-Nadīm has a similar definition in mind, he is portraying a kind, generous and truthful man.

Al-Khaṭīb provides a longer presentation, repeating al-Marzubānī's evaluation *verbatim* and adding a comment on al-Ṣūlī's moral qualities: 'he was sincere in his beliefs, followed good practice, and his advice was respected' (*wa-kāna ḥasan al-iʿtiqād jamīl al-ṭarīqa maqbūl al-qawl*). If we take Ibn al-Nadīm's *murūʾa* as describing private qualities, al-Khaṭīb's *iʿtiqād*, *ṭarīqa* and *qawl* are public, religious ones. In other words, Ibn al-Nadīm's al-Ṣūlī is a good friend, while al-Khaṭīb's al-Ṣūlī is a good Muslim, although, one may already begin to suspect, not a particularly notable transmitter, as he does not deserve the anointment of being called a *thiqa*, a trustworthy source of *ḥadith*. Finally, it is noteworthy that Ibn al-Nadīm is the only source presenting al-Ṣūlī as a chess player.

Voices: the poetry of al-Ṣūlī

As has been noted above, although al-Marzubānī includes al-Ṣūlī in his collection of poets, the *nisba* of poet, *al-shā ʿir* is never attached to his name. Ibn al-Nadīm details his activity as a poetry editor but does not mention his own poetic production. Most later sources, however, starting with al-Khaṭīb, record it briefly: 'Abū Bakr al-Ṣūlī was also the author of much poetry of praise, *ghazal* and other types'. As for samples of this poetry, al-Marzubānī quotes three short pieces which he heard directly from the author; these lines, however, are not of praise or of *ghazal*, and are not found in any of the other profiles. Al-Khaṭīb, on the other hand, quotes five different pieces (one panegyric, the rest *ghazal*), three of which are variations on the same lines, all but one attached to *akhbār* narrated in the first person by al-Ṣūlī. Some of the longer profiles in later sources – Ibn al-Jawzī, Ibn al-Anbārī, al-Ṣafadī, Ibn Kathīr, Ibn Taghrībirdī – quote one or more of these, with or without the attached narratives; Ibn al-Jawzī has an additional poem equipped with a new narrative. These narratives, detailing al-Ṣūlī's relationship with a known vizier, an unnamed one, and a fellow poet respectively, are the only presence of al-Ṣūlī's voice in his biographical profiles. This is not always the case; for instance, the biographical profiles of the grammarian Thaʿlab, found in many of the same sources, are told largely through *akhbār* in his own voice.[64]

Constants: network and the unspeakable death

Two elements remain consistent in all profiles: the list of al-Ṣūlī's teachers and research students,[65] and the circumstances of his death. As the former is part of al-Ṣūlī's scholarly network, it will be investigated in Chapter Three. The latter deserves some attention here because it is treated as a thorny subject. In fact, Ibn al-Nadīm seems to refuse even to mention it at first, saying that al-Ṣūlī's life 'is too well known, famous and close [in time] for us to be necessary to treat it in great detail'. He nevertheless adds later that al-Ṣūlī 'died while in hiding in Basra because he had related a *juz* ʾ on ʿAlī, on him be peace, and the élite and the commoners (*al-khāṣṣa wa-l-ʿāmma*) were after him to kill him'.[66] Later biographers are less forthcoming, mentioning that al-Ṣūlī had left Baghdad because he had become poor (*li-iḍāqa*, or, in some cases, *ḍīq* or *ḥāja*) and had settled in Basra. Ibn Khallikān merges the two snippets of information:

> [He] died in 335 (it is said 336) in Basra while in hiding, because he had related an account (*khabar*) on ʿAlī b. Abī Ṭālib – God be satisfied with him – and the élite and the commoners were after him to kill him, although they did not succeed. He had left Baghdad because of financial difficulties.

This is the portrayal of a dismal situation: while living in Basra in reduced circumstances, al-Ṣūlī had produced a piece of scholarship which had upset many people and was forced to hide. We have details of al-Ṣūlī's financial situation which will be explored in Chapters Two and Three. The problematic *juzʾ*, on the other hand, remains elusive.

The power of stories

Both historical and literary scholarship generally acknowledge that a critical reading of narrative accounts is essential to a correct understanding of premodern texts. Although they often disagree on the implications, they recognize the power of the *khabar* as a narrative tool. Two main points have been made; the first concerns position: as Hilary Kilpatrick put it, 'the context in which a *khabar* or group of *akhbār* is placed enhances its meaning',[67] in that some accounts can be understood better, or only, in relation to each other.[68] The second point concerns manipulation: accounts may be cut, pasted, and merged to fit the author's needs. For biographical profiles in particular, Malti-Douglas identifies techniques such as 'mentioning or omitting incidents, offering excuses or asides, presenting longer or shorter versions or variants of a story or even replacing one story with another, and relating dreams in longer or shorter forms'.[69] These are the tools with which different biographers may highlight specific features of their subject. Yāqūt's profile above, for instance, concentrates on two features, each of which is illustrated by an account: al-Rāḍī's admiration for al-Ṣūlī's chess play highlights his skill at this game, and more in general his work as a boon companion of the caliphs. On the other hand, al-Ṣūlī's bibliophilia is ridiculed by a short invective mocking a scholar who would need to look something up in a book instead of having it committed to memory. These accounts have the further effect of overshadowing an element which was at the forefront of the *Fihrist*'s profile: Yāqūt does provide a bibliography of al-Ṣūlī's books, presumably taken from the *Fihrist*, but it is shortened and inaccurate in places; clearly, authorship is not the focus of Yāqūt's portrayal.[70]

Chess and bibliophilia are persistent strands of al-Ṣūlī's posthumous reputation and evolve over time: in the former case, snippets of information from different sources merge into a coherent story; in the second, two accounts are joined and phagocytized by a more general story. Other accounts have a different fate: al-Ṣūlī's skill at poetic composition and improvization is illustrated by three narratives, all in the first person, two of which appear in only one source, the third recurring with little variation in different profiles. Of the two stories about religious scholarship transmitted by al-Ṣūlī, one is repeated once, unchanged. The highest number and variety of stories is found in al-Khaṭīb al-Baghdādī's *Taʾrīkh Baghdād*. Here, the structure of al-Ṣūlī's profile is very effective at conveying a precise, albeit not necessarily flattering, impression.

How to demolish a scholar's reputation

Having seen above the example of Yāqūt's short, compact profile of al-Ṣūlī, we now delve into the sophisticated portrayal painted by al-Khaṭīb. Profiles in *Taʾrīkh Baghdād* are consistent in structure despite their huge number and their varying length. This is particularly striking because the first impression, dictated by the long *isnād*s and non-committed style, is one of chaotic juxtaposition of accounts. On the contrary, even the order in which information appears is relatively consistent.

The subject's name is given in its fullest possible version, often complete with comments on some links of the genealogical tree and followed by all known *nisba*s indicating geographical location, profession and affiliations of various kinds. If the geographical *nisba*s do not include Baghdad or one of its areas, al-Khaṭīb will usually mention that this person 'came to Baghdad and transmitted *ḥadīth* while there', or that he lived there, stopped there on the way to the Pilgrimage, died there, or any other specification of a connection to the city, often including the subject's address. This will be followed by the list of people on whose authority the subject transmitted *ḥadīth* and other disciplines – often ordered hierarchically – and a list of those who transmitted and related from them. Samples of this transmission work will often be included and critiqued, and sometimes attached to a narrative. These will be followed by accounts illustrating the subject's character or notable events in his life. Finally, when it is available, al-Khaṭīb will report the opinion of his direct authorities on the reliability of the subject in question as a traditionist. Dates of death are usually at the very end, and al-Khaṭīb spends considerable time reporting all different versions of these and trying to evaluate them, even when the difference is a matter of days. Dates of birth, when they are present, are referred to an actual statement of the subject related by his students.

Applied to al-Ṣūlī's life, this structure results as follows:

1 Full name.
2 First presentation: good at *adab*, accounts of rulers, chronicles of caliphs, deeds of great men and classes of poets.
3 List of teachers.
4 Second presentation: an authority for traditions and *adab*, skill in book composition, work as boon companion, topics of book production (but no bibliography), personal qualities, ancestry, poetic production.
5 List of students.
6 List of individuals who transmitted to al-Khaṭīb directly on his authority.
7 *ḥadīth* (with mistake in *isnād*).
8 saying of ʿAlid *imām*.
9 Account from youth with a teacher (first-person, including poetry).
10 Poetry by al-Ṣūlī.
11 Account from adulthood with vizier and another poet, illustrating composition of the above poetry (first-person).
12 Poetry by al-Ṣūlī.
13 Account from old age: al-Ṣūlī's mistake in relating *ḥadīth* (two versions).
14 Account on al-Ṣūlī's library.
15 Poetry on al-Ṣūlī's library.
16 Date and place of death (two versions).

Al-Ṣūlī's profile begins with **[1]** his complete name and **[2]** a brief summary of skills and activities; **[3]** a list of his authoritative teachers illustrating the thoroughness of his education in the fundamental subjects (grammar, *ḥadīth*, poetry, etc.); **[5]** and an equally prestigious list of people who transmitted traditions from him, followed by **[6]** those who transmitted on his authority to al-Khaṭīb directly. The most prominent of these is Abū l-Ḥasan al-Dāraquṭnī (d. 385/995), al-Khaṭīb's main source of opinion on the reliability of traditionists. Between these lists, al-Khaṭīb adds **[4]** a second enumeration of al-Ṣūlī's qualities, activities and genealogy. The source, al-Marzubānī's *Muʿjam al-shuʿarāʾ*, is acknowledged at the end of the profile but does not deserve an *isnād* here.

The profile continues with samples of al-Ṣūlī's activity as a traditionist: first, **[7]** a *ḥadīth* transmitted by al-Ṣūlī, for which al-Khaṭīb points to a mistake in al-Ṣūlī's *isnād*, where a link of the chain is garbled.[71] However, the mistake is not attributed directly to al-Ṣūlī, as it could be ascribed to al-Jawālīqī, the last link before al-Khaṭīb. Immediately lower in importance, and subsequent in order, comes **[8]** the saying of an ʿAlid *imām*, Jaʿfar al-Ṣādiq, transmitted by al-Ṣūlī. This is the only hint of ʿAlid sympathies in this profile, as there is no mention here of the *juzʾ* which caused al-Ṣūlī to go into hiding. The following paragraph introduces a cluster of more mundane narratives illustrating episodes from different times in al-Ṣūlī's life: **[9]** in a first-person account, he relates that he was once late for a class held by Abū Khalīfa al-Faḍl b. al-Ḥubāb al-Jumaḥī (d. 305/917–18) where al-Ṣūlī was presumably to act as teaching assistant. When he realized that the servant would not let him in because the class had already started, he composed two lines complaining that Abū Khalīfa would prefer the company of uncouth pupils to his own refined one. Once he read the lines, Abū Khalīfa let him in and responded with two lines by the grammarian al-Tawwāzī (d. 233/847). This account introduces the first piece of poetry in the profile and legitimizes al-Ṣūlī as a poet in a specific field: in the episode, Abū Khalīfa is teaching the work of his famous uncle, Ibn Sallām al-Jumaḥī (231/846), on pre-Islamic poets, for which he is the authorized transmitter (*rāwī*). However, the short, entertaining lines he exchanges with al-Ṣūlī are in the style of the Moderns.

The following episode **[10]** is set later, during al-Ṣūlī's time at court in Baghdad, involving an unnamed vizier and displaying al-Ṣūlī's poetic skills in producing variations on a theme. Al-Khaṭīb begins by quoting two lines of poetry by al-Ṣūlī in the *basīṭ* meter, describing how the lover's body, weak and ill, imitates the beloved's eyelids fluttering languidly:

All who resembled him, for his sake, I loved
'cause everything from the beloved is loved
Even with my body I mimicked his eye
as if stealing languor from his lids

This is followed by **[11]** al-Ṣūlī's first-person account, attached to a different *isnād*, providing context to the poem:

A vizier one day recited to us a line by al-Buḥturī and began repeating it, saying how good it was. The line was (*kāmil*):

It's as if my body had
the languor of your eyes[72]

I pulled out the inkwell and composed on the spot (*basīṭ*):

All who resembled him, for his sake, I loved [. . .]

The vizier appreciated this and gave me a present of money. Later, a *kātib* known as al-Raḥūnī claimed these two lines for himself. When I confronted him, he insisted: 'Come on, give the lines to me [so I can work them into a poem]!' I replied: 'I'm afraid you couldn't compose something this nice if you tried'. 'Compose it yourself then!' he replied; and so I did, on the spot (*basīṭ*):

When I complain about my passion, he says it's a lie,
but the witness of tears has spoken on my cheeks.
The fire of my heart is ablaze in the body,
it's busy with the body, otherwise it would burn.
You, whose eyes are sleeping, you do not know what befalls
an eye which has to bear tears for you, and sleeplessness.
My body is reduced to almost nothing,
as if stealing languor from your lids

Al-Raḥūnī swore that he would never claim the two lines for himself again.

While examining this episode with an eye to structure, one should also keep in mind the other operation which al-Khaṭīb has carried out imperceptibly under the reader's eye: a transition from religious scholarship to poetry on mundane subjects, and presently, in the last and longest piece, the most secular of themes, wine. The poem **[12]** is not equipped with a narrative, but it is introduced by an *isnād* and followed by clarifying remarks: 'I heard from ʿAlī b. al-Qāsim [al-Najjād] this short poem except four lines. Aḥmad b. Aṣram al-Shaḥrī recited all of it to me in Mecca on the authority of ʿAlī b. al-Qāsim'.

The fact that in al-Khaṭīb discusses the *isnād* of this poem as if it were a *ḥadīth* makes the contrast even sharper, and the transition to the following narrative more significant. At this point, al-Ṣūlī's reputation is already shaking, and al-Khaṭīb can start attacking his reliability as a religious scholar. The next account **[13]** concerns an episode from al-Ṣūlī's old age when, before his students in Basra, al-Ṣūlī misread and mistransmitted a *ḥadīth*.[73] The story is particularly significant if we consider that one of the authorities for the episode is the above-mentioned al-Dāraquṭnī who, instead of delivering a general assessment on al-Ṣūlī's reliability, narrates an episode illustrating the contrary.

A final blow comes with the mention of al-Ṣūlī's library. In the *Fihrist*, Ibn al-Nadīm does not attach any negative judgement to the fact that al-Ṣūlī owned many books; on the contrary, al-Khaṭīb juxtaposes **[14]** the description of al-Ṣūlī's library to **[15]** the mocking poem, thus giving the reader the key to a particular interpretation of the description – in other words, enhancing its meaning: it is clear that, although al-Ṣūlī claimed to have a *samāʿ* for each of the books he owned, i.e. to have heard them directly from the authors or from authorized *rawīs*, this was not enough to make his memory reliable, as it was known that he needed to look up his books before answering a question. As has been seen above, Yāqūt presents the same combination of description and invective and, because there is no *isnad*, the narrative seems continuous.

If we go back to the initial list of topics in al-Khaṭīb's profile, we can now re-read it as follows:

1–6 Name, presentation, teachers, students.
7–8 Sample of (imperfect) transmission work.
9– Youth: relationship with teacher, skill at modern poetry.
10–12 Adulthood: relationship with vizier and with fellow poet/courtier/*kātib*, skill at modern poetry.
13– Old age: unreliable as traditionist.
14–15 Library: possibly unreliable as scholar.
16– Death.

The reader, lulled into a false sense of security by the initial descriptions and *ḥadīth*, is slowly led to understand al-Ṣūlī's little value. While doing this, al-Khaṭīb provides different kinds of entertainment in the form of poetry and witty remarks. The resulting image is that of a frivolous man with no solid knowledge, but good for the entertainment which his stories provide, and a respectable poet.

Two of the later profiles, Ibn al-Anbārī and Ibn al-Jawzī, present al-Ṣūlī with the same material. The former has shortened versions of the incorrect *ḥadīth*, the library description, and the first of the poems; the latter quotes both poems with no attached narrative, but provides a different first-person account, in which al-Ṣūlī receives a present of money from the vizier ʿAlī b. ʿĪsā (d. 334/946) for composing four lines, in each of which the second hemistich is from the *muʿallaqa* of Imruʾ al-Qays.[74] None of these sources provide a bibliography, and chess is ignored altogether. This, however, is not al-Ṣūlī's definitive portrayal: another strand develops in parallel, as shown in Yāqūt's profile and, more extensively, Ibn Khallikān's.

On chess, mathematics, and, incidentally, on al-Ṣūlī

Al-Khaṭīb's *Taʾrīkh Baghdād* and Ibn Khallikān's *Wafayāt al-aʿyān* are amongst the more widely used medieval biographical sources, and also amongst the most studied in modern times. The *Wafayāt*, in particular, is considered to introduce a new type of collection, the 'universal biographical dictionary', highly selective in its choice of subjects and much more open than its predecessors in dispensing with source-quoting and reshaping its material. Two elements are always found in the same position in each profile: the full name of the person at the beginning of the entry, and a final endnote section, containing mainly explanation and spelling of words, identification of place names, and information on individuals who are mentioned within the profile.

In a typical profile, the full name is followed by several qualifications and a summarizing evaluation, usually without source attribution. Lists of teachers and pupils are sometimes mentioned but, especially the latter, not always in detail; often just a remark such as '[the subject] had many students' suffices. Scholars' profiles usually contain a bibliography, often taken from the *Fihrist*. Death, and possibly the place of death and burial, and date and place of birth, are often found towards the end of the entry, just before the footnotes. Sometimes, the stories connected to the profile's subject generate a long digression. Together with endnotes, these digressions are distinctive of Ibn Khallikān's narrative style. Endnotes strengthen the idea of accuracy and precision, clearing inconsistencies and answering possible questions without interrupting the narrative flow; they are, in other words, a critical apparatus. Digressions, on the contrary, do interrupt the narrative flow, inserting clusters of information at times only loosely connected with the subject of the profile. Both endnotes and digressions may develop into sub-profiles on the current subject's father, teacher, friend or enemy, complete with dates, genealogies and stories. To retrieve such sub-profiles one cannot use simple alphabetical order but must resort to temporal, social or scholarly connections reminiscent of earlier, non-universal biographical collections, which are arranged by discipline, excellence or generation. Through these devices, Ibn Khallikān can include in the *Wafayāt* individuals whose date of death is uncertain, or narratives without a clear protagonist, which otherwise would have been left out.[75] These are, then, a *second class* of individuals and narratives, worth including in a comprehensive work even though they are not consistent with the general criteria of the work regarding excellence and alphabetical order.

The main stylistic point distinguishing the *Wafayāt* from the *Taʾrīkh Baghdād* is its narrative cohesion: where the latter presents its material as a series of juxtaposed *akhbār*, each attributed to a source, the former organizes it into seamless stories which make sense on their own, because the context is provided, or at least cited, through endnotes and digressions. Abridgements make sure that all asperities of different *akhbār* put together from different sources are smoothed into a coherent narrative. In short, Ibn Khallikān leaves little to his reader's intuition and knowledge of the context.

Al-Ṣūlī's entry in *Wafayāt al aʿyān* is the longest of all the ones reviewed here. However, the space properly devoted to al-Ṣūlī is not very large. Although his other abilities are recognized, al-Ṣūlī becomes here the symbol of chess, and almost an excuse to talk about this and other topics. The general structure is as follows:

1 Full name and qualifications.
2 Teachers and students.
3 Presentation: profession as *nadīm*.
4 Bibliography.

5 Evaluation: *nadīm* and historian, good authority, character qualities, best chess player of his time.
6 Digression on the origin of chess, to correct the mistaken belief that al-Ṣūlī himself invented it.
   a. Backgammon and chess.
   b. The marvellous reward requested by Ṣiṣṣa from the king of India for inventing chess.
   c. Sub-digression on how to calculate Ṣiṣṣa's reward.
   d. Cross-reference to another profile, where the reader can find how to calculate the circumference of the Earth.
7 Account on the caliph's admiration for al-Ṣūlī's game of chess.
8 Account on al-Ṣūlī's arrival at court as a chess-player.
9 Account on al-Ṣūlī's library, including poetry.
10 Death.
11 Endnote: cross-reference to his uncle's profile, where the ancestry is explained.
12 Endnote: Ṣiṣṣa.
13 Endnote: Ardashīr.
14 Sub-endnote: Persian dynasties.
15 Endnote: Balhayt.

The first part of the entry **[1–5]** contains the usual information: name, occupation, teachers and students, connections, books, skills. However, a few details are peculiar of Ibn Khallikān's portrait. Firstly, al-Ṣūlī's skill at chess has made it into his name and has become a *nisba, al-shiṭranjī*. Secondly, Ibn Khallikān follows Yāqūt in providing a shortened and somewhat inaccurate bibliography of al-Ṣūlī's works, lacking, most notably, his books on chess. This is all the more remarkable because, from this point on, al-Ṣūlī's proverbial game of chess comes to the fore: to this day, says Ibn Khallikān, whoever excels at chess is said to play like al-Ṣūlī. This is the starting point of a long digression on the origins of chess, and a second one on one of the most famous mathematical puzzles in the world:

> **[6]** I met many people who believed that al-Ṣūlī is the inventor of chess, but this is wrong. The one who invented it was the Indian Ṣiṣṣa b. Dāhir. The name of the king for whom he invented it was Shihrām, with a *kasra* under the *shīn*.

Ibn Khallikān then explains how, in the same period, the **[6a]** Persian emperor Ardashīr had invented backgammon (*nard*). Chess was found to be preferable because, being based on skill and not on luck, 'it is an instrument for learning about war, a glory for religion and this world and the basis for every justness'. The wisdom of Ṣiṣṣa in inventing chess is expanded upon by a second story **[6b]** detailing the reward he requested from the king: he asks to be given the amount of wheat grains resulting from putting one on the first square of a chessboard, doubling it on the second square, doubling that amount on the third, and so on until the sixty-fourth and last square. The story ends with the stereotypical amazement of the king when he discovers that there is not enough wheat in the whole kingdom to satisfy Ṣiṣṣa's request.[76] At this point, Ibn Khallikān inserts himself in the narrative to explain **[6c]** how the calculation – a practical example of arithmetical progression – is carried out, and how an unnamed Alexandrian mathematician explained it to him personally once. In the course of his explanation, the mathematician mentions the maximum number of cities in the whole world, which can be assumed because the circumference of the Earth is known. This calculation is also briefly explained, and **[6d]** a reference is given to the profile of the Banū Mūsā brothers for a more detailed explanation.[77]

The narrative, then, has moved three steps away from al-Ṣūlī: the story of chess, the mathematical calculation, and the circumference of the Earth, including a cross-reference to another profile. Only now does attention return to al-Ṣūlī:

> We digressed beyond the original intention, but it was not in vain because this way of reasoning is unusual. I wanted to record it for those who refuse to believe what has been said on the doubling on the chessboard, so that they can think about it, and know that it is correct, and that this is an easy way of demonstrating it.[78]

While the story of the inventor of chess and the grain of wheat must have been circulating in Arabic for some time,[79] the discussion with the Alexandrian accountant graphically illustrates a conversation which seems vivid in the author's memory. The impression is that al-Ṣūlī's existence is now a prelude to this interesting encounter with a wise man who found an effective way of explaining some mathematics. The following two episodes **[7–8]** return to al-Ṣūlī, but they still concern chess, and specifically two caliphs' admiration for al-Ṣūlī's game. Both narratives, the first of which is also used by Yāqūt, are quotations from al-Masʿūdī's (d. 345/956) *Murūj al-Dhahab*, where they appear as the principal information on al-Ṣūlī. Ibn Khallikān follows the original source in arranging the two accounts in reverse chronological order, first recording the admiration of al-Rāḍī, the last caliph al-Ṣūlī served, and then illustrating his arrival at court:

> When al-Ṣūlī began his service for al-Muktafī (r. 289–95/902–8), who had been told of his chess training, the caliph's favourite player was al-Māwardī[80] [. . .]. Thus, when [al-Ṣūlī and al-Māwardī] played together in the presence of al-Muktafī, the latter, influenced by his friendship, supported al-Māwardī, to al-Ṣūlī's initial surprise. However, as the game progressed and al-Ṣūlī collected all his strength of will, confronted al-Māwardī and took the lead so that it would hardly be possible to recover, the beauty of al-Ṣūlī's game became clear to al-Muktafī, who no longer supported al-Māwardī – in fact, he told him: 'Your rosewater has become urine!'[81]

This account closes the cluster on chess in this profile, while helping to refocus the reader's attention on al-Ṣūlī. However, such attention is no longer on a scholar and courtier, but specifically on a chess player – in fact, this last account makes it clear that al-Ṣūlī's point of access at court was not through his scholarship, ancestry or administrative skills, but through chess.

The final account **[9]** concerns al-Ṣūlī's bibliophilia, and it is a perfect example of how information can be processed over time. As has been seen, al-Khaṭīb provides two separate accounts with different *isnād*s: the first, narrated by Abū Bakr b. Shādhān, describes how al-Ṣūlī's library was arranged, and the second quotes al-ʿUqaylī's poem satirizing al-Ṣūlī's habit of looking up everything in his books. In his version, Yāqūt cuts all *isnād*s and inserts a connecting sentence: al-ʿUqaylī composed his short poem *because he had heard al-Ṣūlī send for his books whenever he was asked a question*. Finally, Ibn Khallikān uses the same material as al-Khaṭīb and Yāqūt but merges it into one account and attributes it all to al-ʿUqaylī, who is now mentioned at the beginning of the *khabar*. Moreover, the frame shifts the focus: while al-Khaṭīb's focus is al-Ṣūlī's use of books, Ibn Khallikān's point is that even the best of men can attract criticism: 'despite al-Ṣūlī's acknowledged qualities [. . .], there was still a detractor who lampooned him, although gently. It was Abū Saʿīd al-ʿUqaylī; he saw that [al-Ṣūlī] had a house full of books [. . .]'.

Except for a reference to al-Ṣūlī's ancestry, all of the endnotes **[11–15]** concern names and places found in the chess stories. Thus, the structure above may be summarized as follows:

1–5 Name, presentation, education, bibliography.
6–8 Chess; al-Ṣūlī and chess.
9– Library: detractors.
10– Death.
11–15 Endnotes.

It is clear that the real protagonist of the profile is chess itself.

Strands

It is hopefully clear by now that, while providing very similar basic information (anagraphical details, professional and scholarly presentation), al-Khaṭīb and Ibn Khallikān represent two different versions of al-Ṣūlī through their selection and arrangement of narrative accounts. The two profiles have only two accounts – merging into one – in common, regarding al-Ṣūlī's bibliophilia, but even this shared story is used to different effects. Indeed, excepting this latter element, the accounts remain clustered together in later profiles: one group portrays al-Ṣūlī as a poet and (possibly unreliable) scholar, the other as a chess player. To my knowledge, only al-Ṣafadi uses narratives from both strands in the same profile.[82] All other biographers choose either of these representations: as has been seen above, Ibn al-Anbārī and Ibn al-Jawzī follow al-Khaṭīb. Later, the short profile in Ibn Kathīr's *al-Bidāya* quotes the poem inspired by al-Buḥturī's lines, with no attached narrative. The chess strand is followed by al-Yafiʿī, who quotes the whole of Ibn Khallikān's profile, and Ibn al-ʿImād.

To be sure, it may be argued that not all biographers had access to all earlier sources, and that therefore their portrayals simply depend on the material at their disposal. In turn, I would point out that, by the seventh/thirteenth century, most if not all scholars had direct or indirect access to, at least, the works of Ibn al-Nadīm, al-Khaṭīb and Ibn Khallikān, and the question was which of these they chose to consult. In other words, it is a question of focus and interests.

Although these different strands and the resulting portrayals are not necessarily in conflict and may well be provided concurrently, it seems that one strand of information does prevail in the long run and eventually makes it into popular culture: the symbolic arrival point of its journey may be *al-Kanz al-madfūn*, a composite work of uncertain authorship written between the eighth/fourteenth and the tenth/sixteenth century. It contains a list of the ninety-two most prominent men since the beginning of Islam, each man being the best in one particular field. In the eighty-ninth place, al-Ṣūlī is included as the best chess player.[83] Indeed, to this day Abū Bakr al-Ṣūlī may well be better known outside the field of medieval Arabic studies as one of the earliest chess players known to have really existed.[84]

Person or persona?

At this point, it is worth checking what we have found against what is extant of al-Ṣūlī's own work. Al-Ṣūlī, whom Canard describes as 'un homme de lettres d'une vanité parfois insupportable, naïvement convincu de sa propre supériorité et de l'excellence de ses vers, qu'il proclame toujours les meilleurs de tous ceux qui ont jamais été écrits',[85] misses no occasion, in his *Kitāb al-Awrāq*, to record his own successes. The part of the *Awrāq* covering al-Ṣūlī's own times, and which therefore probably contains most autobiographical notations,[86] make it clear that al-Ṣūlī was quite concerned with being remembered by posterity as an excellent scholar, as well as a favourite of the powerful. Still, none of this material end up in the biographical profiles, where only two *akhbār*, one of which a *hapax*, are told in the first person, and only one vizier and two caliphs are mentioned by name; on the other hand, there seems to be no mention of chess in the extant parts of the *Awrāq*.[87] To be sure, later sources may not have had access to the book. However, although al-Ṣūlī's writings on chess go equally unmentioned in these later sources, his reputation as a chess player increases over time on the basis of two elements: an origin story which has nothing to do with his life, and two generic accounts found in al-Masʿūdī's *Murūj*, who does not cite his source.

While al-Ṣūlī's own poetry might have been of a lower quality than its author realized, his activity as a poetry editor and poets' biographer is well documented, even, as we have seen, within the biographical collections reviewed here. Still, despite his pervasiveness, this role is almost absent in the biographical profiles, with the partial exception of *Taʾrīkh Baghdād*. Al-Ṣūlī's scholarship in the field of chancery, which is part of his name in the earlier sources (*al-kātib*) and evident from the titles of his written production, disappears altogether.

In short, al-Ṣūlī's *persona*, that of the chess player, has become detached from his documented activity, although this still exists and is used in other contexts. The existence of 'autobiographical' material and of his own work does not necessarily influence the development of his biographies. On the contrary, the material used for the biographies rarely coincides with the autobiographical material. These two aspects remain separated and serve different purposes, to the point that a person and a *persona* seem sometimes to coexist within the same book. The person is an *adīb* and a source for poetry and poets, often mentioned in other people's biographies, and sometimes as the narrator of events of which he was the protagonist, but rarely mentioned within his own profile. The *persona*, a legendary chess player, occupies al-Ṣūlī's profile, which is mostly narrated in the third person and has little to do with autobiographical material.

2

In his own Words

Keine der Autobiographien ist aus dem Bewusstsein eines Eigenwertes des einmalig Persönlichen entstanden; sondern alle, besonders deutlich die wenigen, die sich über die Form des blossen Lebenslaufes erheben, verfolgen sachliche Zwecke, die dem gesamten übrigen Schaffen der Verfasser weitestgehend kongruent sind.[1]

Franz Rosenthal

As has been noted in Chapter One, biographical profiles of al-Ṣūlī include a few first-person accounts. These illustrate al-Ṣūlī's poetic production, and in particular his ability to improvise modern poetry in a social setting, narrating interactions with a teacher, a fellow poet and two viziers. As may be expected, they all show al-Ṣūlī in a good light. However, in Chapter One we have seen that first-person accounts are a very small part of al-Ṣūlī's afterlife; indeed, his later portrayals contain a great deal of extraneous material which is only loosely connected with his life, resulting in a profile with a defined silhouette but very fuzzy features. On the contrary, al-Ṣūlī's work is peppered with personal details: he has much to say on events of his life, his personal and professional character, and his connections; he is liberal with opinions and complaints on himself, other people, and current events. In this chapter, we shall use this material to define al-Ṣūlī's features.

Terminological traps

If 'biography' is a loaded word in premodern Arabic culture, 'autobiography' is even more ambiguous. The generic concept is not difficult to tackle: not only have examples of premodern Arabic autobiographies been recorded and studied by modern scholars since the beginning of the twentieth century; Reynolds et al.'s seminal work outlines an 'autobiographical subgenre' in the form of the *tarjamat al-nafs* ('self-entry'), a profile within a biographical collection which is narrated in the first person. A cluster of material that 'presents itself as a description or summation of the author's life, or a major portion thereof, as viewed retrospectively from a particular point in time', they argue, is an autobiography.[2]

While providing a solid framework for the analysis of works – or sections of works – devoted explicitly to portraying the life of their authors, Reynolds et al. see such works as one development of the uses of the first-person *khabar*. As we know, however, a *khabar* is an independent unit that can be placed in different contexts and stitched together with other *akhbār* depending on the compiler's specific purpose. Whether or not there existed an original continuous narrative by the same individual relating events in their life, what we have in many cases is separate *akhbār* scattered across different works, related in the same voice. To make matters more complicated, the vast majority of *akhbār* are narrated in the first person by an eyewitness. Does this mean, one could paradoxically ask, that most Arabic historical accounts are autobiographical in nature? Or, much less paradoxically, that there is no distinction between different types of narration except the ways in which *akhbār* are arranged?

Hilary Kilpatrick comes to our aid. Introducing the notion of 'fragments of autobiography' within large classical Arabic literary works, she suggests a way to 'add a missing piece to the puzzle of Arabic autobiography': to look at *akhbār* narrated in the first person by one individual within large compilations, biographical or otherwise, where the speaker is not just a witness but is significantly involved in the events he or she narrates.[3] Kilpatrick notes that there is no way of recovering what collectors and successive compilers have discarded: compilers act, she argues, as 'producers' of the lives they report – indeed, we have seen that the producers of al-Ṣūlī's life choose to discard most of the first-person material. On the contrary, one may add, it seems reasonable to assume that the personal information and opinions which an author chooses to share in his own works, as well as their placement in such works, are the result of a conscious authorial decision. In fact, in his monograph on biography in Arabic literature, Iḥsān ʿAbbās explicitly mentions al-Ṣūlī's information on himself as one of several manifestations of autobiography.[4]

There are further terminological hurdles to address and overcome, or rather to sidestep, because they are imposed by the appropriation of 'autobiography' as a technical term on the part of scholars of modern European literature, who have established a (not unanimous) starting date for 'proper' autobiography, as well as necessary components of an autobiography, which they have then arbitrarily attributed to some, but not all, cultures. Arabists have engaged in this discussion, and even accepted its premises, to varying degrees. It is especially important to take such categorizations seriously and argue against them when they concern modern and contemporary autobiography, where cultural stereotyping may have political and downright racist consequences. In the present investigation, a couple of points, stripped of their ideological context, may be useful as signposts for discussion.[5]

Firstly, individuality: Rosenthal's passage at the beginning of this chapter illustrates the traditional orientalist view that there is little individuality in Muslim culture.[6] Indeed, even though such a sweeping statement is clearly unacceptable, biographical collections are universally understood as records of a community as much as of single lives, as has been discussed in Chapter One. All this, however, has to be reconciled with the omnipresence of first-person *akhbār* not only to relate events but also to evaluate the specific features of a person's character, scholarship and even physical appearance. While such assessments help to collocate a person within his or her community, it is also significant that they are presented as the opinions of specific, authoritative *individuals* who in turn have been evaluated by others.

A second point of debate concerns introspection: the standard modern distinction between an autobiography and a memoir is determined by its focus: a memoir records an individual's public role and their relations with their contemporary; autobiography, on the contrary, concentrates on their inner life and spiritual development.[7] The traditional view sees any classical Arabic narration of one's own life firmly in the camp of the memoir and lacking any serious introspection, any representation of the supposedly 'true self'. Here, again, such view disregards ways of expressing one's inner life other than the straightforward description of feelings and thoughts. The obvious example is dreams, which are often related – naturally, in the first person – as important elements in personal and professional decisions. Similarly, as shall be seen in Chapters Three and Five, conversations with authoritative individuals may be described as turning points in one's understanding of specific questions.

To summarize: first-person accounts are a prevalent form of Arabic narrative. In such accounts, the narrator may be a witness or an involved participant. Accounts of the latter type may form independent clusters, be nested within a longer profile in a biographical collection, or be separate units scattered across the author's own work. In all cases, narrators have techniques at their disposal to express both their individuality and their introspection – in other words, they have the means to raise above what Rosenthal calls 'die Form des blossen Lebenlaufes'. One may feel justified, therefore, in disregarding sweeping statements about the existence, or lack thereof, of classical Arabic autobiography, and concentrate on the more interesting question of the fragmented autobiography of al-Ṣūlī. Whether or not one agrees with the concept of fragmented autobiography, and whether or not one decides that autobiographical material in al-Ṣūlī's work may be disregarded for the higher purposes of solid historical research, its presence and effect have to be investigated. In Chapter Five, we shall see the effects of al-Ṣūlī's autobiographical accounts on his historical scholarship. Here, we shall look at what such accounts tell us about his own image of himself.

Motivations, intended readers and time

> I have now said what I had to say of my personal situation (*dhikrī ḥālī*), relating true facts, and how they evolved, to those with discernment, hoping to find some comfort and relief in complaining to people. Now, God willing, I shall return to illustrating events (*sharḥ al-ḥawādith wa-mā jarā*).[8]

When we descend from the general into the particular, two more issues emerge: al-Ṣūlī's motivation for including autobiographical material in his historical work and, secondly, whether he naively considers his life equally worthy of attention as major historical events. Al-Ṣūlī answers these questions himself in the passage above, near the end of the annalistic part of the *Awrāq*, in the chronicle of the year 330/941–2. The passage implies that the writer is well aware of the difference between historical events (*al-ḥawādith wa-mā jarā*) on the one hand, and what happened in his own life (*dhikrī ḥālī*) on the other. He also gives us highly personal motivations: in his present depressing circumstances, he wishes to confide in the reader, to unload his sorrows in the hope of relief. In other parts of his work, written in earlier, more prosperous times, other factors are involved, such as the need for self-promotion. These evolving factors reflect a change in al-Ṣūlī's intended reader from a current or potential employer to, presumably, a group of students unlikely to provide him with a lavish salary. This evolution is best illustrated by three sets of accounts found in different parts of the *Awrāq*, all dealing with al-Ṣūlī's work as a teacher at court.

In 312/924–5, al-Ṣūlī became part of the teaching staff for two children of the caliph al-Muqtadir, Abū l-ʿAbbās, who was later to become caliph as al-Rāḍī, and Abū ʿAbdallāh. The event is mentioned in the chronicle for that year; later, two episodes set in the same period are found in the chronicle for the year 322/934–5, the beginning of al-Rāḍī's caliphate. The first of these episodes[9] is composed of three parts: a description of the pupils' proficiency and the subject they studied with al-Ṣūlī; how, through the children's intercession, he obtained an additional income from the vizier; and a *qaṣīda* poem where al-Ṣūlī asks the two princes to intercede on his behalf. While one cannot presume to know al-Ṣūlī's intentions in recording this account, which was written while al-Ṣūlī worked as table companion under al-Rāḍī, we may observe its effects: it praises the current caliph for his intelligence, reminds him of his past generosity, and promotes al-Ṣūlī as an excellent teacher and poet.

The second *khabar* is nested within the account of how al-Rāḍī's chamberlain, Muḥammad b. Yāqūt (d. 323/935) marched against the army of Hārūn b. Gharīb and brought the latter's head back to the capital. Al-Ṣūlī mentions al-Rāḍī's conflicted feeling towards his grandmother Shaghab, who was Hārūn's sister. The episode, which is a continuous prose narrative, recounts the then-prince's angry outburst about Shaghab's taste for trashy fiction.[10]

The third set of accounts[11] follows a poem in which al-Ṣūlī congratulates the caliph on the death of the Daylamite leader Mardāwīj b. Ziyār and asks al-Rāḍī for a gift, reminding him of the suffering he endured for the caliph's sake. To explain the poem, he relates the circumstances of this suffering, in three parts: an outline of al-Ṣūlī's syllabus and his teaching experience, culminating in being told in no uncertain terms that the caliphal household did not appreciate this learned curriculum; his resignation from the teaching post and fear that he would be given a bad reputation if the story became known; and a poem with a particularly difficult rhyme, which he had composed on al-Rāḍī's request at the end of his teaching tenure.

The first time, then, the topic is tackled as one of the events of the year; in the other two cases, it is used to illustrate and explain later events. The second and third episodes were written after the death of al-Rāḍī, when al-Ṣūlī must have felt free to show the caliph's father and grandmother in a bad light, venting his disappointment at them. The three clusters are different not only thematically but also stylistically: contrary to the first, the second and third episodes are mostly related as direct speech between al-Ṣūlī and other individuals. Finally, the poems in the first and third clusters deserve special attention: they certainly belong to a similar genre, but their function seems different: in the former, the original addressee coincides with the present intended reader; in the latter, the addressee, al-Rāḍī, is no longer alive to read. There must be a new intended reader – in fact, al-Ṣūlī himself makes it explicit:

> I am only reporting part of my poetry on al-Rāḍī, when it is necessary to explain the sense of its composition; otherwise [there would be too much], as I have composed a lot of poetry on him. In my chronicle of the caliphate of al-Muqtadir I have reported some of it, in the hope that the *udabā'*, God willing, not disapprove of it, seeing as it is correct and pure, has a difficult rhyme, and is nevertheless free from any exceptionable affectation or contemptible silly expressions.[12]

In other words, even when a reward is unlikely, self-promotion remains a motivation for inserting al-Ṣūlī's own experience and work within the narrative, because his intended readers are not only, or no longer potential patrons, but also colleagues and prospective students.

The concept of fragmented autobiography, then, acquires more layers. Going back to the basic definition of autobiography as a cluster of material that 'present itself as a description or summation of the author's life, or a major portion thereof, as viewed retrospectively from a particular point in time', we should add that, in a fragmented autobiography, the latter element has in itself a dynamic dimension reflected in the evolution of motivations, aims and intended readers. To muddle the terminological waters further, one may say that a fragmented autobiography shares some characteristics with the diary, in that it is a record kept intermittently.

Within al-Ṣūlī's extant work, autobiographical material is mainly found in chronicles of the caliphates of al-Muqtadir (296-320/908–32), al-Rāḍī (322–9/934–40), and al-Muttaqī (329–33/940–4). As has been seen in the example above, references to the present time in the text tell us fairly precisely when that part of the text was composed. Thus, we are not only able to put events in his life in chronological order; we are also able to trace, if not a spiritual journey, a change in attitude and life expectations.

Al-Ṣūlī's voice

Al-Ṣūlī's career is easily summarized: he served at court for several decades, in different capacities and varying degrees of closeness to the inner chambers. During this period, he was patronized by members of the caliphal family as well as viziers and chamberlains, at times receiving concurrent salaries and pensions for fulfilling different – real or nominal – roles. After being dismissed, together with the other courtiers, by the new caliph al-Muttaqī, he was briefly attached to various military leaders. Eventually he moved to Basra, where he ended his days working as a teacher. In the *Awrāq*, al-Ṣūlī records these roles and activities mostly through accounts of direct or indirect interactions with colleagues or patrons, often involving direct speech and/or poetry, and often leading to specific results. These can be on a personal level (a promotion or demotion, a present, a period of disgrace) but may also have more important implications, such as decisions taken on al-Ṣūlī's advice.[13] In the course of the narration, but at times also as an isolated comment, al-Ṣūlī may also express his opinion on a certain matter or person, in relation to himself personally or in general.

Sometimes, al-Ṣūlī's autobiographical insertions are in the form of one short *khabar*, relating circumstances in his life contemporaneous with the historical events he is recording. For example, when describing the accession of al-Muqtadir in 296/908 and the presents the caliph gave out to the various members of his household and army, al-Ṣūlī notes that nobody had recited any poetry. He continues:

> I had composed some lines for this occasion, beginning thus [...], so I recited some of it. The boon companion (*al-nadīm*) Yaḥyā b. ʿAlī

> [al-Munajjim] had also composed a *qaṣīda* which began thus [. . .]. We were given a present of 10,000 *dirham*, which we split between us. Then came Mutawwaj b. Maḥmūd b. Marwān, who belonged to the rank of the boon companions (*wa-kāna bi-rasm al-julasāʾ*) offering a *qaṣīda* and dedicating it to the Stewardess Fāṭima. He was given a present of 200 *dīnār*.[14]

By attaching himself to a specific event, al-Ṣūlī provides a sample of his own work, also recording its worth – throughout the *Awrāq*, he is always specific when he mentions the amount he was paid, or promised, as a regular salary or as occasional retainers.

Some autobiographical remarks involve recollections from the past. For instance, in the year 323/934–5, al-Rāḍī has Jaʿfar, son of al-Muktafī, arrested. At the request of Jaʿfar's mother, al-Ṣūlī and his fellow *julasāʾ* plead with the caliph until he is released. It was his duty, says al-Ṣūlī, 'for the sake of al-Muktafī, who had singled me out and favoured me'.[15] Other clusters, such as the three sets of accounts illustrated above on al-Ṣūlī's experience as a teacher at court, are much more complex; in particular, the third and longest story is worth investigating in detail, as it provides examples of most of the elements described above: it portrays al-Ṣūlī in different formal and informal roles, as well as his interactions with colleagues, inferiors and superiors through different means of communication; it shows how these interactions have consequences for the people involved; and it links the present of the narrative to its past. The cluster may be divided thematically into three parts.

- **Main event**: in the year 322, the Daylamite leader Mardāwīj b. Ziyār is killed by his *ghulām* Bajkam (d. 329/941).[16] Al-Ṣūlī recites to the caliph a fifty-four-line-long congratulatory poem, which is quoted in full.[17] In the second part of the poem, al-Ṣūlī asks for a reward, saying that he is al-Rāḍī's first companion (*jalīs*) and that he has gone through misfortunes for his master.
- **Flashback**: illustration of the misfortune alluded to in the poem, equipped with a second poem.
- **Junction**: rationale for including this second poem: it explains the meaning of the poem on Mārdāwij's death. The chronicle then continues with other events.

A first observation must be made on the main event, which in turn may be divided into three parts: firstly, a short account of how Mārdawīj had been acquiring power and cooperating with the Qarmaṭī leader to march against Baghdad; secondly, an account of how, on the news reaching the capital that Mardāwīj had been killed by his lieutenants, the chamberlain Muḥammad b. Yāqūt had claimed that this was the result of his own correspondence with the *ghulām*; this introduces the account of how, on hearing the news, the courtiers use poetry to congratulate the caliph: first the Munajjim brothers (al-Ṣūlī's colleagues and rivals), who are with the caliph on a Thursday; then, on the Saturday, al-Ṣūlī. These successive items localize the event, bringing it from the place where it happened, Iṣfahān, to the capital, and finally into the inner circle of the caliphal entourage. Al-Ṣūlī's congratulatory poem serves as a junction, providing the hook to which the flashback is attached or, more precisely, providing a motivation for including a second poem. In other words, the first poem is part of the events of the year, the flashback explains the first poem, and a second poem is included as part of the flashback. With a final paragraph illustrating his rationale, al-Ṣūlī seals the flashback and goes back to the events of the year 322.[18]

The flashback, then, is effectively framed by two long pieces of poetry, both by al-Ṣūlī, both addressed to al-Rāḍī. Its content, narrated as a single long *khabar* with al-Ṣūlī providing the only viewpoint, may in turn be broken up into separate units:

1 When al-Ṣūlī is assigned by the chamberlain Naṣr al-Qushūrī (d. 316/928) to tutor the two princes twice a week (in the year 312, although the date is not mentioned here), he finds them intelligent but ignorant due to the negligence of their main teacher, Ibn Ghālib. Under al-Ṣūlī's guidance, the children thrive: they collect a library with works on jurisprudence, poetry, lexicography and history. Eventually, al-Ṣūlī introduces them to the study of *ḥadīth*, engaging the reputed religious scholar Ibn bt. Manīʿ (d. 317/929) to recite his best transmissions, which al-Ṣūlī copies down for the pupils. When he asks for some money to be presented to Ibn bt. Manīʿ, al-Ṣūlī is told that the princes' mother does not intend to disburse anything, nor does she wish for the lessons to continue. Al-Ṣūlī then informs the Chamberlain, who uses his own money to pay the religious scholar.

2 After witnessing a lexicography lesson, some eunuchs tell the caliph and his mother that al-Ṣūlī is teaching the children the names of genitals. Al-Muqtadir asks Naṣr to investigate, and Naṣr in turn summons al-Ṣūlī.

The latter explains that lexicography is a discipline essential for jurists and judges. Al-Muqtadir is placated.[19]

3 When al-Rāḍī attends a reception hosted by his grandmother, al-Ṣūlī suggests that he should be particularly attentive to the religious scholar al-Mahāmilī (d. 330/942). After meeting the child, the scholar says to another guest, al-Khiraqī, that he has never known members of the caliphal family who are so versed in *ḥadīth*, that this is all the work of al-Ṣūlī, and that the *qahramāna* Zaydān should be asked if anything had been done to reward such a great tutor.[20] When al-Ṣūlī asks al-Khiraqī what Zaydān's reaction was, he is sorely disappointed: the message to al-Ṣūlī is that the caliphal household does not wish for their children to become scholars. Al-Ṣūlī relates the affair to Naṣr, who despairs of ever being able to educate the children properly. Al-Ṣūlī intends to leave the post, but Naṣr advises he should continue for a while, otherwise he risks not being paid at all.

4 In the meantime, Ibn Abī l-Sāj (d. 315/928), the governor of Azerbayjān, Armenia and Arrān, is in Wāsiṭ, preparing to attack the Qarāmiṭa. Al-Ṣūlī has addressed an epistle (*risāla ṭawīla*) to him, suggesting that he wait. In his reply, the governor commiserates with al-Ṣūlī for his treatment, quoting Zaydān's words *verbatim*.[21] Al-Ṣūlī, concerned that this has become a widespread rumour and that he may be blamed for originating it, confides in Naṣr. The latter reassures him: some eunuchs in the palace service are spies for Ibn Abī l-Sāj, and this is how he must have been informed.

5 Al-Ṣūlī leaves his post as a tutor but the princes remain attached to him.

6 As al-Rāḍī had promised to present al-Ṣūlī with a ring, the latter addresses a poem to him asking for it. In exchange, al-Rāḍī requests a poem rhyming with *faṣṣ* (ringstone). The poem is quoted in full (forty-eight lines). Al-Rāḍī sends the ring together with a present of money (*ṣila*) and a note expressing his affection and admiration for al-Ṣūlī.

This cluster can be interrogated in several ways. From the point of view of general historical data, it provides incidental details on the organization of education in the caliphal household, the teaching curriculum and the hiring, economic treatment, and working conditions of staff. It also describes the cultural environment and the different attitudes to learning coexisting at court.

On a more personal level, it shows al-Ṣūlī in three formal roles – *jalīs*, teacher, and, perhaps most surprisingly, political advisor – as well as the informal role of confidant, both of the prince and of the chamberlain. These topics will be explored further in Chapters Three and Five. From a narrative point of view, the cluster illustrates several means of communication: direct and indirect speech, verbal messages, written notes, and poetry. The succession of events is not strictly chronological: both al-Ṣūlī's letter to Ibn Abī l-Sāj and al-Rāḍī's promise of a ring are antecedents to the event of the flashback. Finally, events span over years: while we know from the first story that al-Ṣūlī was appointed tutor in 312/924, the letter to Ibn Abī l-Sāj can be dated to 315/927, when the latter was actually in Wāsiṭ. These narratological elements will be investigated further in Chapter Five.

However, this is not all: if we go back to the initial questions of this chapter, the account of al-Ṣūlī's personal experience conveys three levels of content. Firstly, it provides his perspective as a qualified witness – his assessment of events and his evaluation of people. Secondly, it recommends him as a professional by quoting his work and mentioning its payment. Thirdly, through all of the above it reveals traits of his own character, of his vision of the world and of himself in it. While it seems safe to assume that the first and second level of content are deliberate, there is no way to determine al-Ṣūlī's intentions in the third. All the same, what transpires cannot be reduced to Canard's portrayal of a vain scholar, naïvely convinced in his own excellence as a poet.[22]

Indeed, it is worth reflecting on the role of poetry, not only in al-Ṣūlī's work, but also in his scholarly and artistic persona. If it is true that he often remarks on the beauty of his poetry in the *Awrāq*, it is also true that al-Ṣūlī, who is a renowned poetry editor, has left no trace of a *dīwān* of his own.[23] His poetic production is mainly found in the *Awrāq* and, like the pieces in this passage, it is an integral part of the narrative – part of the record, so to speak. As such, it belongs to al-Ṣūlī's narrative style and technique, but not automatically to a supposed personality trait. In fact, all of al-Ṣūlī's autobiographical insertions, not only those in the cluster above, may be thought of as functional to the historical narrative, not as the expression of personal vanity: they all contribute to establishing al-Ṣūlī as a credible source – an eyewitness, or otherwise well informed through his connection – and as a competent historian, possessing the scholarly tools to interpret and assess events. On the one hand, then, al-Ṣūlī acknowledges the difference between historical events and events in his own life. On the other, he is able to use the latter to corroborate the former.

'Der blosse Lebenslauf' and beyond

What, then, of al-Ṣūlī's fragmented autobiography? To be sure, so much of al-Ṣūlī's work remains lost or undiscovered that we may never expect to put together a complete picture. Still, even with these limitations, the personal material al-Ṣūlī shares with his readers is vast and, as far as his curriculum vitae goes, it has in fact been reassembled. In his translation of the *Akhbār al-Rāḍī wa-l-Muttaqī*, Canard puts in chronological order the information al-Ṣūlī provides in that work.[24] Elsewhere, material from other works has been added to trace his career at court and afterwards, following his financial misfortunes as well as his movements.[25] However, there is more: as may already be seen in the few examples above, we know more about al-Ṣūlī's introspection, development and image of himself than about most of his contemporaries.

The first point of note is that, in the *Awrāq*, the main descriptor al-Ṣūlī uses for himself is *jalīs*. He explicitly does so, as has been seen above, in the congratulatory poem to al-Rāḍī on the death of Mardāwij, where he claims to have been the caliph's first *jalīs*.[26] The same role is implied in other places, such as the celebrations on the accession of al-Muqtadir. Moreover, when al-Rāḍī organizes his first reception after becoming caliph, al-Ṣūlī helps him in selecting appropriate *julasāʾ* (*man yaṣluḥu an yujālisanī*) and eventually sits next to him.[27] Finally, in his account of the ill-fated coup against al-Muqtadir in 296/908, al-Ṣūlī is amongst the *julasāʾ* summoned by Ibn al-Muʿtazz. It is worth noting that, on this latter occasion, the only person to answer Ibn al-Muʿtazz's summon is 'al-Ḥasan b. Ismāʿīl the judge', i.e. the traditionist al-Mahāmilī. This illustrates how '*jalīs*' describes a broad group of individuals who sit with the caliph with different frequency and whose other professional activities are by no means homogeneous. And indeed, while al-Ṣūlī did hold a formal role as table companion to al-Rāḍī with a specific timetable and salary, the word *jalīs* also includes his earlier activity as a tutor, as well as a general idea of being adjacent to power and providing advice and commentary on the basis of poetry, historical precedents, religious tradition, and chancery etiquette.[28] This less regimented role as a learned man at the service of the court and administration is implied throughout the *Awrāq* and manifested in several ways, for some of which we have already seen examples:

1 The composition or recitation of poetry as commentary to current – private or public – events.
2 The composition of prose works, at times unsolicited – such as the epistle to Ibn Abī l-Sāj mentioned in the episode above – other times on commission, such as the treatise on youth which was requested by the vizier al-ʿAbbās b. al-Ḥasan on the accession of the thirteen-year-old al-Muqtadir.[29]
3 The practice of religious scholarship, for example, as an employee of the general Bajkam in Wāsiṭ.[30]
4 The collection of successive caliphs' poetic production, which al-Ṣūlī records in the *Awrāq* at the end of the chronicle for each caliphate.

It seems to this reader, on the basis of the above, that the image al-Ṣūlī wants to convey is not that of a great poet; it is, rather, that of a knowledgeable and trusted advisor and instructor who employs various tools to express his guidance. More examples of this will be seen in a later chapter. Here, it is worth mentioning that, on several occasions, al-Ṣūlī claims to have had a hand in somebody's education. For instance, on the early death of the judge ʿUmar b. Muḥammad in 338/939, he says that he had been 'like a teacher' (*ka-l-murabbī*) to the young ʿUmar, son of the great judge Muḥammad b. Yūsuf (d. 320/932–3);[31] earlier, in an obituary for Muḥammad, son of al-Muqtadir's chamberlain Naṣr, he says that he had tutored him (*rabbaytuhu*).[32]

Rights and wrongs

In his capacity as advisor and instructor, al-Ṣūlī presents himself, of course, as an excellent judge of character. Indeed, he explicitly asserts his own impartiality and disinterest:

> My only purpose is to tell the truth and provide sincere advice. In everything I relate and write, God preserve me from praising a friend because of his

> friendship, or a superior because of his benevolence, nor accuse an enemy because of his hostility or the hate I think he harbours against me. He who attaches himself to the truth is safe, now and in the future.[33]

However, despite this claim, it seems that al-Ṣūlī never completely succeeds at distancing himself from his personal experience with the individuals he assesses.[34] In the narratives described above, it is never in doubt which of the protagonists the reader should support: the caliph al-Muqtadir and his female household are the villains, ignorant and insensitive to the importance of culture; the two princes are the object of everybody's interest; different teachers and scholars are committed to varying degrees; spies are a real danger; and al-Ṣūlī and his protector, the chamberlain Naṣr, are the heroes. Within this framework, al-Ṣūlī provides a character assessment for both princes: the children, he says, were 'intelligent, clever, and sensible [. . .]. Al-Rāḍī was the more intelligent of the two, and the more eager to learn.'[35] Of Naṣr he says, elsewhere, that he was 'perspicacious, intelligent, trustworthy, and, despite his stranger's tongue, magnanimous and generous' (*wa-kāna mā ʿalimtu ḥasan al-fahm min ashbāhihi, ṣaḥīḥ al-ʿaql, wāfir al-amāna, wa-in kāna aʿjamī l-lisān, wa-kāna wa-llāhi maʿa dhalika jawwādan karīman*).[36]

Al-Ṣūlī never wavers from his fondness for al-Rāḍī and Naṣr, recording the financial benefits he received from them, and justifying their occasional shortcomings with contingent reasons. Of al-Rāḍī, he says that his coldness towards the end of his life was due to illness.[37] When Naṣr tried to save al-Ḥallāj from being executed in 309/922, al-Ṣūlī says that he was taken in by the clever charlatan.[38] On the contrary, al-Ṣūlī is ruthless with people who, in his opinion, have wronged him. Al-Rāḍī's successor, al-Muttaqī, who dismisses all his *julasāʾ*, has, according to al-Ṣūlī, no understanding of his role:

> Some eunuchs had told us: 'this one is not like al-Rāḍī; he does not want *julasāʾ*.' 'If it is like you say,' I replied, 'it is as bad for us as it is for you and, what's worse, it is bad for the caliph and will bring consequences contrary to what he expects and hopes for.'[39]

Al-Ṣūlī's prediction is inevitably fulfilled a few years later, when al-Muttaqī is deposed. Mercilessly, al-Ṣūlī enumerates the caliph's many mistakes, wondering at how he could think that he had nothing to blame himself for.[40]

In other cases, al-Ṣūlī's assessment seems more detached. Of the *kātib* al-Ḥasan b. Hārūn, who was in charge of the negotiations leading to al-Muttaqī's deposition, he says that, besides his bureaucratic skills, he was fearless, valiant, and a good horseman (*rābiṭ al-ja'sh, qawī al-shujā'a ḥasan al-farūsiyya*). Still, his assessment is not completely neutral, as it is based on an appreciative statement made by al-Rāḍī.[41] At the other end of the spectrum, on the death of Muḥammad b. Īnāl the Interpreter, in 332/944, al-Ṣūlī says that 'in general, he was a coward, a troublemaker, changeable, a miser, short-sighted, and made bad choices'.[42] Here, too, a personal reason may be detected: the Interpreter had been able to acquire al-Ṣūlī's old estate for a pittance, after al-Ṣūlī had lost all possession when the Daylamites ransacked his house in the year 329/941 because it was close to that of the Interpreter.[43]

On the one hand, then, it seems reasonable to agree with Canard that we cannot expect from al-Ṣūlī a totally objective account of events, because his point of view is too personal.[44] On the other, this personal point of view is precisely what organizes al-Ṣūlī's fragmented autobiography into an arc: his story is that of a wronged man who, having survived his benefactors, is treated unfairly by the current powers that be, so that his disappointment and bitterness tinge even the sweetest recollections. Al-Ṣūlī's constant attention to financial matters only reinforces the arc: he mentions occasional retainers and pensions during the caliphate of al-Muqtadir, a regular salary and frequent lavish gifts during the caliphate of al-Rāḍī, and an unending quest for funds in later years. The end of the arc is clear: since the misfortunes that befell him in the year 329/941, he says, he is poor, has no regular income and has nobody to give him gifts or advantages: 'I live on the prices of my notebooks and the proceedings from the sales of a garden of mine which was my life and heaven'.[45]

Person, persona and an arc

In Chapter One, we have seen two distinct aspects to the life of al-Ṣūlī: on the one hand, the persona of a legendary chess-player; on the other, the person of an *adīb*, scholar, and expert on poetry who worked as a courtier and died in Basra in reduced circumstances. The material reviewed in this chapter provides a further element: an arc, putting events in al-Ṣūlī's life into a specific perspective so as to form a story. It is a story with no happy ending: in the latter part of the *Awrāq*, al-Ṣūlī becomes progressively bitter and resentful and, as has been seen above, admits to using his chronicle as a way of venting his disappointment with life and other people. On this basis, Rosenthal's statement at the beginning of this chapter appears completely incorrect: far from having practical objectives, al-Ṣūlī's autobiography is borne out of his awareness of his self-worth.

Within this framework, reading parts of the *Awrāq* as a fragmented autobiography not only makes sense for our understanding of his life, but can also help to interpret the events to which the autobiographical fragments are attached. In particular, the following points deserve exploration:

- Al-Ṣūlī's autobiographical material is mainly conveyed through accounts of interactions with other people, the majority of whom are easily identifiable and are often themselves authors. Investigating al-Ṣūlī's social and intellectual network will shed light on the specific environment to which he belonged.
- Perhaps one of the most distinctive features of the *Awrāq* is the amount of poetry it contains, and especially al-Ṣūlī's own poetry. If we dismiss simple vanity as his only criterion, we must assume that this poetry has one or more functions. Some examples have been seen in this chapter, but it is worth going into more detail.
- However dismissive posterity may be of al-Ṣūlī's historiographical style and of his personal insertions in the *Awrāq*, several of his younger contemporaries praise his work precisely because he is an eyewitness to many events. They also praise him because he organises material in his books in the best of orders. Do autobiographical accounts have a specific function in the organization of historical material?

The next chapter will investigate the first of the above questions.

3

In his own Time

The view deriving from literary texts threatens to transform this lively and changing social environment into a tableau vivant of well-known roles: the absolute prince, the suave boon companion, the scheming courtier, the wise advisor, and the honest jester.[1]

Jeroen Duindam

In the passages from the *Awrāq* discussed in Chapter Two, we encounter individuals in different formal and informal roles, and with various degrees of involvement in the events. Al-Ṣūlī describes his interactions with them (in person, in writing or through intermediaries), mentioning the material aspects of such interactions (money, gifts, jobs), and occasionally providing an explicit opinion on an individual. In the resulting tableau, each character has specific traits but also functions as the representative of a category. On a formal level, several components of the court are introduced: the chamberlain, the harem (*qahramāna*, Queen mother, eunuchs), the young princes and the courtiers. Intellectually, there is a clear distinction between positive role models – the chamberlain, the traditionist, al-Ṣūlī himself and his young wards – and negative ones – the children's other teacher, the harem in its entirety and, implicitly, the caliph. Each category has an intermediary figure – the eunuchs, al-Ṣūlī's fellow *jalīs*, and Ibn Abī l-Sāj. At the core of the cluster is al-Ṣūlī's certainty of what the children's curriculum should be.

This typification of individuals as representatives of a group is far from unusual – indeed, Duindam's comment above lists some of these very characters. However, the implied criticism does not necessarily apply here. One obvious reason is that al-Ṣūlī's account describes a personal experience and is not related through a transmitter or extrapolated from its original context, as may be a case in an *adab* collection, a biographical profile, or a manual.[2] Secondly, and more generally, while the previous chapters have argued the individuality of life writing, there is no question that Arabic sources provide plenty of information on networks, communities, and societal structures in general, not only through biographical collections, but also through the standard practice of attaching a chain of transmitters going back to the original source to any account of a past event.

It is an aspect that modern scholarship has always explored. Indeed, classic monographs of the twentieth century, such as Pellat's on al-Jāḥiẓ,[3] typically devote a section to the intellectual milieu of their subject, relying both on narrative material and on more standardized data such as lists of teachers and students. More recently, new questions have emerged, and the attention has shifted from the individual at the centre of a milieu to the very fabric of such milieu and its intellectual development.[4] Monique Bernards, for instance, has applied the tools of social network analysis to data extracted from biographical collections, reconstructing grammarians' circles of learning on the basis of their lists of teachers and students. Her approach builds on her own and earlier quantitative work discussed in Chapter One, but the investigation goes into different aspects, such as the importance of key individuals for the advancement and dissemination of certain subjects, or the connection and influence between disciplines.[5]

Another type of investigation looks into textual and narrative clues. One example is Shawkat Toorawa's criterion of 'proximity', which he uses to contextualize the life of Ibn Abī Ṭāhir Ṭayfūr (d. 280/893). Drawing on Hilary Kilpatrick's work, he suggests two ways of identifying relations between individuals that are not explicitly stated: firstly, the arrangement of profiles in biographical collections and, secondly, the arrangement of sources within texts. In the simplest of terms, individuals whose profiles are adjacent, or individuals who are quoted as sources in clusters, are likely to have been associates. Toorawa's argument follows an important premise: while twentieth-century scholarship has devoted much attention to individual outliers (such as al-Jāḥiẓ), concentrating on a less exceptional figure is a better means to illustrating a cultural context in more general terms – this being, in the case of Ibn Abī Ṭāhir, the cultural changes brought about by the arrival of paper and the shift from an oral/aural to a writerly mentality.

A third, more diachronic approach centres on lineage. Classical Arabic culture offers plenty of families, often described as dynasties, whose members were prominent in one or more professions across generations. One obvious example is that of the Ṭāhirids, whose literary, political and scholarly importance was investigated by C.E. Bosworth and Mongi Kaabi in the latter half of the twentieth century.[6] More recent research has looked into how certain families are recorded in the sources. Bray's study on the Buhlūl-Tanūkhīs, where she identifies a religious founding myth recurring as a leitmotiv in the portrayal of all family members, is particularly interesting because some of the sources on which it is based are authored by a member of the family, the well-known al-Muḥassin b. ʿAlī al-Tanūkhī (d. 384/994).[7]

In short, classic twentieth-century studies concentrate on outstanding personalities and paint a milieu around them; social network analyses, and quantitative history in general, identify important connections and nodes of communication; studies based on textual analysis reconstruct clusters of individuals in a shared cultural environment. Additionally, broader studies on specific cities, social groups or concepts will often contain a survey of specific cultural milieus.[8]

As it happens, al-Ṣūlī's lifetime is one of the better-investigated periods in Islamic history. It is interesting to students of most disciplines because it combines political and military turmoil with cultural vivacity, as well as an abundance of extant narrative sources. Already in the early twentieth century, essential chronicles and *adab* works were published and translated into other languages. Based on these, Bowen's volume on ʿAlī b. ʿĪsā and, on a larger scale, Massignon's monograph on al-Ḥallāj, offered detailed descriptions and narratives on the Baghdadi social and intellectual environment of the time. Adam Mez's portrayal of the so-called Renaissance of Islam has inspired studies on the intellectual history of the second half of the fourth/tenth century. More recently, studies on court culture and education have appeared. In the words of a respected Islamicist, the third and fourth centuries have been done.[9] This chapter investigates whether al-Ṣūlī can contribute to this already detailed picture, and how.

Whatever their methodology, investigations on cultural milieus draw from a similar mix of materials: anagraphical information from biographical profiles (dates and places of residence, lists of teachers and students, known associates); narrative accounts from biographical profiles, chronicles, or *adab* works, describing interactions between contemporaries; and the names of the individuals who are the sources for said accounts. From what has been seen so far of material *by* al-Ṣūlī and *on* al-Ṣūlī, it is clear that there is enough content to test and cross-check all these approaches. Again, what sets al-Ṣūlī apart is the autobiographical element of the *Awrāq*. So far this has been contrasted with material from his biographical profiles and tested against an abstract concept of autobiography. Here, we shall set it against the background of his scholarly and professional environment.

The classroom

Al-Ṣūlī got angry when the guest
  broke [fast], saying *bismillāh*
Then when the guest got chewing
  from distress he almost collapsed
He said to the guest: 'smell
  the scent of bread
And get my thanks', but the guest
  answered: 'I'd rather have food and your blame!'[10]

These few lines mocking al-Ṣūlī's avarice are found in Yāqūt's biography of the respected scholar Abū Sahl al-Qaṭṭān (d. 349/960–1), as one of the less terrible pieces of his 'dull, silly poems'.[11] The setting of the four lines, obviously a meal hosted by a miserly al-Ṣūlī, highlights one of the places of cultural production and dissemination: the home of a scholar. This is where, at least before the institution of the *madrasa* around the fifth/eleven century, part of a scholar's teaching was carried out.[12] The poem is also interesting as it helps to illustrate the complexity of information contained in biographical collections. While it implies familiarity between author and his addressee, it is the only trace of such familiarity left in the sources: al-Qaṭṭān does not appear in al-Ṣūlī's profile, nor is he cited in what survives of al-Ṣūlī's work. Nevertheless, there are tools to investigate and contextualize a personal connection. Al-Qaṭṭān will be our *fil rouge* in the first part of this chapter, illustrating different ways of recovering links through names in the most straightforward components of a scholar's network: his scholarly pedigree.

The two earliest biographers of al-Ṣūlī, al-Marzubānī and Ibn al-Nadīm, do not provide a list of teachers, but al-Khaṭīb al-Baghdādī lists eleven names under the rubric 'he transmitted from (*ḥaddatha ʿan*)'. Al-Khaṭīb's consistence in providing names of teachers and students, as well as complete *isnād*s, makes him the ideal source for investigating connections through cultural content. His list is as follows:

1 Abū Dāwūd al-Sijistānī (d. 275/889), author of one of the six canonical books of Traditions.[13]
2 Abū l-ʿAbbās Aḥmad b. Yaḥyā Thaʿlab (d. 291/904), leader of the Kufan grammatical school (*madhhab*).
3 Abū l-ʿAbbās Muḥammad b. Yazīd al-Mubarrad (d. 285/898), leader of the Basran grammatical *madhhab*.
4 Abū l-ʿAynāʾ (d. 283/896).
5 Abū l-ʿAbbās al-Kudaymī (d. 286/899).
6 Abū ʿAbdallāh Muḥammad b. Zakaryā b. Dīnār al-Ghallābī, the Baghdadi historian (d. 298/910–11).
7 Abū Ruwayq ʿAbd al-Raḥmān b. Khalaf al-Ḍabbī (d. 279/892).
8 Ibrāhīm b. Fahd al-Sājī.
9 ʿAbbās b. al-Faḍl al-Asfāṭī.
10 Aḥmad b. ʿAbd al-Raḥmān al-Hajarī/Hijrī.
11 Abū l-Muthannā Muʿādh b. al-Muthannā al-ʿAnbarī (d. 288/901).

Al-Khaṭīb's list is the longest; most of the later biographers mention the first four names, or a selection thereof. The rationale is easily recognizable: al-Khaṭīb provides the names of those religious scholars from whom al-Ṣūlī received *ḥadīth* as a young man,[14] adding the most notable of his other teachers. Other biographers, who are more interested in al-Ṣūlī's literary scholarship, concentrate on the latter, only mentioning the most important from amongst the religious scholars, i.e. Abū Dāwūd al-Sijistānī. Indeed, as has been seen in Chapter One, Abū Dāwūd is the source for the one example of *ḥadīth* provided by al-Khaṭīb in al-Ṣūlī's profile. The other prominent teachers are Thaʿlab and al-Mubarrad, the most important grammarians of their generation, and the poet and *adīb* Abū l-ʿAynāʾ. This pedigree confirms that al-Ṣūlī was educated in Basra and Baghdad,[15] but does not say much about his standing as a student, nor about how much he disseminated his masters' teachings to the next generation – in fact, al-Khaṭīb only lists al-Ṣūlī among the students in the profiles of al-Mubarrad and Abū l-ʿAynāʾ, while his name does not appear amongst the important students of the other scholars.[16] The list is also not exhaustive: for instance, al-Khaṭīb's very profile of al-Ṣūlī, as has been seen in Chapter One, contains an episode set in the classroom of Abū Khalīfa al-Jumaḥī (d. 305/917–18), where al-Ṣūlī appears to have a higher role than that of a simple pupil.[17] And, although al-Ṣūlī is not listed amongst Thaʿlab's students in the latter's profile, *within* the profile he relates an episode set in Thaʿlab's classroom.[18]

Elsewhere in *Taʾrīkh Baghdād*, fifteen profiles include al-Ṣūlī amongst those who disseminated the work (*rawā ʿan*/*ḥaddatha ʿan*) of their subject. These are, in rough chronological order:

1. Al-Mughīra b. Aḥmad (d. 278/891–2), *adīb* and historian (*adīb akhbārī*).[19]
2. The poet al-Buḥturī (d. 284/897).[20]
3. The latter's son, Abū l-Ghawth Yaḥyā b. al-Buḥturī.[21]
4. Abū Mālik ʿAwn b. Muḥammad al-Kindī, *adīb*, story-teller and historian (*akhbārī ṣāḥib ḥikāyāt wa-ādāb*).[22]
5. The poet, prince and attempted coup plotter Ibn al-Muʿtazz (d. 296/908).
6. Abū l-Faḍl Maymūn b. Hārūn (d. 297/909–10), an *adīb* and historian (*ṣāḥib akhbār wa-ḥikāyāt wa-ādāb wa-ashʿār*).[23]
7. Abū Ṭālib al-Mufaḍḍal b. Sulma b. ʿĀṣim, a grammarian belonging to the Kufan *madhhab* and closely connected to Thaʿlab.[24]
8. Yaḥyā b. ʿAlī al-Munajjim (d. 300/912 at 58), an *adīb* and poet who served as *nadīm* for several caliphs.[25]
9. ʿUbaydallāh b. ʿAbdallāh b. Ṭāhir (d. 300/913), head of police in Baghdad, patron of scholars, and a poet and *adīb* in his own right.[26]
10. Muḥammad b. Aḥmad Abū ʿAbdallāh al-Qāḍī al-Muqaddamī (d. 301/914).[27]
11. The court poet Ibn Bassām (d. 302/914).[28]
12. Muḥammad b. al-ʿAbbās Abū ʿAbdallāh al-Yazīdī (d. 310/922), a grammarian and *adīb* who, late in life, became tutor to the children of al-Muqtadir.[29]
13. Aḥmad b. Muḥammad Abū l-Ḥasan al-Asadī (d. 307/919).[30]
14. Abū Mālik Ḥarīz b. Aḥmad al-Ayādī, son of the famous muʿtazilite judge Ibn Abī Duʾād (d. 240/854); al-Khaṭīb specifies that he transmitted stories (*ḥikāyāt*) from his father.[31]

Most of the individuals in this group belong to a younger generation than those listed as al-Ṣūlī's teachers: they are his older contemporaries, often students of the same teachers, and are therefore less valuable in an *isnād*, because they would make it unnecessarily long. This, of course, is less important outside religious sciences, and in fact these individuals are almost exclusively poets, grammarians, and historians – in other words, *udabā*ʾ. Moreover, a majority of them is connected with al-Ṣūlī's work environment at court. For instance, we have seen Yaḥyā al-Munajjim in Chapter Two, reciting a poem in front of the newly-installed al-Muqtadir; and al-Yazīdī was a predecessor of al-Ṣūlī as a tutor of al-Rāḍī and his brother.

Toorawa's concept of proximity can be tested against this list. For instance, al-Ṣūlī and Maymūn b. Hārūn – no. 6 above – are the sources for adjacent stories at least in two places in Yāqūt's biographical collection, in the profiles of Aḥmad b. Muḥammad b.Thawāba (d. 273 or 277/886 or 890) and Ibrāhīm b. al-ʿAbbās (al-Ṣūlī's great-uncle, d. 243/857) respectively.[32] Some trace also emerges of the elusive al-Qaṭṭān: the latter is the only other person mentioned as relating material on the authority of Abū l-Ghawth, son of al-Buḥturī. His connection with al-Ṣūlī, then, is through the study of poetry.

In short, if al-Khaṭīb's list of teachers summarizes al-Ṣūlī's early training in the fundamentals, this collection of individuals from whom al-Ṣūlī related miscellaneous material represents his further education and cultural exchanges as a mature scholar with specific interests. Indeed, al-Ṣūlī's connection with Ibn al-Muʿtazz, for instance, is well documented in his extant written production.

Proximity in life and text

A further survey of *Taʾrīkh Baghdād* provides more connections. Firstly, around thirty individuals who are not named in al-Ṣūlī's profile as his teachers, and whose profiles do not mention al-Ṣūlī as a student, are his sources in the transmission of specific items (poetry, a story, a date of death, etc.). In most cases, these are *udabā*ʾ and poets who are part of longer *isnād*s, but the list includes also occasional sources like the caliph al-Rāḍī.[33] Secondly, al-Ṣūlī is the eyewitness for events concerning the following individuals:

1 *Abū Khalīfa al-Jumaḥī*: the episode in his classroom described in Chapter One.
2 *Tha ʿlab*: two episodes set in the grammarian's home:
   a. Al-Ṣūlī describes Thaʿlab's reaction in 275/888 when, on being informed of the death of the Basran grammarian Abū Saʿīd al-Sukkarī, he recited two lines of poetry. The episode is worth recording because it shows the leader of the Kufan *madhhab* mourning a prominent Basran.[34]
   b. A conversation between Thaʿlab, who is angry with his students, and a scholar who tries to placate him.
3 *Al-Mubarrad*: an episode set at the home of Ibn al-Muʿtazz (no. 4 below) and three episodes set in the classroom, when al-Mubarrad, reacting to a specific situation or answering a question, recites some poetry.[35]
4 *Ibn al-Mu ʿtazz*: A conversation between al-Buḥturī and Abū Muḥammad ʿAbdallāh b. al-Ḥusayn al-Quṭrabbulī, in the presence of al-Mubarrad, at a reception hosted by Ibn al-Muʿtazz in the year 276/889–90, where the poetry of Abū Tammām is discussed.
5 *Al-Buḥturī*: besides the conversation at no. 4 above, al-Ṣūlī relates some lines which he heard being recited back to the poet for verification (*quri ʾa ʿalā l-Buḥturī wa-anā asma ʿ*).[36]
6 *Al-Muktafī*: al-Ṣūlī relates a wise utterance he heard from the caliph.[37]
7 *Muḥammad b. Khalaf al-Ḍabbī Wakī ʿ* (d. 306/918), historian and traditionist. Al-Ṣūlī mentions that he checked the validity of an *isnād* with him (*ḥaddathtu bi-hadhā l-ḥadīth Wakī ʿan fa-qāla*).[38]
8 *Al-Rāḍī*: a story set at court, illustrating the caliph's generosity with his *julasā ʾ*.[39]

There are common traits to these stories. Firstly, in seven out of ten al-Ṣūlī does not participate in the events he narrates; secondly, all but the last three contain poetry and direct speech; thirdly, they serve as illustrations of moral or artistic qualities of their protagonists; finally, the setting is either the court or a scholar's home. Thus, if our first two lists document the subjects of al-Ṣūlī's education and his mature scholarly and artistic interests, this third one fills the outline with details and colours, adding context to data. To illustrate this further point, we shall now look into two of the stories summarized above.

The episode listed above as no. 2a is found in the profile of the grammarian, traditionist and Qur'an reader Abū Sa'īd al-Sukkarī (d. 275/888).[40] It is a short profile but it contains most of the basic features we have seen in Chapter One: his full name, a list of teachers and an assessment of his reliability; the disciplines he practiced; the name of two students; a sample of material he transmitted; his date of death, illustrated with the short *khabar* related by al-Ṣūlī. Here we have a further case of textual proximity: Abū Sahl al-Qaṭṭān is one of the two students of al-Sukkarī, and part of the *isnād* in the *ḥadīth* preceding al-Ṣūlī's story. The two scholars, then, are adjacent but not homogenous: while the former is part of an *isnād* and therefore has a direct link with al-Sukkarī, the latter is an eyewitness, but al-Sukkarī is absent in the event he relates.

Elsewhere, we find a different form of textual proximity, through someone else's work: the poet Ibn Harma (d. 186/792). In the *Fihrist*, Ibn al-Nadīm mentions that 'his poetry on its own consists of about two hundred pages, but in al-Sukkarī's edition it fills five hundred. Al-Ṣūlī had also prepared an edition, but it came to nothing.'[41]

The second episode (2b) is in Tha'lab's profile and is part of a cluster illustrating his teaching style.[42] The protagonist is an exasperated Tha'lab:

> I cite Aḥmad b. Muḥammad b. Aḥmad b. Ya'qūb the *kātib*, citing his grandfather Muḥammad b. 'Ubayd Allāh b. Qufrajjul, citing al-Ṣūlī, who said: one day, when we were at his place, Tha'lab was angry. A *ẓāhirī* scholar with dyed hair told him: 'If you knew your reward for bestowing knowledge on people, you would be patient with the annoyance they bring you.' He answered: 'Were it not for that, I would not suffer this torment.' Then he recited a poem ending thus (*ṭawīl*):

> With their [glances like] arrows they make sport with the lover
> who suffers injustice. Their arrows are never blunted
> But their kisses, they are like honey, for they sweeten their mouths
> with toothpicks of cypress wood or the branch of the *arāk* tree
> Only for such women do I ride a lean camel
> and brave the cold winds of the South.[43]

Here is an example of implied physical proximity: al-Ṣūlī is in Tha'lab's classroom at the same time as an unnamed scholar who dyes his hair and belongs to the *ẓāhirī* legal *madhhab*, led by the son of the founder, Ibn Dāwūd al-Iṣfahānī (d. 294/909). Any student of classical grammar will know that only one person answers to this description: Abū ʿAbdallāh Ibrāhīm b. Muḥammad b. ʿArafa, known as Nifṭawayh (d. 323/935).[44] Not much is left of this scholar's apparently vast written work – on grammar, poetry and Qur'anic science – but biographical collections are abundant with details about his life and character, and he is cited as source by a few contemporary authors. Of Nifṭawayh's many quirky traits – his chosen name and his dyed hair, for instance – two are relevant here. First, he is described as a miser like a few other grammarians, such as his master Thaʿlab and his fellow student Ibn al-Anbārī (d. 328/940). The avarice that al-Qaṭṭān imputes to al-Ṣūlī, then, is either a recurrent trait in this circle or a frequent topic for a joke, or maybe both: misers in these profiles have little to do with the unrealistic *bukhalāʾ* described, for example, by al-Jāḥiẓ. On the contrary, their avarice is ordinary, and therefore believable, but hardly entertaining unless it is accompanied by a joke.[45] And indeed, whether al-Ṣūlī deserves al-Qaṭṭān's satire or not, it is undeniable that in the *Awrāq* he constantly refers to wealth, money and income.

The second element of note is that, like his friend Ibn Dāwūd, Nifṭawayh is a *ẓarīf*, and one of the main sources for poetry in the manual of refinement of his contemporary al-Washshāʾ, who also uses many of al-Ṣūlī's teachers as sources. Al-Ṣūlī himself is mentioned only once in the *Muwashshā*, as the source for poetry. Thaʿlab is the source cited just before him, and Nifṭawayh is the one cited immediately after.[46]

As we have seen in Chapter One, *ẓarīf*, when used as a specific category, describes an individual in whom certain features of the *adīb* are particularly strong, independent of his social and economic standing.[47] Al-Ṣūlī is also described as a *ẓarīf* in the *Fihrist*, and so are al-Washshāʾ and Ibn Dāwūd – al-Washshāʾ, like al-Ṣūlī, as a refined *adīb*, Ibn Dāwūd simply as a *ẓarīf*. Out of seven *ẓurafāʾ* in the *Fihrist*, then, three, including al-Ṣūlī, are part of the same circle.[48]

So far, our investigation into arguably arid lists of names and in-jokes in biographical collections returns a rather coherent image of an *adīb* with a standard, comprehensive training in all major subjects, culturally active in circles of *udabāʾ* and grammarians. It is worth noting that all the interactions between al-Ṣūlī and people from whom he received knowledge are set in a classroom or at the home of a scholar or poet, including Ibn al-Muʿtazz, where al-Ṣūlī is a spectator as often as he is a participant. In al-Ṣūlī's works, a few of these individuals make appearances as his sources, but it is in the *Awrāq* that some of them are occasionally the protagonist of stories. In this case, however, the stories have a different setting: the court or the home of a high official. Here we are on uncharted – or less-charted – territory: while it is far from unusual to find first-person accounts of interactions within the court in all types of sources including chronicles, the case of al-Ṣūlī, where such accounts are the author's own, is special because we can observe it in its own intended context.

In Chapter Two, we have seen how an event in al-Ṣūlī's life, which he inserts in the narrative to illustrate the relationship between members of the caliphal household, reveals the inner workings of education at court. In Chapter Five, we shall look at how these insertions shape the larger historical narrative and how they provide important details about a courtier's access to people in authority. Here we shall investigate what al-Ṣūlī reveals about his relationship with his colleagues – *julasā*ʾ, teachers, scholars, often overlapping functions – at court.

The court years

I am what the *amīr* desires,
   one of the treasures that profit bring
Secretary, accountant, preacher, orator,
   advisor most sincere
Poet admirable, lighter
   than feather from under a wing[49]
(Abān al-Lāḥiqī, describing the skills of a courtier)

After the death of al-Rāḍī in 329/940, having obtained permission to leave the service of the new caliph al-Muttaqī, who did not like to entertain, al-Ṣūlī went to Wāsiṭ and settled at the court of Bajkam (d. 329/941), then *amīr al-umarā*ʾ, where he was joined by three former colleagues. Bajkam announced that he would set up a regular salary for all, so that they would not regret the passing of al-Rāḍī. However, al-Ṣūlī was not satisfied: it is not right, he said to the *amīr*, that only four out of the seven *julasā*ʾ be paid, as they are all part of the same group. Bajkam then ordered that all *julasā*ʾ, including the three who were still in Baghdad and out of a job, receive a payment.[50]

The seven *julasā*ʾ had been together for a long time: besides serving at al-Rāḍī's table since the beginning of his caliphate, most of them had worked under his father al-Muqtadir, as companions or tutors, and some even for earlier caliphs.[51] All of them appear in the *Awrāq*, and al-Ṣūlī provides details not only on the formal organization of their work at court, but also on their internal power dynamics. It is apparent that, notwithstanding al-Ṣūlī's professed solidarity when negotiating with Bajkam, the working environment around the caliph was at times far from friendly. In particular, two teams, who took turns in sitting with the caliph on alternate days, were clearly in fierce competition. The first team consisted of al-Rāḍī's uncle Isḥāq b. al-Muʿtamid, who had also been *jalīs* to his father al-Muqtadir; Abū Jaʿfar Muḥammad b. ʿAbdallāh b. Ḥamdūn; and al-Ṣūlī himself. The second group consisted of the brothers Abū l-Qāsim Yūsuf and Abū l-Ḥasan Aḥmad (d. 327/939), sons of Yaḥyā al-Munajjim, and their cousin Abū l-Ḥasan ʿAlī b. Hārūn (d. 352/963). All these individuals had ancestors connected to the Abbasid court: Isḥāq was an Abbasid prince; Ibn Ḥamdūn's family had served the caliphs since the time of Hārūn al-Rashīd; and Abū Manṣūr al-Munajjim had been court astrologer for the second Abbasid caliph al- Manṣūr.[52]

The way these relationships are described is interesting both from a stylistic point of view – they often revolve around poetry – and for its contents, because it unveils an intricate network of intellectual, financial and artistic elements to this hostility which cannot be simplified into a series of personal squabbles and therefore should not be dismissed as inane courtly gossip but must be assumed to have a specific function in the historical narrative.[53]

Throughout the chronicle of al-Rāḍī's caliphate, al-Ṣūlī describes episodes where the Munajjim team antagonizes him and his colleagues, trying to turn the caliph against them, or simply acting recklessly for financial gain. One instance of the latter is found in the year 327/939, when Aḥmad b. Yaḥyā seeks to disrupt the regular shifts at the caliph's table, telling al-Rāḍī that he would like to enjoy his company every day. Al-Ṣūlī sees this attempt for what it is, i.e. a desire to enjoy the caliphal gifts that came with every drinking session; all the same, he cannot afford to stay home himself, as he does not want to leave the Munajjim alone with the caliph for too long. Everybody knows that there will be a physical toll to this constant feasting, and to be sure, all the *julasāʾ* fall ill, and Aḥmad dies shortly afterwards.[54] Not, however, before causing damage to al-Ṣūlī's reputation: in this last period of the caliph's life, he tells us, al-Rāḍī would treat him and his colleagues harshly, although he would defend him, when absent, from the basest of the Munajjim's accusations, and would not consent to block al-Ṣūlī's access to him altogether.[55]

There may seem to be very little in these stories beside an insight in al-Rāḍī's weaker character traits and al-Ṣūlī's resentment towards these rivals for the caliph's attention – a resentment which must have continued later in life when, after the death of Bajkam, ʿAlī b. Hārūn al-Munajjim found employment with Ibn Rāʾiq, the new *amīr al-umarāʾ*, while al-Ṣūlī was merely promised a salary which he never got.[56] While this is precious evidence for modern scholars to reconstruct details of the economic history of the period, what is the place of such trivial matters in the internal economy of the text? Is this just the overflowing emotion of a bitter courtier with delusions of grandeur? While this remains a possibility, a story set in earlier times, at the beginning of al-Rāḍī's reign, complicates matters.

The earlier story is set, again, at one of al-Rāḍī's receptions, where al-Ṣūlī and Aḥmad b. Yaḥyā al-Munajjim disagree on the authorship of some poetry. To al-Rāḍī's amusement, al-Ṣūlī claims to have learned these lines, including their attribution, from Aḥmad's own father Yaḥyā al-Munajjim. Having effectively silenced Aḥmad, al-Ṣūlī goes on to recite the lines in questions but changes the last part, which al-Rāḍī may find offensive. When Aḥmad protests that his father had taught him the lines differently, al-Rāḍī retorts: 'I also know that your father taught you his own poetry: "if you are Quraysh, desist"!' The context of this line is not mentioned, but it is enough to put an end to the discussion: al-Ṣūlī explains that the caliph got very angry when he mentioned these lines but was gratified that Ibn al-Muʿtazz had refuted them. Some of this poetry is very good, he adds, but he will not quote it here because it contains slander.[57]

The very fact that al-Ṣūlī does not need to explain the significance of this verse suggests that he assumes it to be evident to the contemporary reader. In fact, not much context is needed to detect a political jab: al-Rāḍī is angered by the memory of a conflict between Yaḥyā al-Munajjim, Aḥmad's father, and Ibn al-Muʿtazz; the reference to the Quraysh suggests that a topic connected to the Abbasid family; al-Rāḍī takes the side of Ibn al-Muʿtazz; and al-Ṣūlī remarks that he is heartened by this sign of appreciation on the part of the caliph, considering that al-Rāḍī's own father al-Muqtadir was almost dethroned by Ibn al-Muʿtazz, who died in the attempt.[58] It is in these events, then, taking place thirty years earlier, that we shall find the missing context, and al-Ṣūlī is again our eyewitness and direct source.

Hostility in poetry and politics

Al-Ṣūlī's personal connections with both the the Ḥamdūn and the Munajjim family went back at least one generation: in his account of the caliphate of al-Muqtadir, he describes interactions with both ʿAbū Muḥammad Abdallāh (d. 309/922), father of Ibn Ḥamdūn, and Abū Aḥmad Yaḥyā (d. 300/912), father of Yūsuf and Aḥmad al-Munajjim. Indeed, he is even formally listed amongst the people who disseminated Yaḥyā's work (he is n. 8 above).

Despite deserving a profile in the *Taʾrīkh Baghdād*, Yaḥyā was only a third-generation Muslim, his homonymous grandfather having converted from Zoroastrianism at the encouragement of the caliph al-Maʾmūn. In fact, al-Khaṭīb only describes Yaḥyā as a poet and *adīb*, highly praised by al-Marzubānī, but does not mention religious scholarship. This is not surprising: not only were Yaḥyā's roots Zoroastrian; his entry point into Islam had been Muʿtazilism, the theological current promoted by al-Maʾmūn but deprecated by the time al-Khaṭīb was writing. Yaḥyā makes various appearances in what is left of the *Awrāq*; in particular, he cuts a controversial figure in the chronicles of the caliphate of al-Muqtadir, where, as has been seen in Chapter Two, he is present from the very beginning, at the celebration on al-Muqtadir's accession in 295/908, reciting a poem and receiving a retainer.[59] Only four months later, he plays a supporting but substantial role in al-Ṣūlī's account of the attempted deposition of al-Muqtadir.

In Rabīʿ I, 296/December, 908, a group of conspirators had al-Muqtadir's vizier al-ʿAbbās b. al-Ḥasan ambushed and murdered as he rode to his garden

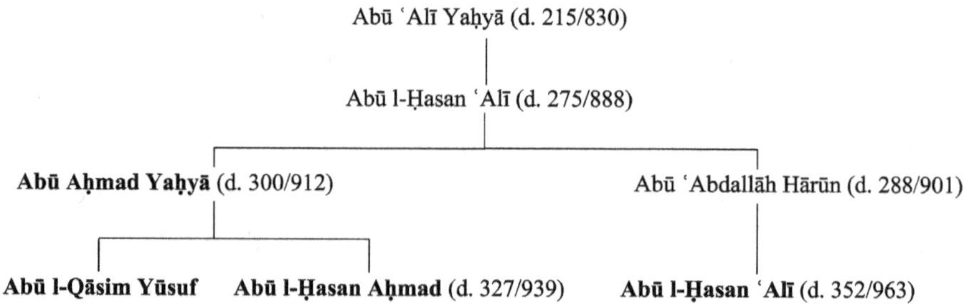

Figure 1: the Banū Munajjim. The individuals who had personal contacts with al-Ṣūlī are in bold.

outside the city. They went on to swear allegiance to Ibn al-Muʿtazz, but the coup was short lived: al-Muqtadir's supporters quickly regained control, and all conspirators were killed or imprisoned.[60] While other historians relate these events in chronological order, al-Ṣūlī, after describing the manner of al-ʿAbbās's death, announces that, before relating the affair of Ibn al-Muʿtazz, he will elaborate on the reasons for al-ʿAbbās's death and relate poetry composed about him. Yaḥyā b. ʿAlī al-Munajjim, who had been part of the retinue riding with the vizier, is the author of three of these pieces, one of which is accompanied by a short narrative:

> One day, [says al-Ṣūlī] after al-ʿAbbās b. al-Ḥasan had been killed, the judge al-Ḥasan b. Ismāʿīl and I visited ʿAbdallāh b. Ḥamdūn. 'I've heard,' he told us, 'that Yaḥyā b. ʿAlī al-Munajjim composed, on al-ʿAbbās's being killed while riding:
>
> Had I been carrying my sword when I was with you
> the vizier would have been safe, and his enemies would have feared me
>
> I swear, if he'd had his sword on him, God would have destroyed everyone else, and nobody would have been safe!'[61]

This first episode divides the fathers along the same lines as the sons: ʿAbdallāh b. Ḥamdūn, friend of al-Ṣūlī, on one side, and Yaḥyā b. al-Munajjim on the other, being derided for his pretend-heroics.

The next episode is set during the brief interlude in which Ibn al-Muʿtazz was recognized as caliph. Immediately after his appointment, Ibn al-Muʿtazz set to organizing a court retinue (*man yujālisunī*). In a scene which is related to al-Ṣūlī, Yaḥyā, accompanied by two of his sons, entered his presence, carrying a sword, and saluted Ibn al-Muʿtazz as Commander of the Faithful. Ibn al-Muʿtazz, annoyed, muttered audibly that this dog had mocked the Prophet and boasted of his foreign people against Ibn al-Muʿtazz's own. Yaḥyā was hastily removed from his presence before the new caliph could think of taking more active measures. Al-Ṣūlī was later present when Ibn al-Muʿtazz continued to rail against Yaḥyā.[62] At this point he drops the story but promises to expand on it later. Indeed, at the end of the account of the coup, the chronological account of events is interrupted, first by a collection of poetry on Ibn al-Muʿtazz's death. One piece by Yaḥyā is accompanied by a comment uttered by ʿUbaydallāh b. ʿAbdallāh b. Ṭāhir (d. 300/913), the aristocratic poet and *adīb*, who says that, rather than an elegy, it is a worse attack than an invective (*hijā ʾ*).[63]

Before returning to the events of the year, as promised, al-Ṣūlī inserts a long flashback (thirteen pages in the published edition) to explain the conflict between Yaḥyā and Ibn al-Muʿtazz. It is a fascinating story on the value of lineage and on the legitimacy of power, told through exchanges of poetry and scholarly discussions, many of which in the presence, or even with the involvement of al-Ṣūlī. One day, he says, Ibn al-Muʿtazz misspelled the name of one of the Arab's pre-Islamic battles because of a copyist's mistake in a book he was reading. Having heard this mistake, Yaḥyā, who used to frequent his receptions, proceeded to gossip about it and then write a *risāla* defending Ibn al-Muʿtazz, to ingratiate himself. Ibn al-Muʿtazz, seeing through this ruse, mistrusted Yaḥyā from then on.

The next part of the story sees al-Ṣūlī himself as the unwitting key player. He explains that he would always have a notebook (*daftar*) on him, where he would write down poetry which he heard recited at receptions and considered beautiful. At times, Ibn al-Muʿtazz would take the notebook and read from it.[64] Thus, one day, he happened upon a poem which al-Ṣūlī had heard recited at one of Yaḥyā al-Munajjim's receptions. There was no attribution, but it did not take long for Ibn al-Muʿtazz to guess that the author had been Yaḥyā himself, despite the latter's attempt to ascribe it to one of the Banū Ṭāhir. The *qaṣīda*, which al-Ṣūlī reports in full, is an invective on the Prophet's family and descendants; it boasts the superiority of the children of Sarah over those of her slave Hagar, and it contains the line we have seen mentioned by al-Rāḍī above: if, as Quraysh, you boast that precedence should be given to lineage in religion, then precedence should go to the foreigners. Angered, Ibn al-Muʿtazz had a rebuttal circulated on the next day, and things quietened down, at least outwardly, for a time. However, Yaḥyā was not finished: he composed more invectives, which he only circulated amongst a few people. Still, it was leaked to Ibn al-Muʿtazz. Yaḥyā suspected al-Ṣūlī and his colleagues at first, but then realized that the spy had been Muḥammad b. Dāwūd b. al-Jarrāḥ (d. 296/908), the author of the *Kitāb al-Waraqa*. Yaḥyā had trusted Ibn al-Jarrāḥ because he, too, had non-Arab, non-Muslim origins. On the contrary, Ibn al-Jarrāḥ had been gathering damning evidence to gain the trust of Ibn al-Muʿtazz, in the hope of becoming his vizier once the coup had succeeded. As al-Ṣūlī's reader well knows, this is indeed what happened: Ibn al-Jarrāḥ became Ibn al-Muʿtazz's vizier and suffered his master's fate shortly afterwards.[65]

The final section of this long excursus focuses on the artistic value of Yaḥyā's poetry. Ibn al-Muʿtazz would discuss its lack of originality, and al-Ṣūlī remarks that he does not know of any person of knowledge who had not attacked Yaḥyā for his first *qaṣīda*. He adds: 'I have strayed from what I wanted to say, but now I will mention some of [these attacks on Yaḥyā], in the same meter and rhyme. This will conclude the affair of Ibn al-Muʿtazz. I shall then, God willing, complete the account of the events [of the year] (*al-akhbār wa-l-ḥawādith*).'[66]

In all, the account of this diatribe between Ibn al-Muʿtazz, an aristocratic poet and literary scholar who briefly played a political role, and an arguably unimportant *jalīs* and scholar, takes up one third of the chronicle of the year. Tempting as it may be, it would be dangerous to read – or altogether skip – these pages as a meaningless distraction from hard historical data: for one thing, in general, we owe it to any author to read their work as the product of conscious choices, independently of inferred personality traits. Secondly, this text in particular provides both direct and indirect evidence of al-Ṣūlī's historiographical method, the macrostructure of the *Awrāq*, the court's and court-adjacent cultural milieu, and the Abbasid family's self-image.[67]

In Chapter Two, we have seen how al-Ṣūlī uses episodes from his own life as flashbacks illustrating and expanding on a statement – for example, the flashback on al-Rāḍī's education explains the statement on the caliph's hostility towards his grandmother. In the present case, the flashback explains the origin of Ibn al-Muʿtazz's dislike of Yaḥyā. Moreover, it has further uses in the macro-structure of the *Awrāq*, which become clear if, as readers, we start from al-Rāḍī's exchange with Aḥmad b. Yaḥyā and move backwards: taken on its own, al-Rāḍī's rebuke of Aḥmad is but an allusion: Aḥmad's father Yaḥyā composed poetry whose sole mention is sufficient to make Aḥmad ashamed, and al-Rāḍī so angry that he takes the side of his father's usurper Ibn al-Muʿtazz. A contemporary reader with knowledge of previous sections of the *Awrāq* may remember a passage devoted to these two people, but even if she does not, she will know to look into the account of the short-lived caliphate of Ibn al-Muʿtazz, which is likely to provide poetry by and on him. Here, she will indeed find the offending verse in its context and understand its full meaning in the later passage. The reader may also wonder whether this mutual dislike had deeper roots in the past. To be sure, in earlier parts of the *Awrāq* she will learn that Yaḥyā's father ʿAlī had been a *jalīs* and active supporter of the caliph al-Mustaʿīn (r. 248–52/862–6), who had been ousted and eventually murdered by al-Muʿtazz (r. 252–5/866–9).[68] Seen from this perspective, poetry and court life are not distractions; rather, they are connecting tissue keeping the *Awrāq* together and helping its reader to navigate it. Al-Ṣūlī himself marks this part of the text – here and in other places, as has been seen in Chapter Two – as different from a standard chronicle (*al-akhbār wa-l-ḥawādith*). We may perhaps compare it with sections on 'further reading' in a modern manual, and of course, if a reader wanted to go deeper into the life and scholarship of Ibn al-Muʿtazz, she would find a long profile and a virtually complete *dīwān* in the section of the *Awrāq* devoted to the members of the Abbasid family who were poets.[69]

Such a comparison may also help reading the political content conveyed through poetry and scholarly discussion, which in the *Awrāq* clearly function as legitimate channels for sectarian and ethnic conflict. In particular, we see here that, with al-Rāḍī, loyalty to lineage prevails on political resentment, while Ibn al-Jarrāḥ puts his political advantage above ethnic belonging.[70] It also seems significant that both the content and the container have an influence: Yaḥyā's *qaṣīda* is not only objectionable because of its meaning, but also because it is bad poetry. Finally, both caliphs involved in these stories are shown to be aware of their family history. This is not unusual: the *Awrāq* reports many conversations between a caliph and a scholar, where the former asks for clarification about an event involving an ancestor, or the latter provides advice on the basis of the actions of a predecessor; but there are also episodes where the caliph himself relates stories passed down in the family.[71]

Settings

So far, we have seen al-Ṣūlī and his colleagues interact before the caliph, at the home of a scholar superior in social standing (such as Ibn al-Muʿtazz and ʿUbaydallāh b. ʿAbdallāh b. Ṭāhir), and at each other's homes. The *Awrāq* also describes interactions in the presence of viziers or other high-level bureaucrats, and a few cases in which two or more *julasāʾ* are waiting to be allowed in a room.[72] Finally, some episodes described in Chapter Two take place in the Princes' quarters of the caliphal Palace. I have used 'reception' as a blanket term to indicate most of these settings.

In his 2010 monograph,[73] Samer Ali uses 'literary salon' to translate *mujālasa*, a gathering in a private home which is both social and literary. Ali contrasts it with *majlis*, which he describes as an assembly at the home of a patron or superior where a clear hierarchy is defined; a *mujālasa*, on the other hand, is usually amongst peers, and it centres around *adab*, and especially poetry, in Arabic. In the *Awrāq*, al-Ṣūlī mostly uses generic language, such as 'I was/arrived at so-and-so's (*kuntu/ḥaḍartu ʿinda/dakhaltu ilā*), and other people were present,' and in fact employs the third form of the root *jls* to describe his service as *jalīs*, giving *mujālasa* the opposite meaning than the one proposed by Ali. Saving this discrepancy in terminology, the settings described by Ali are recognizable, both in their practice and in their content.

An example of the former is what Ali calls the 'Bacchic behaviour' at receptions. In fact, al-Ṣūlī explains that al-Rāḍī had given up the practice of drinking *nabīdh*, formally vowing never to drink again. For the first two years of his caliphate he stuck to his resolution, but eventually he succumbed to the entreaties of his *julasāʾ*, whose drinking was an integral part of receptions. Having written down the text of his vow, he showed it to the jurists, who gave him permission to reverse it. In another episode, al-Ṣūlī relates that al-Rāḍī put a stop to drinking competitions between Ibn Ḥamdūn and Aḥmad al-Munajjim.[74]

As for the cultural content of receptions, Ali's argument helps to give more context to some elements of the stories discussed above, by conceptualizing the performative aspect of poetry and of *adab* in general. For instance, al-Ṣūlī's changing the line of a *qaṣīda* so that it is does not sound offensive to al-Rāḍī is a standard performative practice – adjusting texts to fulfil the expectation of different audiences – which al-Rāḍī understands as such. Moreover, Ali argues that the private, informal setting of *mujālasāt* were 'a pragmatic testing ground for the literary response, value, and the reproduction of value across generations'.[75] In the stories discussed above, Yaḥyā's receptions fulfil precisely this function, offering different levels of circulation and even providing proof of someone's loyalty or betrayal.

A final noteworthy detail is the crucial role played by al-Ṣūlī's trusted notebook (*daftar*) as one of the means of circulation for the controversial *qaṣīda*. This use of notebooks as private written records, which Gregor Schoeler describes as *hypomnēmata*, is well known especially for the field of religious sciences.[76] In this case, however, al-Ṣūlī uses his *daftar*, rather than to record a formal teaching session, to take down the (*impromptu*?) creations of fellow poets. As has been seen in Chapter One, al-Ṣūlī's reliance on written material seems to have been worthy of attention for his time – indeed, elsewhere in the *Awrāq*, al-Ṣūlī makes it clear that his notebooks are amongst his most prized possessions, so much so that he lists them amongst the goods that were plundered when his home was burgled in 329/941.[77] Later in life, these notebooks became his principal source of income, as shall be seen in the next section.

The legacy of notebooks

> I have been poor since [that burglary]. I have no income, no connection with anybody who could give me gifts or advantages. I live on the prices of my notebooks and the proceedings from the sale of a garden which was my life and heaven.[78]

As has been seen in Chapter One, al-Ṣūlī spent his last days in Basra, where he had retreated because of his financial problems. Here, he was able to exploit the cultural currency accumulated throughout his life to earn an apparently modest living. Apart from the above remark, there is little in al-Ṣūlī's voice that refers to this last period of his life: the *Awrāq* as we have it ends with the deposition of al-Muttaqī in Ṣafar 333/October 944, with al-Ṣūlī still trying to regain his footing at court – indeed, he is last seen boarding a *ṭayyār* boat together with the then vizier Ibn Shirzād.[79] The only clear traces of al-Ṣūlī in Basra are recorded by one of his younger students, al-Muḥassin b. ʿAlī al-Tanūkhī (d. 384/994) who, in *al-Faraj baʿda l-shidda*, devotes one long story to his personal involvement with al-Ṣūlī's heirs.[80] Here, al-Tanūkhī specifies that al-Ṣūlī died in Ramaḍān 335/March 947. His permanence in Basra, then, cannot have lasted much longer than two years. With the material we do have, it is possible to reconstruct at least part of the setting, the operative details, and the network of the last six years of al-Ṣūlī's life, from the death of al-Rāḍī to his own.

There are two noteworthy accounts in the *Awrāq* on this topic. The first is set, shortly before the burglary, in Wāsiṭ, where al-Ṣūlī had repaired after leaving the court of al-Muttaqī. Besides employing him as a *nadīm*, he says, the *amīr* Bajkam, at the request of the residents, had asked him to give public lectures (*al-julūs lahum*) on Fridays. Al-Ṣūlī, who had never taught in the Great Mosque at Baghdad, replied that he had already set up two weekly sessions (*qad jaʿaltu lahum majlisayn*) at a mosque next to his house, but Bajkam insisted that he teach in the congregational Mosque.[81]

This episode adds a new cultural setting to those we have seen so far: the public teaching space. It appears from al-Ṣūlī's words that this is an unfamiliar situation for him, and that he is asked to teach because of his scholarly reputation. This latter point is implied in the second account of note, set during al-Ṣūlī's second stay in Wāsiṭ a few months after the death of Bajkam. Al-Ṣūlī was now trying to gain favour with the three Barīdī brothers, who were then at the height of their power.[82] On one occasion, Abū Yūsuf Yaʿqūb (d. 332/943), one of the younger brothers, remarks: 'the people of Basra have asked me to send you to them; they say that all of their sciences are united in you'. However, the elder al-Barīdī, the then vizier Abū ʿAbdallāh Aḥmad (d. 332/944), was hostile to al-Ṣūlī. He would have put a stop to his teaching sessions in the mosque, which he must have reprised on his return, had these not been so well frequented. Besides, al-Ṣūlī adds, it would have been unseemly to forbid the teaching of prophetic Traditions.[83] He then relates a few conversations with the vizier, where the latter interrogates him on *ḥadīth* and pre Islamic history, trying to contradict him and catch him out. On one of these occasions, he demands to see written proof of al-Ṣūlī's claim. Al-Ṣūlī replies that he has no source with him (*mā maʿī aṣl*) but asks the traditionists who frequent his lectures (*man yajiʾunī*) to lend him two specific *ḥadīth* collections (*musnad*). The problem of written sources returns shortly afterwards, when Abū Yūsuf invites al-Ṣūlī to accompany him to Basra. Al-Ṣūlī protests that he must first go to Baghdad because he does not have any sources for *ḥadīth* or any other science (*lā aṣl maʿī min uṣūl al-ḥadīth wa-lā ghayrihi*).

As has been seen in Chapter One, al-Ṣūlī's afterlife has merged descriptions of his library with a short poem mocking his reliance on books. On the contrary, the above episode highlights the importance of the written word not only as aide-mémoire, but as accepted proof that a statement is true.[84]

It is then worth re-examining this description, looking beyond its narrative context, and investigating its sources and their place in al-Ṣūlī's cultural network.

Looking things up

The earliest – and most detailed – description of al-Ṣūlī's library is found in the *Taʾrīkh Baghdād*:

> Al-Azharī says, citing Abū Bakr b. Shādhān: I saw that al-Ṣūlī had a house full of books which he had arranged in rows. Their covers had different colours, one for each row: one row was red, another green, another yellow, etc. [al-Ṣūlī] would say – [Ibn Shādhān] continues – 'All of these books have been checked and corrected by a teacher.'[85]

In this version, the account does not include poetry. The invective piece by al-ʿUqaylī does follow this one but, as has been seen in Chapter One, it is introduced by a separate, independent *isnād*. On its own, then, Ibn Shādhān's description is a neutral observation, divested of its original context and given a new one by al-Khaṭīb. Still, al-Khaṭīb does provide the tools to reconstruct this original context.

Besides being the source for this *khabar*, Ibn Shādhān (d. 383/993) appears at the top of al-Ṣūlī's profile, as one of the people who disseminated his scholarship (*rawā ʿanhu*). The list consists of eight names, only three of which are picked up in later biographies of al-Ṣūlī: al-Marzubānī, who, we have seen, is al-Ṣūlī's earliest biographer and mainly interested in his poetic expertise; Abū l-Ḥasan al-Dāraquṭnī (d. 385/995), one of al-Khaṭīb's main authorities on the reliability of traditionists; and Abū ʿUmar b. Ḥayawayh (d. 382/992).[86] It is in this third name that we find another connection.

Ibn Shādhān's description of al-Ṣūlī's library reaches al-Khaṭīb through Abū l-Qāsim al-Azharī (d. 435/1043), a source he occasionally uses to cite al-Dāraquṭnī and others.[87] Al-Azharī is also al-Khaṭīb's main source for the biographies of Ibn Ḥayawayh and Ibn Shādhān, and the information he provides is consistent in topic, as it concerns the relation between scholars and the written word. Ibn Ḥayawayh, says al-Azharī, had collected many Traditions but was imprecise: sometimes, when he wanted to look up a specific Tradition but did not have his own book at hand (*wa-lā yaqrubu aṣluhu minhu*), he would read from the book of a contemporary he trusted, although he had not been officially authorized to teach it (*wa-in lam yakun fīhi samāʿuhu*).[88] Nevertheless, concludes al-Azharī somewhat inconsistently, he was a reliable traditionist (*thiqa*).[89] In Ibn Shādhān's profile, al-Azharī provides a direct comparison: Ibn Shādhān's reliability was grounded in his memory, while Ibn Ḥawyawayh, whose reliability was grounded in his many books, was imprecise (*kāna Ibn Shādhān thiqa thabatan ḥujja wa-kāna Ibn Ḥayawayh thiqa kathīr al-kutub wa-fīhi tasāmuḥ*).[90]

Neither Ibn Shādhān's short profile in *Taʾrīkh Baghdād* nor Ibn Ḥayawayh's, which is equally short, mention al-Ṣūlī. However, they have a further connection in common: in both profiles, one of al-Khaṭīb's sources is the judge Abū l-Qāsim ʿAlī b. Abī ʿAlī (d. 447/1055), son of the more famous al-Tanūkhī. In Ibn Ḥayawayh's case, he simply confirms the date of death, whereas for Ibn Shādhān he relates another episode connected with the dissemination of Traditions: he was once asked to pass on *ḥadīth* from a certain traditionist but said that he had never studied with him. Having afterwards found a *samāʿ* certification from this scholar, he still refused to teach the material. This may have been because the scholar in question had a dubious reputation, or because Ibn Shādhān would not transmit *ḥadīth* that he did not remember by heart.[91]

The description of al-Ṣūlī's library has now got its original context: a discussion of the ways in which religious scholarship is taught, learned and disseminated. The discussion is applied to three individuals who were part of the same milieu, where al-Ṣūlī was the senior scholar. Taken together, al-Azharī's remarks do not seem to censor al-Ṣūlī's reliance on books – indeed, the neat arrangement of shelves is a clear asset. In turn, Ibn Ḥayawayh's shortcoming is not his reliance on books but his carelessness in using them. Indeed, al-Ṣūlī himself is very critical of Ibn Abī Ṭāhir Ṭayfūr, whose authority he does not trust because he is a *ḥāṭib layl*, somebody who mixes reliable and unreliable material as if he were gathering wood in the dark. He mentions attending two or three lectures by Ibn Abī Ṭāhir but giving up after realizing he was a *ṣaḥafī*, someone who relayed on books exclusively without the aid of a teacher.[92] Ibn Shādhān and Ibn Ḥayawayh, then, take different lessons from their older contemporary: the former uses books correctly, the latter does not.

As for the younger al-Tanūkhī, his connection with Ibn Ḥayawayh and Ibn Shādhān reinforces the idea of a network: ʿAlī b. Abī ʿAlī, a friend of al-Khaṭīb, passes on to him information about his own family as well as its milieu, of which al-Ṣūlī, Ibn Shādhān and Ibn Ḥayawayh are a part.[93]

A final element shows Ibn Ḥayawayh and Ibn Shādhān as part of a network: they are, together with Ibn Shādhān's more famous son al-Ḥasan (d. 426/1034), amongst the main sources for al-Sarrāj's (d. 500/1106) *Maṣāriʿ al-ʿushshāq*, a collection of unhappy stories of chaste love which is related, thematically and philosophically, to the works of al-Washshāʾ and Ibn Dāwūd.[94] In particular, Vadet notes that al-Sarrāj seems to prefer to source his material through Ibn Ḥayawayh's *isnād* rather than citing a book, although he dismisses its value: 'les historiettes de ce dernier devaient plutôt servir à leur entretien quotidien ou à leur *mağlis* familier, celui où il était question de *muḏākara* et non pas de *samāʿ*'.[95] Ibn Ḥayawayh's imprecision is confirmed.

Writing things down

So far, we have investigated al-Ṣūlī's network through two types of works: biographical collections, where we have looked at lists of teachers and students, *isnād*s and individual *akhbār*; and al-Ṣūlī's own work, where we have seen the recurrence of themes, poetry and family ties. The last piece in the puzzle is different, in organization and scope if not in content: al-Tanūkhī's *al-Faraj baʿda l-shidda* and *Nishwār al-muḥāḍara* are collections of thematically arranged stories, partly compiled from earlier written sources, and partly passed on to the author by contemporary informants. Al-Ṣūlī is one of such informants, and through his appearances in al-Tanūkhī's works we can observe the mechanics of how his knowledge was disseminated.

Al-Tanūkhī, the son of an important judge,[96] spent his childhood in Basra. In several places in the *Faraj*, when citing al-Ṣūlī he specifies that he learned the account in Basra in the year 335/946–7. Al-Ṣūlī died later that year, when al-Tanūkhī was just eight years old – as he remarks on one occasion, 'being a big boy (*mutaraʿriʿ*), I understood and memorized what I heard and retained perfectly everything that happened'.[97] Most of the material he relates on the authority of al-Ṣūlī is part of his historical work (*al-Wuzarāʾ* and *al-Awrāq*) and concerns Abbasid caliphs and viziers. In some cases, al-Ṣūlī relates accounts of earlier informants, in others he is an eyewitness. As may be expected, many of the accounts contain poetry.[98]

As well as their origin, al-Tanūkhī also specifies how he received al-Ṣūlī's accounts: while some of the stories are introduced with a simple *akhbaranī*, or mentioning a book title, several begin with a version of 'the following was read back to al-Ṣūlī for verification in my presence and hearing (*quriʾa ʿalā l-Ṣūlī wa-anā ḥāḍir asmaʿ*)'.[99] Elsewhere, the account has reached him through somebody who has been authorized to disseminate it – i.e. in al-Tanūkhī's wording, he had *ijāza*.[100] Other times, al-Tanūkhī had been examined and authorized to disseminate the account himself (*akhbaranī . . . fī-mā ajāza lī riwāyatahu ʿanhu baʿdamā samiʿtuhu minhu*). In one of these latter cases, he adds that he copied the account from a writing in al-Ṣūlī's own hand.[101] As for the setting of al-Ṣūlī's teaching, in one case al-Tanūkhī says that it was in the great mosque at Basra.[102] Finally, some accounts of *Nishwār* reach al-Tanūkhī through his father, who must have had a close relationship with al-Ṣūlī as he was to be in charge of his estate after his death.[103]

Another element of note is that, in two places, al-Tanūkhī mentions *how* he retained the information passed on by al-Ṣūlī. The first is within an episode which al-Tanūkhī witnessed in Baghdad, involving the singing of some poetry. Al-Tanūkhī adds: 'these lines are by ʿAbd al-Ṣamaḍ b. al-Muʿadhdhal [d. 240/854]; they were dictated by al-Ṣūlī with a solid *isnād* which I have written down in my record of what I am authorized to transmit (*fī amālī al-Ṣūlī ʿanhu bi-isnād thābit fī uṣūl samāʿātī*)'.[104] The second story concerns al-Rāḍī's generosity with al-Ṣūlī; al-Tanūkhī introduces it as follows:

> When I was still a boy, I heard Abū Bakr Muḥammad b. Yaḥyā al-Ṣūlī telling my father a long story (*yaḥkī li-abī ḥikāya ṭawīla*) about al-Rāḍī, containing some of his poetry and a narrative. I had not memorized all of it because I was too small, but my father asked him to dictate it, which he did to a friend of my father's, who was sitting with them. The friend wrote the story down on the back of a volume (*ʿalā ẓahr juzʾ*) which he had been reading back to him for verification, and which contained other poetry and narratives, and is now in my possession. With the aid of that I could refresh my memory.[105]

We now have a clearer idea of what al-Ṣūlī means when he writes that he survives on his notebooks, and what these notebooks contain. Al-Tanūkhī's remarks, paired with his own, illustrate three types of dissemination:

- al-Ṣūlī discusses and teaches prophetic Traditions in various mosques and with (actual or potential) employers. As a general rule, he refers to his *uṣūl*, i.e. *ḥadīth* collections written down by him and certified by his teachers with a *samāʿ*. His students follow the same procedure.
- al-Ṣūlī teaches from his own finalized work, dictating texts which are then read back to him by his students for verification.[106]
- Besides teaching in person, al-Ṣūlī may also lend or rent out his books to be copied, as al-Tanūkhī mentions doing on one occasion.[107]

We may assume similar methods of dissemination in Baghdad, and for other types of material which al-Tanūkhī does not name explicitly, such as al-Ṣūlī's technical works and his editions of poetry, as well as content he may not have put into a book himself but simply passed on.[108]

Networks and texts

The above is not a comprehensive account of al-Ṣūlī's intellectual milieu, some elements of which, such as his relationship with people in power and his family, are investigated elsewhere in this volume. This was, rather, an exploration of different tools and the results these may yield, both specifically and methodologically, which in turn may help to read al-Ṣūlī's surviving work.

A few observations can be drawn from the material we examined, some specific and some general, concerning both the content and the way content is presented in the sources. In general, it is apparent that there is no single milieu: al-Ṣūlī belongs to different but intersecting networks, which in turn move between private homes, mosques, and courts. These networks may or may not arrange themselves around disciplines (poetry, *ḥadīth*, history . . .), and may or may not involve remuneration: al-Ṣūlī receives, or hopes to receive, salaries and gifts from his employers, and is certainly paid for at least some of his teaching, but his exchanges with fellow scholars do not involve monetary transactions. As for the mode of these exchanges, remarks in the *Awrāq* and by al-Tanūkhī highlight the importance of writing material: the *daftar* which always accompanies al-Ṣūlī is more than a simple aide-mémoire; it is the record of live sessions which may then be checked, corrected, and finalized as publications, but it is also an immediate means of indirect communications between individuals – in the case discussed above, through poetry. We have also seen use of the written word as proof of a statement. It is an interesting case when contrasted with the account of an earlier example discussed by Schoeler: an Umayyad *rāwī* who, before presenting himself to the caliph, went through his written notes so as to be prepared for any questions without having to consult a book in public.[109] Finally, the written word, accumulated over long years, is precious currency at the end of al-Ṣūlī's life.[110]

Texts, then, reveal the structure of networks and their communications, but the reverse is also true: networks of individuals and milieus serve as connective tissue, as webbing reinforcing a single text and tying it to another: in the case of biographical collections, it helps to navigate otherwise unwieldy material. In the *Awrāq*, we have seen that the portrayal of relationships between people through poetry can be a tool for cross-referencing a long and complex work. This last point in particular has required the examination of both *isnād*s and narratives, as well as lists of students and teachers, as coherent material.

This last point deserves further exploration: Yāqūt's praises al-Ṣūlī for the arrangement of his library; elsewhere, he is praised for the arrangement of material in his books. Chapters Four and Five will be devoted to understanding these evaluations.

4

In his own Books

[. . .] forcing any of the products of human creativity, such as the historical accounts treated here, into neat categories is at best an inexact science; sometimes, indeed, it is so much so, and so possibly misleading, that one questions whether the undertaking is worth the effort. Inevitably, the categories one chooses turn out to be fuzzy around the edges, or bleed into one another, or viewed in a different light can be seen to be in some ways variants of one another [. . .]. I can only hope that readers will keep in mind the taxonomic indeterminacy of much of life and human endeavor, and be charitable.[1]

Fred M. Donner

The analytical quandaries we have encountered in Chapter One are not unique to biographical collections. Since at least the early twentieth century, scholars have been tackling questions of periodization, disciplinary boundaries and literary genres. Indeed, premodern scholars had similar issues: it has been noted that the poets who identified themselves as 'modernist (the *muhdathūn*) and applied literary categories such as style and themes', did not 'apply literary classifications for earlier schools and periods and maintained the chronological convention'.[2] This is not to say that earlier conventions are mindless: on the contrary, scholars such as al-Ṣūlī display acute awareness of issues of classification and disciplinary hierarchy. We find a personal illustration of this sentiment in a long epistle addressed to a benefactor, where al-Ṣūlī expresses his contempt for some contemporary know-it-alls:

> Nowadays someone studies an area of culture (*fann min funūn al-ādāb*), receives his share of it and reaches a certain level. Then he thinks he will not be called a proper scholar or be thought of as a leader in his field without

> attacking other scholars, belittling the dead, and denigrating the living. He becomes so accustomed to voicing these attacks that they become the most important thing he can perform, and they dominate his gatherings (*akthar mā yamurru fī majlisihi*). He is not satisfied with the little bits of knowledge he has acquired but lays claim to it in its entirety. He keeps at bay anyone who would engage him in debate and expose his limited knowledge by besting him in an argument. He achieves this with the aid of people whom he has trained to pounce on those who ask a question or demand an answer. In this way he claims expertise in areas he has never thought of (*min al-ʿulūm mā lam yakhṭur lahu bi-bāl*) or put his mind to, or whose experts he has never met or was even known to have studied with. He thinks that if he does not know everything, he will not be considered a leading and preeminent scholar.[3]

While this classic cry of *O tempora! O mores!* is enhanced and made more personal when read together with al-Ṣūlī's accounts of his fellow courtiers in the *Awrāq*, its interest is also conceptual: on the one hand, al-Ṣūlī uses *funūn al-ādāb* and *al-ʿulūm* in the same paragraph to describe a single general concept which seems to encompass culture in its entirety; on the other, within this general concept he emphasizes the importance of specializing. In fact, he continues, the two greatest grammarians of the previous generation, Thaʿlab and al-Mubarrad, never pretended to be expert in all subjects, nor were they afraid to admit ignorance in the subjects in which they were not expert.[4] These are:

> [. . .] **Ancient sagas**, the rise and fall of dynasties, the study of who was first to do or say a thing, the stories of kings, or the history of Quraysh and the life of the Envoy his mission and campaigns, and knowledge of his kin and Companions. [. . .] The **history and genealogies** of the Arabs, the battles of the pre-Islamic era, the history of Islam, the lives of the caliphs and their viziers, their governors and supporters, the Dissidents, and movements which had sprung up in their own lifetime. [. . .] **Jurisprudence**. [. . .] ***ḥadīth*** and the knowledge of its scholars, methods, transmitters, and their chronology and lifespans. [. . .] The **science of transmitters'** names and teknonyms. [. . .] The sort of **knowledge that would seem to be the preserve of kings**, to wit, which poems were intoned, which poets they are attributed to, the reasons they were composed, and who put which ones to song, as well as the explanation of the songs' modes, genres, and fingering on the lute

> strings. [. . .] The **things kings need and enquire about** when something catches their eye and they expect to be instantly obliged. I mean, for example, questions about various kinds of drinks and their description, and about the best verses composed on the subject; or on the subject of fruits, fragrant herbs, and the seasons; descriptions of palaces and gardens, artificial lakes and literary gatherings, wine-drinking at morning and evening, clear skies and rain clouds, the sun and the moon, the constellations and rain-bringing stars; descriptions of horses and weaponry; and all the other topics of love poetry and so forth. [. . .] The lore of amusing **stories collected for kings or extemporized on the basis of recent events**. [. . .] The study of the **modern poets** and the pioneers from the beginning of the Abbasid dynasty. [. . .] **Prosody and rhyme, genealogy, official and private correspondence, and rhetoric**, and of how to spot when poets plagiarize and borrow from one another, and how to recognize which poets did it properly and which badly.[5]

A question of categories emerges again. In Chapter One, we have seen how the study of biographical writing has at times been hindered by efforts to circumscribe it as a coherent genre. Here, we encounter the issue on a larger scale: al-Ṣūlī's enumeration of disciplines only partly agrees with, for instance, the organization into chapters of the *Fihrist*. In particular, he seems more interested in the purposes for which a discipline is mastered and practised than in the training it requires. Thus, for example, music figures as the discipline of rulers (*ʿilm al-mulūk ka-annahum maqṣūr ʿalayhi*), whereas different aspects and types of poetry appear under separate headings depending on the context in which they are employed. Subjects which today would be classified as either history or fiction are mixed up and pervade every item of the list.

This fluidity has been hard to process for modern scholars – for historians in particular, whose quest for the elusive kernel of truth has at times been clouded by a pre-conception of how truth ought to be conveyed. Thus, while it is acknowledged that 'until well into Ottoman times at least, there was no historical profession in Islam',[6] as late as the mid-twentieth century, Franz Rosenthal could state that poetry within post-*ayyām* historical narratives 'might as well have been omitted in nearly all instances'.[7] We have already seen illustrations of the contrary in Chapters Two and Three, and to be sure, very few twenty-first-century scholars would subscribe to Rosenthal's claim unreservedly. Of course, literary historians have pointed out the problems with this approach, although much work remains to be carried out.[8] This chapter will look at poetry as an essential tool to navigate al-Ṣūlī's scholarship as it is expressed in his written production, its organization and reception. Furthermore, it will contextualize it as one aspect of al-Ṣūlī's organizing rationale.

Career path

Our survey of al-Ṣūlī's network in Chapter Three has highlighted his connections with the earlier generation of scholars and, consequently, the disciplines in which he was trained. We have also seen narratives linking al-Ṣūlī to some of these older scholars; one of them, Abū l-ʿAynāʾ, despite being almost always listed as one of al-Ṣūlī's teachers, does not figure in any story in his biographical profiles. Elsewhere, however, al-Ṣūlī relates an interesting episode:

> One day I went to see Abū l-ʿAynāʾ. He had lost his sight at the end of his life, but he could hear my pen scratching on my notebook. 'Who's there?' he asked. 'It is your servant and son of your servant, Muḥammad b. Yaḥyā al-Ṣūlī.' 'My boy, rather, or son of my brother! What are you writing?' '[. . .] Some grammar and inflection.' He said: 'Grammar in speech is like salt in food: when there's too much it's disgusting. My boy, if you want to be a star at scholarly gatherings you must learn law and Qur'anic lexicography, but if you wish to be the companion (*munādim*) of caliphs, men of value and belles-lettres, you'll have to take a pinch of poetry and spice up *akhbār*!'[9]

There is another version of this saying: like food is not good without salt, so *adab* is not good without grammar.[10] In al-Ṣūlī's telling, on the contrary, there can be too much of a good thing. The story, found in Ibn al-Jawzī's obituary of Abū l-ʿAynāʾ, is passed on through an Abū ʿAbdallāh Muḥammad b. Ibrāhīm of Basra, who uses the formula *akhbaranā*, i.e. he heard this account as it was related to a group of people. Al-Ṣūlī, then, may well have been telling the story in the same classroom or mosque where al-Tanūkhī sat as a child. If this is the case, the remark, in the mouth of one of al-Ṣūlī's most important teachers, is like an origin story for his *curriculum studiorum* and later career: while he did become a competent traditionist, he did not pursue a specialization in religious sciences but preferred poetry and chronicles, which have been an integral part of his career at court as well as his intellectual milieu. This is consistent with al-Ṣūlī's written production and the way it is classified.

Writing and editing

The most comprehensive bibliography of al-Ṣūlī's work is provided, as may be expected, by Ibn al-Nadīm. In the *Fihrist*, however, al-Ṣūlī's written production is not concentrated in one place but fragmented in three parts: a long list of books and poetry editions in his profile; the mention of a further title later in the same chapter; and several individual remarks in the chapter on poetry. In all, he is attributed, thirty-three separate titles, one of which is in turn divided into ten sections. Within al-Ṣūlī's profile, seventeen distinct books are listed:

> Among his books are: **[1]** *Kitāb al-awrāq fī akhbār al-khulafāʾ wa-l-shuʿarāʾ* (Book of the leaves on the accounts of the caliphs and poets), which he did not complete [description of the ten extant parts]. His other books are: **[2]** *Kitāb al-wuzarāʾ*;[11] **[3]** *Kitāb al-ʿibāda*; **[4]** *Kitāb adab al-kuttāb* (this is its correct title), **[5]** *Kitāb tafḍīl al-sinān*, which he wrote for Abū l-Ḥasan ʿAlī b. al-Furāt; **[6]** *Kitāb al-shubbān*; **[7]** *Kitāb al-anwāʿ* (the types of poetry), which he did not complete;[12] **[8]** *Kitāb suʾāl wa-jawāb Ramaḍān*, addressed to Abū l-Munajjim; **[9]** *Kitāb Ramaḍān*; **[10]** *Kitāb al-shāmil fī ʿilm al-Qurʾān*, which he did not complete; it contains rare forms interesting for the scholars, but this is not the place to discuss it; **[11]** *Kitāb manāqib ʿAlī b. Muḥammad b. al-Furāt*; **[12]** *Akhbār Abī Tammām*; **[13]** *Kitāb akhbār al-Jubbāʾī b. Abī Saʿīd*; **[14]** *Kitāb al-ʿAbbās b. al-Aḥnaf* and a selection of his poetry; **[15]** *Risāla fī l-saʿāda*; **[16]** *Kitāb akhbār Abī ʿAmr b. al-ʿAlāʾ*; **[17]** *Kitāb al-ghurar*, a book of dictations (*amālī*).[13]

Later, in the same chapter of the *Fihrist*, al-Ṣūlī is listed as one of the 'chess players who wrote books on the game of chess'. He is attributed a **[18.1]** *Book on Chess*, first recension (*al-nuskha al-ulā*); and a **[18.2]** *Book on Chess*, second recension.[14]

The majority of these eighteen books has not come down to us,[15] but their titles are enough to understand that al-Ṣūlī's written production fits Abū l-ʿAynāʾ's instructions perfectly: a few of the titles are connected to religious studies (nos. 3, 8, 9, 10) and grammar (e.g. no. 16, which is devoted to an important grammarian, d. 154/770); some are – probably short – treatises or epistles (e.g. nos. 5, 6, 15, 18). The rest concern *akhbār* and poetry, mostly at the same time. Two of the books have an explicit dedication, one to the vizier Ibn al-Furāt (d. 312/924), who is also the object of a book of praise, and another, presumably, to a colleague belonging to the Munajjim family. In fact, we know from internal evidence that there were other dedications. For instance, al-Ṣūlī mentions that, on the accession of al-Muqtadir, the vizier al-ʿAbbās b. al-Ḥasan commissioned him a treatise on youth (no. 6 in the list above), to honour the new caliph's young age. After al-ʿAbbās's death during the attempted coup against al-Muqtadir, al-Ṣūlī finished the book and simply addressed it to the new vizier, Ibn al-Furāt, presumably in the hope of receiving payment.[16] Another piece of internal evidence helps us to establish that title no. 13 does not concern the Muʿtazili theologian Abū Hāshim al-Jubbāʾī (d. 321/933), but the Qarmaṭī leader Abū Saʿīd al-Jannābī (d. 300/913), as al-Ṣūlī refers to this book in his account of the sack of Basra in 311/923.[17] Two titles, nos. 12 and 14, are accounts of the life of Abū Tammām (d. 232/846) and al-ʿAbbās b. al-Aḥnaf (d. 192/807) respectively, equipped with samples of their work. This type of work has been considered by modern scholars closer to biography than to literary criticism and has been aptly translated as 'life and times'. However, they contain important remarks about the poetic production of their subjects.[18]

At the end of the profile, Ibn al-Nadīm devotes a separate list to al-Ṣūlī's activity as an editor: he collected and arranged in alphabetical order [by rhyme] (*ʿalā ḥurūf al-muʿjam*) the *opera omnia* of: **[19]** Ibn al-Rūmī (d. 283/896); **[20]** Abū Tammām; **[21]** al-Buḥturī; **[22]** Abū Nuwās (d. 198/813–200/815); **[23]** al-ʿAbbās b. al-Aḥnaf; **[24]** ʿAlī b. al-Jahm (d. 249/863); **[25]** Ibn Ṭabāṭabā (d. 322/934); **[26]** Ibrāhīm b. al-ʿAbbās al-Ṣūlī, his great-uncle; **[27]** Ibn [Abī] ʿUyayna (d. mid-third/ninth century); and **[28]** Ibn [probably Abū] Shurāʿa (d. after 255/869).[19]

In the chapter on poetry, al-Ṣūlī appears in the profiles of some of these and other poets, often with additional details, as follows:

- **[22]** Abū Nuwās: al-Ṣūlī 'arranged the *dīwān* in alphabetical order and purged it of wrongly attributed poetry (*ʿalā l-ḥurūf wa-asqaṭa l-manḥūl minhu*)'.[20]
- **[29]** Muslim b. al-Walīd (d. 208/823).[21]
- **[30]** Diʿbil (d. 246/860).[22]
- **[31]** Diʿbil's nephew Muḥammad b. ʿAbdallāh b. Razīn (Abū l-Shīṣ, also called Abū Jaʿfar, d. *c.* 200/915).[23]
- [23] al-ʿAbbās b. al-Aḥnaf.[24]

- [20] Abū Tammām: 'his poetry had remained unpublished (*lam yazal shiʿruhu ghayr muʾallaf*) until the time of al-Ṣūlī, who organized it alphabetically'.[25]
- [21] al-Buḥturī: 'his poetry had not been organized alphabetically until the time of al-Ṣūlī'.[26]
- [19] Ibn al-Rūmī. Again, al-Ṣūlī was the first to organize it alphabetically.[27]
- **[32]** Khālid al-Kātib: 'arranged alphabetically' (d. 269/883).[28]
- [26] Ibrāhīm b. al-ʿAbbās al-Ṣūlī.[29]
- **[33]** al-Ṣanawbarī (d. 334/945).[30]

To sum up, al-Ṣūlī is attributed seventeen books and fifteen editions of *dīwāns*. He is also said to have intended to edit the *dīwān* of Ibn Harma (d. late second/eighth century),[31] and to have been falsely attributed the edition of Khubz Aruzzī's poetry (d. *c.* 327/938).[32] No mention is made, in al-Ṣūlī's profile or in the poetry chapter, of a *dīwān* of his own: although his poetry populates both his biographical profiles and his own books, it does not exist as a stand-alone body of work. This is consistent with what has been observed in previous chapters: al-Ṣūlī, who has collected and edited the *dīwān* of so many poets, does not consider himself a poet; his verses exist as an integral part of his writing style – they belong, in the summary above, to the material 'extemporized on the basis of recent events' for the use of persons in authority. In the words of al-Thaʿālibī, his poetry 'belongs to the poetry composed by authors of books'.[33] Interestingly, this reinforces his standing as a poetry scholar rather than diminishing it – as he explains in the introduction to the *dīwān* of Abū Nuwās, the greatest experts on poetry and rhetoric, the greatest *kuttāb*, are not necessarily the greatest poets.[34]

Some of al-Ṣūlī's younger colleagues openly criticize this use of poetry. ʿArīb (d. *c.* 370/980), who quotes al-Ṣūlī extensively in his chronicle, says that he maintained some of the poetry '[...] to infer, from al-Ṣūlī's intimacy with [the Abbasids], his knowledge of their accounts and his memory of what happened in their times'.[35] On the other hand, a couple of generations later Hilāl al-Ṣābiʾ (d. 448/1056) expresses a different opinion in his *Taʾrīkh al-wuzarāʾ*: reviewing previous vizieral histories, he says that he has seen al-Ṣūlī's, 'but he filled it with unnecessary stuffing and obscured it with his silly poetry'.[36] On the contrary, in the original context of al-Ṣūlī's oeuvre, poetry is far from unnecessary, as it plays a pivotal role in its organization.

The well-organized mind

Ibn al-Nadīm specifies that al-Ṣūlī's editions of poetry are arranged alphabetically. This is not a universal standard: for Abū Tammām and al-Buḥturī, for instance, Ibn al-Nadīm also lists editions by al-Ṣūlī's younger contemporary Ḥamza al-Iṣfahānī (d. 360/970); these group the poetry according to type (*ʿalā l-anwāʿ*). In fact, al-Ṣūlī's organization is more complex: as he explains in the introduction to the *dīwān* of Abū Nuwās, he arranges the poetry in ten thematic groups, within which he employs alphabetical order.[37] Such remarks on the arrangement of material are frequent across al-Ṣūlī's work. In the introduction to the *Akhbār Abī Tammām* quoted above, he continues his tirade complaining against chaotic scholars:

> Some things I dictated long ago about the motifs that poets contend with one another over had not been given a proper and systematic arrangement (*muṣannafa mubayyana*) before I made them available [. . .]. Now I see that some individuals have broken them up and have made them available in a piecemeal fashion, strewn throughout their dictated lectures with no organization at all.[38]

In fact, al-Ṣūlī's attention to matters of organization, classification and arrangement is recognized by his contemporaries: in particular, his student al-Marzubānī praises his 'skill in composing books and collocating each of their elements in its proper place'.[39] This is not limited to works on poetry or *dīwān* editions: the way poetry is classified has an impact on the micro- and macrostructure of al-Ṣūlī's historical narrative.

The first clue of poetry's role is in the book's very title: according to al-Ṣafadī, it was called the *Book of the Leaves* in opposition to Ibn al-Jarrāḥ's *al-Waraqa*, a poetic anthology where the profile of each poet occupied a single leaf of paper.[40] And indeed, Ibn al-Nadīm gives the full title as *Book of the Leaves on the Accounts of the Caliphs and Poets*. He lists its subsections as follows:

> **[1.1]** Chronicles of the Caliphs (*akhbār al-khulafāʾ*) in its entirety; **[1.2]** Poetry of the Caliphs' children and of their fathers, from [the reign of the first Abbasid] al-Saffāḥ [r. 132–136/749–54] to the days of Ibn al-Muʿtazz; **[1.3]** the poetry of the other Abbasids who were neither caliphs

> nor children of caliphs [i.e. descendants but not sons (*li-ṣulbihi*)]. This [part of the book] begins with the poetry of [al-Saffāḥ's uncle] ʿAbdallāh b. ʿAlī [d. 147/764] and ends with the poetry of Abū Aḥmad Muḥammad b. Aḥmad b. Ismāʿīl b. Ibrāhīm b. ʿĪsā b. al-Manṣūr. After this follow: **[1.4]** the poetry of the Ṭālibids descending from al-Ḥasan and al-Ḥusayn [b. ʿAlī b. Abī Ṭālib]; of the descendants of al-ʿAbbās b. ʿAlī; of ʿUmar b. ʿAlī; and of Jaʿfar b. Abī Ṭālib. After that comes **[1.5]** the poetry of the descendants of al-Ḥārith, son of ʿAbd al-Muṭṭalib, [uncle of the Prophet]; then **[1.6]** the life and times of Ibn Harma [d. 176/792, of Quraysh lineage] and a selection of his poetry; **[1.7]** the life and times of [modern *shīʿī* poet] al-Sayyid al-Ḥimyarī [d. between 173/789 and 179/795] and a selection of his poetry; **[1.8]** the life and times of Aḥmad b. Yūsuf [d. 213/828] and a selection of his poetry; **[1.9]** the life and times of Isḥāq b. Ibrāhīm [al-Mawṣilī, d. 235/850] and a selection of his poetry; **[1.10]** the life and times of Sudayf [b. Maymūn, d. 147/764] and a selection of his poetry.

Ibn al-Nadīm states that the *Awrāq* was left unfinished, so it is not possible to draw definitive conclusions, but it is clear enough that the *Awrāq* is organized along two intersecting lines. The first is rank – caliphs, then children of caliphs, then members of the caliphal families, then ʿAlids, etc.; the second is the production of poetry – caliphs and their poetry, then those related to the caliphs who composed poetry, down to the most distantly related. Section 1.1, although its title does not mention poetry, is part of this structure, as al-Ṣūlī illustrates in the introduction to section 1.2:

> We have finished with the poetry of the caliphs and their accounts (*ashʿār al-khulafāʾ wa-akhbāruhum*). Here is the poetry of children of caliphs and their accounts, then we will follow this with the poetry of the other Abbasids, then the poetry of the Ṭālibids, then the rest of the Hashemites.[41]

Later, he goes into more granular detail on his criteria in dealing with family ties: 'When we mention a poet who had [other] poets in his family, we mention them all immediately after his profile so that the reader who looks them up can have the information in one place'.[42]

In other words, poetry is not only worth recording in the *Awrāq*, but also a principle along which to organize historical accounts.[43] If we see the *Awrāq* from this point of view, it becomes difficult to situate the first section in a different category from the rest – as a 'history', for instance, followed by anthologies of poetry. On the contrary, all sections follow the same rationale and use the same organizational tools.[44] We go back to the idea of a single pool of material which may be selected and arranged for different purposes but does not substantially differ in nature. Focusing on this first section of the *Awrāq*, further details may be observed.

The effects of poetry

Three segments of section 1.1 of the *Awrāq* have come down to us: the first one covers the years from the accession of al-Wāthiq in 227/842 to the death of al-Muhtadī in 256/870; the second segment covers the reign of al-Muqtadir (296–320/908–32) up to the year 318/930, and the third goes from the accession of al-Rāḍī in 322/934 to the death of al-Muttaqī in 333/944. These three segments have different textual histories but are consistent in style and structure: at the beginning of each reign al-Ṣūlī explains the circumstances of the death of the old caliph and the selection of the new one, describing his character and physical features through eyewitness accounts, and quoting poetry on the caliph himself or on particular events. This general description is followed by annals and equipped with a selection of the poetry by the caliph, if he composed any. Within this overall structure, the space is distributed differently: for the earlier period, most of the narrative accounts and poetry are concentrated on the initial and final part, while the annalistic section is short and often contains only names of notable deaths and leaders of the Pilgrimage, infrequently accompanied by poetry. In the second segment, covering the period for which al-Ṣūlī is himself an eyewitness, the narration of events is provided within the chronicle of each year, and poetry is distributed more evenly. Much of it is al-Ṣūlī's own and was composed, as has been seen in previous chapters, as a commentary on current events or at the request of a patron. The amount varies: the chronicles of al-Muqtadir, which were written during the caliphate of his lettered son al-Rāḍī, contain the most poetry; al-Rāḍī's years, which were written when al-Ṣūlī was no longer attached to the caliphal court, has less; in the final section on al-Muttaqī there is still much less. As for the caliphs' own poetry, al-Rāḍī's selection is by far the longest, as may be expected, given that al-Ṣūlī collected it himself shortly before the caliph's death and prepared it for dissemination.[45] It has been noted that al-Rāḍī is the last caliph whose poetry was recorded in this way – a sign of the loss of relevance of the Abbasid court as cultural centre.[46]

We may divide the poetry in the annalistic part of the *Awrāq* into two main types: occasional pieces within *akhbār*, by al-Ṣūlī and others, and selections of poetry by caliphs at the end of their reign. The latter, as we have just argued, is one of the main organizational criteria of the *Awrāq* and is crucial in connecting this first part to the rest of the work. As for poetry within the narrative, its effects are manyfold. They may be roughly divided as follows:

- After relating the death of prominent individuals, al-Ṣūlī may add verses composed on them as part of their obituary. We have seen an example of this in Chapter Three, with the death of al-ʿAbbās b. al-Ḥasan.
- One or more pieces may be included as a commentary within accounts of specific events. Al-Ṣūlī's own poetry is mainly directed at people in authority and praises their successes while hinting at their generosity; it may be followed by an account of the addressee's reaction. One such case has been seen in Chapter Two, where al-Ṣūlī congratulates al-Rāḍī on the death of the Daylamite leader Mardāwīj and asks him for a gift.
- Al-Ṣūlī also mentions other people's poetic takes on some events, such as, in Chapter Three, al-Munajjim's lines on the murder of al-ʿAbbās b. al-Ḥasan; verses by authors other than al-Ṣūlī may on occasion be less flattering or downright critical.[47]
- Finally, poetry may be a part of a discussion or debate. In Chapter Three we have seen a complex exchange across generations between Abbasid caliphs and the Munajjim family; there are many simpler conversations fully or partly carried out through the quotation or composition of poetry. Some examples will be seen in Chapter Five.

There is a discernible rationale for the insertion of poetry. To be sure, self-promotion is involved in many cases, and in others al-Ṣūlī's appreciation of a poem takes precedence over narrative pace. This is, after all, what Abū l-ʿAynāʾ means with 'spicing up *akhbār* with poetry'; it is a version of the *adab* purpose of instructing while entertaining. Vanity, too, may be a factor, as has been seen in Chapter Two. In any case, while we can only speculate on al-Ṣūlī's intentions, we may observe the effects of this poetry on the narrative. Elegies, for instance, help to characterize the deceased person and their relationship with their contemporaries – we have seen how al-Munajjim's verses on the death of al-ʿAbbās b. al-Ḥasan are judged to be an invective in disguise. Commentary on current events is often a shorthand for the mood of the population, or of certain power groups, and may add details to the prose; and exchanges of poetry are a full-fledged channel of communication. Finally, poetry is rarely static: not only does it clarify and inform; it also advances the narrative, triggering actions and reactions and framing and highlighting events. In other words, it is one of the tools – arguably one of the most important – that al-Ṣūlī uses to organize his text.

Chapter Five will reflect further on the microstructure of the *Awrāq* and the role of poetry in it. Here, it is important to point out that al-Ṣūlī's organizational skills are not isolated but have a complex and multifaceted context.

The well-organized life

One last issue is worth examining, as it illustrates the connection between aspects which so far have been looked at individually. The last section of the *Awrāq*, as listed in the *Fihrist* (1.10), is a work on the life and times of the Meccan poet Sudayf b. Maymūn (d. 147/764; *Akhbār Sudayf wa-mukhtār shiʿrihi*).[48] Ibn al-Nadīm, however, adds a troubling remark:

> But in composing this book, [al-Ṣūlī] relied on the book of al-Marthadī, *On Poetry and Poets* – in fact, he copied it word by word and claimed he was the author. I myself saw [al-Marthadī's] original copy (*dustūr*), which had been taken from the library of al-Ṣūlī, so he was exposed.[49]

Ibn al-Nadīm makes the same accusation in the profile of al-Marthadī (d. 286/899), a *kātib* who had been in the employ of the regent al-Muwaffaq (d. 279/892); here, he says that al-Ṣūlī relied on al-Marthadī's book on the poetry of the Quraysh (*Kitab ashʿār Quraysh*). The book was attributed to al-Ṣūlī, but Ibn al-Nadīm had seen the original copy 'in al-Marthadī's hand'.[50]

This is no small shortcoming; while it is well accepted that plagiarism in medieval Arabic culture did not have the same wholly negative value which it would have for a modern author, relying on a scholarly work without attribution is not acceptable.[51] Indeed, in the *Akhbār Abī Tammām* al-Ṣūlī himself complains that something similar had been done to him by the universally disliked Abū Mūsā al-Ḥāmiḍ (d. 305/918), who had insulted him and his work publicly: after his death, it was found that al-Ḥāmiḍ had in his possession some of al-Ṣūlī's work written down in his own hand at al-Ṣūlī's dictation, which he would use as sources for teaching (*ittakhadhahu uṣūlan*) without acknowledgement.[52]

Ibn al-Nadīm's remark highlights the physicality of al-Ṣūlī's library. However many sources he may have taken with him to Wāsiṭ and then Basra, and however many notebooks may have been lost in 329/941, when his house was robbed by the retreating Daylamite troops,[53] quite a few of his books must have remained in Baghdad, neatly arranged in multi-coloured rows. Perhaps Muḥammad b. Īnāl acquired them when he bought al-Ṣūlī's house, or perhaps they were sold separately. In any case, traces of this library were still identifiable half a century later, when Ibn al-Nadīm was able to source a book back to it and thus discover al-Ṣūlī's plagiarism.[54]

A well-organized time

The cultural production of al-Ṣūlī's lifetime, and of the fourth/tenth century in general, has been associated with an intellectual trend towards the standardization, classification and organization of knowledge which has at times been called encyclopaedism. Such a notion, which has been studied and conceptualized for other periods of Islamic history, has remained undefined for the fourth/tenth century, both in its precise timeframe and in the type of works it encompasses. All the same, many works of this period are casually referred to as encyclopaedias or, even more vaguely, as being encyclopaedic.[55] It would be easy to contextualize al-Ṣūlī's efforts within this framework: it may be argued that his use of poetry as an organizational tool, such as has been described here, is one version of what Hilary Kilpatrick describes as an *adab* encyclopaedia.[56] On its own, however, this reading would cut out important elements. In fact, it has been argued that using 'encyclopaedism' as an analytical category can lead us, on the one hand, to conflate different phenomena into one, and, on the other, to ignore other developments that took place in this period, in the history of the book in particular, some of which are not intellectual but practical.

What Schoeler describes as a shift from a 'literature for the school' to a 'literature for the reading public' in religious scholarship, became mainstream during al-Ṣūlī's lifetime.[57] Texts became easier to navigate without a teacher's guidance, and this involved physical as well as intellectual tools: not only were books arranged with an understandable rationale; it became easier to access their contents randomly, i.e. to look up one specific item of information without reading from the beginning. This was possible not only through hierarchical structuring and topical chapter divisions, but also chapter-headings, chapter lists or tables of contents at the beginning – in other words, through physical tools.[58] A simple example in al-Ṣūlī's work is the introduction to his *Adab al-kuttāb*, where he specifies that, at the beginning of each of its three parts, he will provide a list of its chapters so as to make it easier to find what is needed.[59]

This is not all: al-Ṣūlī's case helps us to understand that these physical tools were not confined to the contents of books but extended to, and may be guided by, external circumstances. Indeed, al-Ṣūlī is praised not only for the organization of his texts; he is also remarked upon for the physical organization of his colour-coded library. Al-Ṣūlī himself provides an example of book arrangement when he relates how he helped the caliph al-Rāḍī to rationalize his own collection of classical poetry:

> Begin by arranging the editions of poetry (*ʿamal al-ashʿār*), starting with the Muḍar tribe, then Rabīʿa, then Yaman. What is not there, your servants will bring to you from their own stock. Whatever they have as lecture notes (*mā kāna samāʿan li-ʿabīdika*), and whatever they cannot replace, the copyists you appoint will copy it and the binders of the library will bind it.[60]

This attitude involves other aspects: beside criticizing, as has been seen above, the disorganized teaching of some colleagues, he also comments on their precision in other matters. For instance, in *Adab al-kuttāb* he remarks that 'careful people (*ahl al-waraʿ*)' avoid counting the days of the month backwards because it is imprecise, as a month can have either twenty-nine or thirty days.[61]

In short, al-Ṣūlī's case illustrates that we cannot discuss a vague idea of 'encyclopaedism' in isolation. We must consider a wide range of activities, encompassing the organization of knowledge (e.g. classifications of sciences or disciplines), of information (e.g. biographical data, or poetry), and of practical, physical elements (the contents of notebooks, books, or documents, but also how such books and documents are stored). This is particularly important for the period and place of al-Ṣūlī's lifetime, for which we have very little material evidence left in comparison with other periods and places in Islamic history.[62]

Al-Ṣūlī's ability to organize objects, both physical and intellectual, in the proper order, is both part of the culture of his time and exceptional for its comprehensiveness. In the next chapter, we shall see whether it translates into a stylistic marker in his historical work.

5

Insight and Hindsight

[Le] manque de sens historique [d'al-Ṣūlī] . . . l'empécha cependant d'observer, avec la rigueur que l'on pourrait attendre d'un témoin aussi bien placé, le déroulement des événements auxquels il se trouva mélé.[1]

Dominique Sourdel

As has been seen in Chapter Four, the presence of poetry in the *Awrāq* has made this work difficult to classify and evaluate, for pre-modern and modern scholars alike. Chapter Four argues that it is pointless, and may be downright counterproductive, to single out the first part of the book from the rest – on the contrary, the fact that all sections contain the words *akhbār* and *ashʿār* in their title is the most obvious case for their uniformity. We have also observed the purposes poetry serves in the book: connective tissue, as a reading aid and navigation tool between sections; channel for communication and debate; bargaining tool; commentary on specific individuals and events; and means to convey concepts.

Still, accepting that poetry is a legitimate part of al-Ṣūlī's historical narrative does not automatically acknowledge him as an enlightened historian and critical thinker. While specific verses may add some morsels of information to our knowledge of events, some historians will argue, their importance is mostly literary and stylistic, not factual. Conversely, modern historical scholarship alternates between surprise and scepticism when confronted with literary readings of classic historiographies: they may be interesting, but their use is limited at best.[2]

This chapter will look at how al-Ṣūlī's work contributes to our own historical insight, challenging Sourdel's claim that he is mostly useful as a naïve eyewitness and arguing that, on the contrary, he presents us with a mature and coherent vision of the past, and that poetry and autobiographical details are two of the tools he employs to convey such vision.

The clueless observer

Posterity generally acknowledges al-Ṣūlī's value as an eyewitness: 'The eyewitness', ʿArīb expounds in describing his work, 'is superior to the one who, having been absent, [only] hears'.[3] This is also the main point of praise on the part of al-Masʿūdī (d. 345/956), who says that al-Ṣūlī 'mentions rare information that no one else had been given, and things he alone knew because he witnessed them himself'.[4] This emphasis, however, raises two issues: first, it disregards the parts of al-Ṣūlī's work that concern earlier periods; second, it does not comment on al-Ṣūlī's ability to read and interpret the events he witnesses. This is the sense of Sourdel's modern criticism, which is reinforced by Kennedy with a specific case:

> A typical example of this concerns the appointment of Ibn Rāʾiq as *amīr al-umarāʾ* in 324/936; as Miskawayh (and probably Thābit b. Sinān before him) saw, this represented the real end of the political power of the Abbasid family. For al-Ṣūlī, however, it is simply another incident in court life, the same as the appointment of any other official. If the Abbasid caliphs were surrounded by courtiers with al-Ṣūlī's narrowness of vision and essentially frivolous attitudes, it is not, perhaps, surprising that they lost their political power.[5]

Indeed, Ibn Rāʾiq's entrance in Baghdad as the first *amīr al-umarāʾ* is part of a decade of turmoil which will only end in 334/946, with Aḥmad b. Būya's appointment in the same position and the beginning of the Buyid century.[6] However, while it is true that most historians portray this period as a gradual descent into chaos, they differ in isolating a symbolic point of no return. In particular, both al-Ṣūlī and Miskawayh (d. 421/1030) relate the events leading to the appointment of Ibn Rāʾiq, but, as Kennedy remarks, while the latter pinpoints it as the moment when it all went wrong, al-Ṣūlī does not appear to regard it as especially significant. There is no competition between the two versions: Miskwayh's account of this period, made accessible in print decades earlier than al-Ṣūlī's, provides *both* events *and* their interpretations—it makes the past make sense, and therefore it is the history of record.

An event where two sources, while agreeing on the basic facts, do not give them the same importance, is an ideal case study to investigate the value of al-Ṣūlī's insight – or lack thereof, by contrasting his narrative with Miskawayh's.

Time and space

We have encountered several of the protagonists of these events in Chapter Three, but here we see them five years earlier, during al-Rāḍī's lifetime. Baghdad and Iraq are already in turmoil: military commanders and bureaucrats are appointed and dismissed quickly, and move up and down the Tigris, trying to gain (or re-gain) control of key towns and districts. The caliph observes these conflicts uncomfortably, never sure of how much revenue is going to be sent to Baghdad after each new takeover.

Miskawayh begins his chronicle of the year 324/935–6 with two actions undertaken by the current vizier, Ibn Muqla (d. 328/940): he releases al-Muẓaffar, son of the general Yāqūt, who had been imprisoned in the palace, and dispatches a new head of security to Egypt. Then he briefly notes: 'In this year, Muḥammad b. Rā'iq stopped transmitting the revenue which he farmed in Wāsiṭ and Basra to the capital, alleging the necessity of spending the money he had collected on the troops'.[7] This remark is followed by a long account of the intrigue through which al-Muẓaffar b. Yāqūt, once free, endeavoured to get the vizier Ibn Muqla arrested and replaced. This plot involves several parties, including, on the same side as Muẓaffar, the caliph al-Rāḍī and the *Ḥujarī* troops, one of the few sections of the army that still answered to him directly.[8] Two points are of note in this long *khabar*. Firstly, the *Ḥujarīs* have the caliph go out to the Friday Mosque, an obsolete practice in al-Rāḍī's time, and deliver a sermon where he shows his support by mentioning them specifically. Secondly, there is debate about how to deal with Ibn Rā'iq's insubordination. The vizier, Ibn Muqla, suggests that the caliph go out to Wāsiṭ himself to expel Ibn Rā'iq. He begins to take steps in this direction. On his part, Ibn Rā'iq sends a secret message to the caliph, offering to take over the government and pay all necessary expenses and revenues. At this time, the caliph does not take up Ibn Rā'iq's offer, nor does he march against him because, shortly thereafter, the vizier Ibn Muqla is arrested and replaced. Miskawayh describes the downfall of Ibn Muqla and a quick succession of new viziers, all unable to keep the administration running financially.

At this point, the narration moves abruptly away from Baghdad: 'In this year, [the general] Yāqūt [father of the above-mentioned al-Muẓaffar] was killed at ʿAskar Mukram'.[9] This brief remark introduces a long narrative involving the three Barīdī brothers, the emerging Buyid family and, occasionally but only tangentially, the central authority in Baghdad, which is deemed increasingly irrelevant. Miskawayh highlights this irrelevance through a conversation between two of the Barīdīs, who decide that they will not try to get to the capital because it is going to ruin, and the caliph, far from being a source of wealth, is trying to seize wealth from them.[10] At the end of this long account (eleven pages in the published edition), the narrative returns to Baghdad, where the situation is unchanged: Ibn Rāʾiq is still withholding payments, and no vizier is able to manage the financial situation. The turning point comes when the caliph takes action: al-Rāḍī has no other choice (*dafaʿat al-ḍarūra al-Rāḍī*) than to send for Ibn Rāʾiq, asking if his offer is still valid and inviting him to the capital. After describing Ibn Rāʾiq's arrival, Miskawayh concludes:

> From this time the power of the viziers ceased. The vizier no longer had control of the provinces, the bureaux or the departments; he had merely the title vizier, and the right of appearing on ceremonial days at the Palace in black with sword and belt. But he stood there in silence. Ibn Rāʾiq and his secretary had control of the whole business of state, and the same has been the case with all who have been *amīr al-umarāʾ* from the time of Ibn Rāʾiq to this date.[11]

This is the final reference to Baghdad for 324/935–6: subsequent accounts concern the new ruler of Kirmān, the Buyids in the east and the Barīdīs in the south. Thus, while Miskawayh describes events in Baghdad and comments on them as crucial, more than half of the narrative for this year is devoted not only to *events* taking place outside Baghdad but is also told from a *perspective* which is outside Baghdad. This is reflected in Miskawayh's commentary: he sees the appointment of Ibn Rāʾiq as a defeat for caliphal power, for Baghdad and for the civil administration – a class, incidentally, to which he himself belongs. Finally, he makes it equally clear that the failure of the central administration lies in its inability to feed the population and to pay the troops.

Al-Ṣūlī's account of the year 324/935–6[12] is shorter than Miskawayh's but contains much of the same information. The difference lies in the style and perspective in which such information is related. The first noticeable element is that al-Ṣūlī gives his information month by month, thus fragmenting the narrative without giving an overall view of events.

Al-Ṣūlī opens with reports of unrest in Baghdad and of the vizier starting to collect the land tax (*kharāj*) already in the month of Muḥarram, which caused an outcry. He then mentions individuals who died in the same month; amongst these is a Baghdadi official, whose coffin arrived in the capital from Syria. After the obituaries, al-Ṣūlī returns to the unrest in Baghdad, where the populace protested against rising prices. As a remedy, the vizier allowed the use of old and damaged *dirham* coins. The following month, Ṣafar, sees a moment of conflict, swiftly resolved, between the *Ḥujarīs* and the other branch of the Baghdadi army, the *Sājīs*,[13] and the appointment of al-Ḥasan b. ʿAbdallāh al-Ḥamdānī (the future Nāṣir al-Dawla d. *c.* 357/968), to the governorship of Mosul. Here begins a long account on the death, in Rabīʿ I, of the caliph's brother Hārūn, who had been, together with al-Rāḍī himself, al-Ṣūlī's pupil. Al-Ṣūlī describes the caliph's bereavement, the conversations they had about the deceased, and inserts an elegy which he had composed in honour of the dead prince. This account, which is four pages long, is followed by the first mention of a rumour according to which Ibn Rāʾiq wanted to come from Wāsiṭ to Baghdad, and that he had exchanged secret messages with the caliph: 'The caliph then wrote to Ibn Rāʾiq that he should not come'.[14] Unlike Miskawayh, al-Ṣūlī does not relate a definite version of events but speaks of a rumour without confirming or denying it, limiting himself to state this rumour's consequences. Immediately afterwards, in the month of Rabīʿ II, al-Ṣūlī mentions the death of a respected *kātib* who was the father of Ibn Rāʾiq's current secretary.

After mentioning the arrival in Baghdad of an old Samarran *muḥaddith* who had an excellent *isnād*, al-Ṣūlī goes back to the financial crisis and the vizier's futile attempts to raise the money to pay the troops: having tried unsuccessfully to obtain loans from the city's main merchants to pay the army, he confiscated some money from a flour merchant and expropriated the homes adjacent to the city walls, with the intent of selling them. In the meantime, help arrived from abroad: 'Al-Ḥasan b. ʿAbdallāh [al-Ḥamdānī] sent one hundred *kurr* of flour to be distributed in Samarra and Baghdad amongst the Hashemites and the poor. People rejoiced, many merchant boats went down [the Tigris], and prices went back to normal'.[15]

At this point, in Jumādā II, al-Ṣūlī reaches the events leading to the downfall of the vizier Ibn Muqla. The main points coincide with Miskawayh's account, but there are important differences. To begin with, while Miskawayh points to a specific individual, al-Muẓaffar b. Yāqūt, as the instigator of events, as a revenge on the vizier who had imprisoned him, al-Ṣūlī does not initially mention al-Muẓaffar. His narrative is composed of two sequential events: firstly, there is unrest amongst the Baghdadi troops and al-Rāḍī, at their request, goes out to the mosque to preach; secondly, the troops become discontented with the vizier Ibn Muqla, who cannot pay them, and contrive to have him arrested. Moreover, al-Ṣūlī describes al-Rāḍī's sermon in some detail, having been in the audience, and also relates that the caliph asked for his opinion on his performance, quotes the poetry he composed to celebrate the event, and mentions the caliph's reward to him. Only at the end of the account does al-Ṣūlī say that al-Muẓaffar b. Yāqūt was re-arrested for plotting to depose the caliph. Several remarks, nested within the appointments made by the new vizier and the interrogation and fines extracted from Ibn Muqla, mention food shortages, epidemics and fluctuation of prices in Baghdad. Amongst these short reports, including obituaries, al-Ṣūlī mentions that the troops had heard that the caliph was planning to go to Mosul, but this had not materialized.

In Rajab, Ibn Muqla's successor was deposed. This time it is al-Ṣūlī who attributes this deposition to a conspiracy on the part of a rival *kātib*, Ibn Sanjala. This is followed by a series of short *akhbār* reporting deaths and arrests with extraction of money from several government officials. The death of Yāqūt, to which Miskawayh devotes eleven pages, is related here in a few lines: 'The news arrived in Ramaḍān that Yāqūt had been killed. In seeing the emotion of the *Ḥujarī* troops, al-Rāḍī swore that he was sorry and that this had been done without his consent'.[16] Again, the event is portrayed as news arriving in Baghdad and having consequences in the city.

The appointment of Ibn Rā'iq in the month of Dhū l-Ḥijja is the last item for 324/935–6. It is related as a series of events and not commented on: the embassy that had been sent to Ibn Rā'iq returns to Baghdad and is immediately sent back to him with the offer to become *amīr al-umarā'*. Ibn Rā'iq enters Baghdad and his first action is to ask the caliph to go to Wāsiṭ, 'in order to carry out his plan to rid himself of the *Ḥujarī* troops'.[17] The plan immediately comes to fruition and is the first event described for the following year: during al-Rāḍī short stay at Wāsiṭ (2 Muḥarram–8 Ṣafar 325/20 November–26 December 936), Ibn Rāʾiq, with the help of his then general Bajkam, completes the dismantlement of these troops.[18] He also has the caliph meet with Abū l-Ḥusayn ʿAlī b. Muḥammad al-Barīdī and officially award him and his brothers the governorship of al-Ahwāz, which they were already holding without transmitting any revenue to Baghdad. The account of Ibn Rāʾiq's appointment is sealed by the news of the death of a famous traditionist, but before this al-Ṣūlī reports that, on his arrival in Baghdad, Ibn Rāʾiq had appointed his long-time secretary al-Nawbākhṭī to oversee affairs.

Contrasting al-Ṣūlī's chronicle of the year 324/935–6 with Miskawayh's throws light on several points. Firstly, al-Ṣūlī's account contains narratives in his own voice relating situations in which he was personally involved. Such accounts by no means represent the majority of the narrative: as we have seen, there are two instances where al-Ṣūlī interacts with the caliph, on the occasion of his brother's death and his preaching at the Friday Mosque respectively. These are long passages, clearly marked by al-Ṣūlī through the use of his own poetry as well as mention of presents he received from the caliph. The rest of the chronicle, although it does not present al-Ṣūlī as a protagonist, does maintain his distinct voice and perspective: the narrative stays with him and relates what he sees and hears from his standpoint in Baghdad. Miskawayh, on the other hand, provides multiple perspectives and moves his narrative wherever the action is. This difference in perspective has consequences: on the one hand, al-Ṣūlī is able to elaborate on the details of the financial and economic crisis in Baghdad as well as providing information on its cultural life; on the other, Miskawayh provides a wider view of events and more detailed information on what happened outside Baghdad. Of course, a wider view does not automatically mean a greater understanding.

A second difference lies in the arrangement of information: Miskawayh divides the year into several major events and attaches each single *khabar* to one of these; thus, his account consists of a series of coherent narratives, often accompanied by the author's commentary. On the other hand, al-Ṣūlī narrates events in what appears to be the strictest chronological order, month by month. While this may give the impression of a more short-sighted chronicle, it does succeed in conveying not only the political and economic instability of the time, but also the state of anxiety and insecurity in which the Baghdadi population found itself during this time – the recurrent references to price fluctuations and its effects on daily life, for instance, serve as a sort of refrain to the narrative, casting a grim light on any other item of news. The question, then, is not one of insight but one of perspective: al-Ṣūlī, who by the time of writing may already be in Wāsiṭ or Basra, nevertheless writes from a Baghdadi perspective and records events based on the effects they produce in the capital. Within this local framework, the arrival of one individual is less important than the departure of another, as shall be presently seen.

Perspectives and principles

> [. . .] these texts are more than somewhat biased, but generally unproblematic representations of the past: they are complex narratives which have to be understood by taking into account the authors' positions in social and intellectual terms.[19]
>
> Konrad Hirschler

In his comparative study of Ibn Wāṣil and Abū Shāma, Konrad Hirschler uses Hayden White's theory of emplotment to analyse the strategies of these two Mamluk historians.[20] We may think of a comparison between al-Ṣūlī and Miskawayh in similar terms if we go back and reconsider Kennedy's remarks: it is correct that Miskawayh attributes to Ibn Rāʾiq's appointments a finality which it does not have for al-Ṣūlī; however, it must also be acknowledged that it is easier for Miskawayh to see such finality: al-Ṣūlī, who writes a mere decade after the event, may still be hoping for a restoration of caliphal authority. Leaving aside the time of writing, then, which gives Miskawayh the benefit of hindsight, the fundamental difference between the two authors is that al-Ṣūlī does not provide an explicit assessment of the situation and its significance. This does not mean that there is no assessment at all. Rather, it is to be found elsewhere and it is formulated on the basis of different principles. In the first place, social standing must be considered: as a bureaucrat himself, Miskawayh deplores the end of the old vizierate. Al-Ṣūlī, on the other hand, deplores the end of the old ways of the caliphate and its capital. In other words, their personal circumstances are parallel to their narrative choices – as Hirschler argues in the passage above.[21]

It is worth emphasizing that al-Ṣūlī's choice of focus cannot be casual or naïve, because it is specific. As the author of a book on viziers – now all but lost – and of a manual for *kuttāb*, he must be aware of the importance and role of administrators and has given an important contribution to shaping the character of the ideal *kātib*.[22] Nevertheless, in the *Awrāq* his point of reference is the caliph.[23]

Seen in this light, the two stories in which al-Ṣūlī is part of the action he describes appear not as arbitrary, self-promotional insertions but as affirmations of the caliphal role. While mourning the death of his brother Hārūn with al-Ṣūlī, al-Rāḍī compares his grief to that of his ancestor al-Maʾmūn: 'Al-Maʾmūn did not have as much love for his brother Abū ʿĪsā as I did for Hārūn'.[24] This is clearly a stylistic exercise, not an expression of genuine grief, as in the same conversation al-Rāḍī reminisces that Hārūn had constantly conspired to unseat him. The important point is to establish a link to a meaningful ancestor. In the case of al-Rāḍī's sermon at the Friday Mosque, the connection is even clearer: the caliph performs what used to be a standard religious duty for his predecessors, thus managing to command the loyalty of his troops. On both occasions, al-Ṣūlī encourages and advises his master on how to follow the caliphal tradition. In other words, different parameters are at play: for Miskawayh, a competent and honest administrator is the foundation of a

***Amīr al-umarāʾ*, 324-334/936-945**

al-Rāḍī (322-329/934-940)
- Ibn Rāʾiq (324-326/936-938)
- Bajkam (326-329/938-941)

al-Muttaqī (329-333/940-944)
- Kurankij (329/941)
- Ibn Rāʾiq (329-330/941-942)
- Ibn Ḥamdān, Nāṣir al-Dawla (330-331/942-943)
- Tūzūn (331-334/943-945)

Figure 2: list of the first five generals who held the office of *amīr al-umarāʾ* for the caliphs al-Rāḍī and al-Muttaqī

strong caliphate; for al-Ṣūlī, the deciding factor is a caliph who is versed in the history of his family and adheres to the duties attached to his role. Within this framework, al-Ṣūlī's assessment comes later, starting with the chronicle for the year 326/938, when Bajkam unseats his former master Ibn Rāʾiq and replaces him as *amīr al-umarāʾ*.

In Dhū l-Qaʿda 326/September 938, Ibn Rāʾiq, having lost the support of the caliph, resolves to leave the capital, carrying everything he can; as he passes, people cry: 'This is God's punishment for appointing al-Kūfī your secretary and giving him full authority!' Al-Ṣūlī goes on to explain:

> [Ibn Rāʾiq] had made [al-Kūfī] secretary, dismissing al-Ḥūsayn b. ʿAlī b. al-ʿAbbās al-Nawbakhṭī, after the latter's judgement and guidance had allowed him to get where he was – it was al-Nawbakhṭī who had orchestrated the ruin of the *Sājī*s and managed the affair of the *Ḥujarī*s![25]

A few days later, Bajkam enters Bagdhad with his troops and is appointed *amīr al-umarāʾ*. When he receives the ceremonial robes of honour, Bajkam declares that his only request is that his troops receive their pay. Here, al-Ṣūlī adds a significant item: it is suggested to al-Rāḍī that he put his chamberlain Dhakī at the head of troops independent from those of Bajkam, and that he keep track of the number of soldiers in Bajkam's army so as to establish the precise sum that is to be paid to them. The caliph acts on the first suggestion but ignores the second, with the consequence that, within two months, Bajkam's army has grown so much that it requires 20,000 additional *dīnār* a year or more. Disregarding this advice, remarks al-Ṣūlī, 'is one of the faults al-Rāḍī has been blamed for'.[26]

Contrary to other instances we have seen, al-Ṣūlī does not insert himself in the narrative of these two events, nor does he highlight their importance with a distinct personal remark. Nevertheless, his assessment emerges clearly: through the cries of the crowd, he illustrates the crucial success of Ibn Rāʾiq – the dismantlement of the caliphal army – his secretary's key role in it, and the consequences of dismissing the latter.[27] Through an unattributed remark, he blames al-Rāḍī for not understanding the importance of keeping an independent army and controlling the manpower of his *amīr* as long as he had the slightest chance to do it. All the elements of Miskaway's assessment are present, though not packaged into a tight paragraph. In his account of subsequent events, al-Ṣūlī shows the results of these mistakes.

Persuasion

> The approach to poetry and poets was not at all unequivocal. On the one hand, poetry was straightforwardly regarded as a political weapon, and the role of a poet as that of a servant. The utilitarian approach prevailed, but poetry and poets had rights and privileges of their own. Poetical form enabled the poet to express ideas, inadmissible or improper when said in prose. According to the old traditions of nomadic democracy in ancient Arabia poets were excused an audacity otherwise intolerable. [...] Poetry fulfilled a social function, which was at other times and in other societies achieved by quite different means. [...] The ruling clique headed by the caliph and the social élite paid to poetry the tribute of love, respect and fear not only because of traditions, education and habits, but also owing to the poet's power to influence political and financial decisions.[28]
>
> Anas B. Khalidov

We have already seen several instances in the *Awrāq* where poetry functions as a means of – peaceful or conflictual – communication, alone or mixed with conversations, oral messages and written notes. Al-Ṣūlī also uses his own compositions to plead his case before a person of authority, asking for more access or more presents. In the chronicle for the year 327/938–9, we see poetry used for political persuasion and mixed with another powerful device, direct speech.[29]

The situation is similar to that of 324: in Mosul, al-Ḥasan b. ʿAbdallāh b. Ḥamdān has been withholding the revenue that he is farming there. Despite advice to the contrary from many parties, including al-Ṣūlī and the head judge ʿUmar b. Muḥammad, al-Rāḍī establishes that it is necessary to accompany Bajkam to Mosul. Al-Ṣūlī also mentions that the population of Baghdad is not happy about the caliph's leaving to confront Ibn Ḥamdān, as the latter has been generous to the poor of the city in the past, sending flour and money in periods of famine. Moreover, his brother ʿAlī (the future Sayf al-Dawla, d. 356/967) has been active on the Byzantine frontier, leading the traditional summer campaign (*ṣāʾifa*) and other military feats. In other words, the Ḥamdānid brothers have been carrying out traditional caliphal duties.[30] The caliph's party, including al-Ṣūlī, other courtiers, and the head judge, sets out in Muḥarram 327/October 938. By the time it reaches Samarra, there is already news of unrest in Baghdad, where Ibn Rāʾiq has reappeared and is rallying supporters. The consensus, says al-Ṣūlī, is that the caliph should stay in Samarra, let Bajkam go forth to Mosul, and join him only if strictly necessary (*in iḥtāja ilayhi*): 'Tongues were loosened in advising him not to quit Samarra. The most insistent that he should not leave were the judge ʿUmar b. Muḥammad and the chamberlain Dhakī. We were all in agreement'.[31] In the meantime, Ibn Ḥamdān, having heard of the expedition, begins to send messages from Mosul, offering conditions which al-Ṣūlī considers better than expected. Al-Ṣūlī claims he had direct access to these exchanges, because the messages were delivered through the judge ʿUmar b. Muḥammad, who would let him read everything. At this point, al-Ṣūlī uses the first-person plural again: 'After al-Rāḍī had been in Samarra for a few days, we wished him to go back. I agreed with the judge that we should take it in turns to talk to him when we found him alone'. The opportunity to stage an intervention comes one day, when al-Ṣūlī enters the caliph's presence before the rest of his colleagues arrive. He records the conversation as a word-by-word account:

> 'Commander of the Faithful, the loyal servant does not conceal from his master anything that is in his heart, nor does he store away his advice to him. Likewise, there is nothing wrong for the master in hearing out his servant's words: if he is right, the caliph will approve, and if he is wrong, he will do as if he had not heard him.' He laughed: 'Tell me what you have.' 'From what we've been told, [Ibn Ḥamdān's] army, against which you have started this expedition, is much more similar to the true armies of Islam (*ʿasākir al-islām*) than the army you are marching with, which is little disposed to obey your orders. [Ibn Ḥamdān's] is more like the armies of your ancestors than yours is. They say that al-Ḥasan [Ibn Ḥamdān] has offered much more than was expected of him. You would do well to accept his proposition and go back to the capital, to dispel the fear of revolt on the part of Ibn Rāʾiq [. . .]. Moreover, Ibn Ḥamdān has addressed the man who is most dear to you, your judge, making him his intermediary and guarantor. The judge will speak to him and will obtain everything he wants. And there is something else.' 'What is it?' asked the caliph. 'If Ibn Ḥamdān despairs of the caliph accepting his offer, he will probably turn to someone else, gaining his good graces in exchange for much less than he is offering you now. This someone will make him his creature, his source of fortune and support of his power. This someone, to whom Ibn Ḥamdān will turn, will speak in his name to you and will require that you grant him what he wishes. You will grant him his

> request and give him satisfaction. It is he – Bajkam, the one I am speaking of – who will enjoy the advantages we want to obtain.'[32]

Al-Ṣūlī interrupts the dialogue to add that the caliph had pondered his words for a long while; but he is not finished. 'As for prose,' he adds, 'the argument is covered, but I have composed a *qaṣīda* on the subject which I'd like to recite, with my lord's permission.' The poem praises al-Rāḍī as its addressee, as well as Ibn Ḥamdān, whose offer should be accepted; the chamberlain Dhakī who, al-Ṣūlī says, had been listening in on part of the conversation; and the city of Baghdad, because the caliph had been saying that he intended to quit it for good and reside in Samarra. The caliph promises to consider al-Ṣūlī's argument and dismisses him. When his turn arrives, the judge offers similar advice, but to no avail: al-Rāḍī, far from being persuaded, does quit Samarra but, rather than going back to Baghdad, heads for Takrīt, about 60 kilometres north of Samarra along the Tigris. There, the cycle is repeated: there are news of Ibn Rāʾiq gathering troops and followers in Baghdad, while Ibn Ḥamdān keeps sending conciliatory messages. However, al-Rāḍī overhears some of Bajkam's Daylamite troops disparaging him amongst themselves. The caliph's advisers see an opening:

> While he was talking, Dhakī made a sign at me. Thinking that, after overhearing the Daylamites, the caliph would change his mind, I said: 'Commander of the Faithful, Baghdad is the seat of government, the home of the caliphate; there is no going back if you abandon it!' 'It used to be so,' he replied, 'when the Treasury had millions of *dīnār* at the time of al-Muʿtaḍid, and twice as much at the time of al-Muktafī. Now that the Treasury is empty it is like any other place.'[33]

In other words, al-Rāḍī seems to share the opinion which Miskawayh attributes to the Barīdī brothers in 324/935–6, that Baghdad is no longer worth fighting for. Al-Rāḍī does not seem to see the implication, that without Baghdad his own importance is questionable. Al-Ṣūlī, however, has other arguments:

> 'But there is something more precious than money in Baghdad, the two princes [. . .], the caliph's women and their treasures!' [My fellow *jalīs*] al-ʿArūḍī spoke up to support my argument, but the caliph got angry with him so he stopped talking. Then al-Rāḍī approached me: 'How often you give me advice when I have not asked for it!' 'Your servant is guilty my lord, but only out to fear for you. I shall not say one more word.'

The episode is sealed by a final conversation, where al-Ṣūlī complains to Dhakī: 'You gestured for me to speak and see what I got!' Dhakī replies that the subject should not be mentioned again.

Indeed, the caliph continues for Mosul and only returns to Baghdad after accepting an unattractive deal with Ibn Ḥamdān, negotiated, as al-Ṣūlī had warned, by Bajkam, who may not be entirely honest about the deal he has struck. Still, al-Rāḍī, now completely dependent on Bajkam financially, has no choice but accept. During all this time, the caliph remains cold with al-Ṣūlī, overlooking him at receptions in favour of his Munajjim rivals. A *qaṣīda* where al-Ṣūlī seeks to get back into the caliph's graces, going as far as praising Bajkam, merely elicits a mild reaction.[34] Eventually, however, on the eve of his return to the capital, al-Rāḍī summons al-Ṣūlī alone and tortuously acknowledges that he should not have gone to Mosul. Once again, al-Ṣūlī relates the exchange as a word-by-word conversation:

> 'You seem to think that I have made a mistake and have abandoned the rightful way.' 'I swear by God,' I replied, 'this idea has never crossed my mind because I am too absorbed by pain and will remain so until I see my lord back in his capital, enjoying the durable happiness that you are used to.' 'Did you not tell me that Yaḥyā b. Khālid al-Barmakī said: I do not congratulate myself on an idea that was wrong even though it was then revealed to be right, because my first idea was wrong, as I did not know what the consequences would be. Conversely, I do not blame myself for a project which had been right, although it later revealed itself to be wrong. It is the same for me: I was right in my first conception of the project, but I did not know what is hidden from our eyes.'[35]

Al-Rāḍī concludes the conversation by giving al-Ṣūlī a present of money, thus sanctioning the end of his anger.

In the chronicle for the year 324/935–6, we have seen that the arrangement of accounts creates a sense of anxiety in the narrative, and that al-Ṣūlī's autobiographical insertions contribute to affirming the centrality of the caliph. In the case of the expedition to Mosul, the key role is played by dialogue between al-Ṣūlī and the caliph, which advances the action and frames the whole enterprise. It must be noted that, while dialogue is a common device in the historiography of this period, al-Ṣūlī only uses dialogue when he himself is part of it or has witnessed it directly.[36]

From a stylistic point of view, these exchanges do not simply punctuate the narrative but rather dominate it, suffusing it with a sense of hopelessness and impending doom: everybody around the caliph sees what should be done but no argument can persuade him. Moreover, the conversations firmly ground al-Ṣūlī's opinion in two key principles: first, the caliph must have a trusted army whose leader is prepared to perform the duties connected to this role: fighting the non-Muslim enemy and providing for the population. Second, in order for the caliph to remain relevant, he must stay in Baghdad, the seat of his authority.

Al-Ṣūlī's attention to the caliph's role becomes evident when we compare his account with Miskawayh's: the latter, who devotes only a few short pages to the expedition to Mosul, portrays it mainly as a conflict between Ibn Ḥamdān and Bajkam. Al-Rāḍī is indeed shown to have some agency, both in planning the trip and in resisting Ibn Ḥamdān's offer, but he is mostly marginal to the narrative. The only additional titbit concerns al-Rāḍī's army: while in Takrīt, some of the troops had deserted and gone back to Baghdad to join Ibn Rāʾiq, at which point the caliph had hastened to Mosul by land, afraid that they would march against him.[37] While this partly explains al-Rāḍī's decision to proceed to Mosul, it is consistent with al-Ṣūlī's argument: it would have been better to go back to the capital from Samarra, before Ibn Rāʾiq could gain more supporters, rather than rely on troops whose loyalty was doubtful.

Arguments

After reading al-Ṣūlī's account of the expedition to Mosul, the reader is sure to side with the author: the caliph's decision was unreasonable, and it would have been better to go back to Baghdad from Samarra. Still, in the last conversation al-Rāḍī maintains that his initial decision had been correct based on the information available to him at the time. The reader does not know what al-Rāḍī's rationale had been, because al-Ṣūlī has not described it yet. Only a few pages later, when discussing the situation in Baghdad on al-Rāḍī's return, he mentions that, before beginning the expedition, the caliph had explained his motives, again in a conversation which al-Ṣūlī relates as direct speech. Al-Rāḍī had said that Baghdad and its territory could not sustain both Bajkam's army and the caliph's own maintenance. Al-Rāḍī hoped to seize Mosul, a prosperous region, and use its revenue for Bajkam's troops, so that, with the revenues of the caliphate's other territories, he would be free to pay for all remaining expenses. Al-Ṣūlī's counterargument at the time had been that Mosul was prosperous because of the Ḥamdanids' good administration, and that it would go to ruin without them, just as Fārs and Iṣfahān had done after the fall of ʿAmr b. al-Layth and Abū Dulaf respectively.[38]

Even though he eventually shows us the caliph's argument, then, al-Ṣūlī undermines it immediately. Ultimately, however, he leaves the last word to al-Rāḍī: in the collection of the caliph's poems at the end of the narrative, two are invectives against Ibn Rāʾiq, and three lament the necessity of his journey, his regret of having to leave Baghdad, and his contempt for Mosul.[39] The caliph, after all, had been paying attention, and the careful reader should already know that his political intelligence was never in doubt, as we shall see presently.

There are two further elements of note in al-Ṣūlī's account of the expedition to Mosul: on the one hand, although the conflict is ultimately about revenue, administrators play a minor part in the negotiations.[40] On the other, there is an important factor, which is not explicit in the conversations between al-Rāḍī and al-Ṣūlī but recurs in the narrative and seems to be an argument directed to the reader rather than the caliph: the welfare and mood of the population. We have seen two instances of the latter above, firstly in the cries accompanying Ibn Rāʾiq's exit from Baghdad. These cries represent Baghdadi public opinion and are a device to communicate the unpopularity of Ibn Rāʾiq and his new secretary. Later, the population (*al-ʿāmma*) is unhappy with the caliph's decision to march against Ibn Ḥamdān; here, al-Ṣūlī uses public opinion to plant his argument for Ibn Ḥamdān early on in the narrative. On the contrary, during the caliph's absence, 'scoundrels (*al-ʿayyārūn*) ruled Baghdad', going so far as to 'steal people's clothes from mosques and streets'. Only after Ibn Rāʾiq's departure, the new head of police had many criminals arrested and 'there was quiet in Baghdad, after great unrest'. The caliph had a letter read out in the city, assuring the population that nobody would be punished for recent events and that 'he would not leave Bajkam free rein over them'. People, says al-Ṣūlī, were placated.[41]

The welfare of the population is a concern throughout the expedition. Al-Ṣūlī relates how Bajkam's troops wreaked havoc wherever they passed, from the very outset of the journey when, being a little ahead of the caliph's party, they 'abused people (*al-nās*), which aggrieved al-Rāḍī'.[42] Later, when Bajkam is temporarily in control of Mosul, his men terrorize the population. Bajkam and his troops behave in such a despicable way that the caliph complains, and Bajkam has to order his men to stop.[43] On the way back from Mosul, conditions are so difficult that several of Bajkam's men drown. 'People,' adds al-Ṣūlī, 'said that this was their punishment for attacking the inhabitants of Mosul.' Once in Baghdad, the caliph has a general pardon proclaimed for clashes between soldiers and civilians. This reassures the population (*sakana l-nās*).[44]

Parallel to the conversations between al-Ṣūlī and the caliph, then, it seems that there is an implicit dialogue between al-Rāḍī and the population: the former strives to protect and provide for his subjects, everywhere he goes but especially in the capital, where the inhabitants recognize him as their highest authority. Within this framework, we can identify a metanarrative argument, suggesting a causal link between the prosperity of Baghdad and the caliph's presence in it, and in turn, between caliphal authority and the support of the population.

This argument is made explicit in al-Ṣūlī's account of the caliphate of al-Muttaqī. During his short reign (329–33/940–4), the latter goes on two long expeditions, the second of which results in his deposition. Al-Ṣūlī, who has no direct contact with this caliph, cannot rely on dialogue as a means to conveying internal discussions, but he can still show the effects the caliph's absence has on Baghdad. During al-Muttaqī's first expedition, the population of the capital suffers at the hand of the Barīdīs and their troops, who go so far as entering the caliphal apartments. Al-Ṣūlī relates the words of a Baghdadi eyewitness, who thinks the best solution would be 'to send a thousand horsemen, promising them some money, to take the caliph and Ibn Rā'iq back. The caliph would retake his palace, a large allowance would be given to him for his expenses, those of his household and his court'.[45] Eventually, after the caliph's deposition, he comments that 'his first senseless, reckless mistake was leaving the seat of his rule (*dār mamlakatihi*) and going out, [...] when there was no reason compelling him to do that'.[46] This assessment is all the more trenchant because it is not followed by a selection of the caliph's poetic compositions—in al-Muttaqī's case, al-Ṣūlī has the last word.

Looking at al-Ṣūlī's account of the expedition to Mosul reinforces our reading of the chronicle for 324/935–6: through various stylistic and narrative devices – poetry, arrangement of accounts, dialogue – al-Ṣūlī conveys not only the succession of events, but also a mature reading of the past based on firm principles.

Preparation

So far, we have examined the expedition to Mosul as a closed temporal unit, confined within the year 327/938–9. However, the attentive reader does not reach these events unprepared: al-Ṣūlī has planted an interpretive key much earlier, in the year 322/934–5, when Bajkam is first introduced in the narrative at the head of the rebel officers who killed the Daylamite leader Mardāwīj b. Ziyār. As has been seen in Chapter Two, news of Mardāwīj's death sets off a flashback on the education of al-Rāḍī, after which al-Ṣūlī continues with the sequential narrative. This, however, is not the only interruption: 322 is the first year of al-Rāḍī's caliphate, and there seems to be a need to provide background to events which, in isolation, would be difficult to contextualize.[47] Thus, not long after the flashback on al-Rāḍī's education, al-Ṣūlī introduces successive flash-forwards where al-Rāḍī and Bajkam express their opinion on one another. We start with the caliph:

> Al-Rāḍī told us: I understand that people are saying: 'How can this Caliph be happy that a Turkish slave manages his affairs, disposing of public money and holding all power?' But they don't know that everything had already gone to hell before I became caliph, and that others threw me in when I didn't want to! I was put in the power of *Sājīs* and *Ḥujarīs*, who tyrannized me, demanded an audience many times a day and came to look for me even at night. Each of them wanted to be preferred to the others, and wanted the Treasury all to himself, and to keep myself afloat I didn't dare deceive them. Eventually the Lord got them out of my way! Then Ibn Rāʾiq came to power – in terms of money he was more brazen than the others, and in terms of drinking and partying he was unique [. . .]. When I gave an order, no one obeyed; it was neither carried out nor passed on. It almost always happened that one of those dogs asked me something, and I was not the master of refusing it [. . .]. But when this slave [Bajkam] came, I got someone who never said to me 'I made you', or: 'I put you on the throne', as the other had said: on the contrary, with him I can raise my voice, because he is my creature. And I have seen that when one of his men goes

> wrong, he is not happy if he does not kill him or punish him, even too severely. And if the news comes that the enemy has invaded a province, he rushes in and meets it in no time, without grabbing me by the neck or demanding money, and without expecting arrears. Of course I'm happy with him! He serves me better and makes himself loved, more than those before him. Of course, I would prefer it all to be in my hands, but my fate did not want it to be so![48]

Al-Ṣūlī illustrates al-Rāḍī's statement with the description of an audience between the two. He then jumps further forward and relates a conversation between himself and Bajkam in Wāsiṭ, after the caliph's death. The two look back at the events leading to Bajkam's appointment and his relationship with the caliph:

> I then related to him al-Rāḍī's words: 'I understand that people are saying . . .' He laughed and said to me: 'al-Rāḍī was smart, shrewd, and extremely flattering, (at least that is what Bajkam meant, even if he did not use these expressions exactly), but I blamed him for being too weak; he let the voice of pleasure and desire speak louder than that of reason'. I admired Bajkam's intelligence: indeed, he had found the only two faults of al-Rāḍī.[49]

When the reader reaches the events of the year 327/938–9 and reads about the expedition to Mosul, then, she will be equipped with two framing arguments: a short-term one – explicit conversations between the caliph and his entourage during the expedition to Mosul – and a long-term one which, being at the beginning of the chronicle, helps to shape the reader's understanding of all subsequent events. A similar observation can be made for the appointment of Ibn Rāʾiq in 324/936: events will be read with the knowledge that the caliph will soon come to regret his decision.

Access

Having identified al-Ṣūlī's specific reading of the expedition to Mosul, we must acknowledge that there is another level to the narrative: while the account may, and indeed should be read as the chronicle of historical events, it is also the story of al-Ṣūlī's period of disgrace with the caliph. This *personal* level of the narrative should not be ignored, as there may be tactical considerations in how, on the *authorial* level, al-Ṣūlī assesses events and accounts for his own behaviour. For instance, at the time of writing Bajkam may already be dead and incapable of any retribution for an unflattering portrayal. On the other hand, al-Ṣūlī may be seeking to gain the favour of the Ḥamdānids; portraying this family as the defenders of Islam is sure to help. Chapter Two has argued that this personal level of the narrative may be thought of as a 'fragmented autobiography', which is in turn functional to al-Ṣūlī's style. Here, an implication of this argument will be considered: for al-Ṣūlī to obey such tactical considerations only make sense if we assume that he expected his writings to reach, and possibly influence, the individuals he was seeking favour from. In other words, even after leaving the court, al-Ṣūlī may still have access to potential benefactors, at least as intended readers. Whether he has still access to information is more doubtful.

Caliph management

Of course, that a *jalīs* such as al-Ṣūlī should have access to people of power, including the caliph, is obvious and well recorded. The story of his arrival at the court of al-Muktafī is described in several of his biographical profiles and is also mentioned in the *Awrāq*. At least in one instance, he also claims to have had a direct effect on this caliph's actions, advising him on the choice of a successor.[50] There are even traces of contacts with an earlier caliph, al-Muʿtaḍid, when al-Ṣūlī was still in his twenties; and during the reign of al-Muqtadir, although he did not hold a regular post as a *jalīs* of the caliph, al-Ṣūlī still had occasional access to him. For much of al-Rāḍī's reign, contact is constant and al-Ṣūlī is careful to highlight instances when his own intervention influenced the caliph's political decisions.[51] So far in this volume, we have mostly seen al-Ṣūlī attempt to influence a decision for his own advantage – to obtain a reward or a favour of some sort – or to affect a specific issue in which he was directly involved – such as the education of the young princes, or indeed al-Rāḍī's expedition to Mosul. In these cases, al-Ṣūlī typically bases his advice on precedent and principle but also demonstrates a thorough knowledge of the current situation. These episodes suggest that al-Ṣūlī, whatever his authority and personal power as a *jalīs*, had access to confidential information through a network of people who trusted and confided in him. The account of the expedition to Mosul provides an illustration of this element, too.

While al-Rāḍī was away from Bagdhad, Ibn Rāʾiq, in open rebellion, had looked into the possibility of appointing a new caliph and had contacted al-Ḥasan and al-Ḥusayn, elderly grandsons of al-Maʾmūn, for this purpose. The plan had come to nothing because Ibn Rāʾiq did not have the funds to pay for the usual donations on the accession of a new caliph.[52] Before leaving Mosul, al-Ṣūlī had received news of this, as had other members of the caliphal party. At the same time, al-Rāḍī's troops, led by the chamberlain Dhakī, were clamouring for their pay, threatening to go back to Baghdad and pledge allegiance to Ibn al-Maʾmūn. In one episode where al-Ṣūlī is alone with al-Rāḍī, the caliph complains about the situation: 'Look here, your neighbour Ibn al-Maʾmūn has been made to sit on the throne! They were uncertain, but eventually they chose the elder. I will feed their flesh to the birds!' al-Ṣūlī tries to reassure al-Rāḍī that it will all come to nothing, mocking the two brothers' ineptitude.

> When [al-Rāḍī] laughed, I felt more at liberty to speak: 'They have many enemies and are slandered terribly. Perhaps this is a rumour spread by their enemies'. But the caliph showed me part of a letter mentioning what he had just said. [My colleague] Muḥammad b. Ḥamdūn arrived at this point; the caliph repeated what he had said to me, but Ibn Ḥamdūn's reply was similar to mine, and the caliph was placated. After I left, Dhakī asked: '[. . .] have you received a letter saying what his lordship mentioned?' I said I had, and so had he. He gave me his letter and I handed over mine, then he threw both letters in the Tigris.[53]

Three of the people mentioned in this episode – al-Rāḍī, al-Ṣūlī and Dhakī – and possibly the fourth one, Ibn Ḥamdūn, are in possession of the same information, which they have obtained separately by letter. However, the courtiers go to great lengths to downplay the situation with the caliph, concealing their own knowledge of the truth, presumably for fear that al-Rāḍī may react irrationally and make matters worse. Again, dialogue is both a narrative device and a means of persuasion. In this case, it is complemented by a physical element, the destruction of the letters.

This episode also highlights the importance of external information received and shared between members of the court, including written communication. There is another instance earlier in the story of the expedition, when al-Ṣūlī says that he knew the details of the negotiations with Ibn Ḥamdān because the judge ʿUmar b. Muḥammad let him see the content of Ibn Ḥamdān's missives. In both cases, al-Ṣūlī and others attempt to use their knowledge of outside information to manage the caliph's decisions, steering him in a specific direction. The enterprise is not always successful because, amongst other things, the caliph has his own separate channels of communication; after all, as we have seen, the original appointment of Ibn Rāʾiq in 324/936 is the result of a secret exchange of messages between the latter and al-Rāḍī.

Confidence

This image of courtiers banding together, and sharing information to bend the ruler's will, is hardly original. On the contrary, it is consistent with the portrayal of al-Ṣūlī as an historian of court gossip, valuable as an eyewitness but useless as an interpreter of events. Such a portrayal, however, confuses correlation with causation: that there is a personal level to the *Awrāq* does not necessarily imply that al-Ṣūlī's vision is clouded. A practical example of this can be seen juxtaposing *akhbār* on the same subject found in different places in the *Awrāq*.

Chapter Two has illustrated how the matter of al-Rāḍī's education, which is only briefly mentioned in the chronicle of al-Muqtadir's caliphate, is expanded on later in the book, presumably after al-Rāḍī's death, when al-Ṣūlī is free to be considerably more dispassionate in his evaluation of al-Muqtadir's ignorance. One of the main characters in these stories is the chamberlain Naṣr, who was in charge of organizing the children's schooling.

At the beginning of his chronicle of al-Muqtadir's reign, al-Ṣūlī devotes a long section to the virtues of the young caliph. Within the general positivity, a careful reader may identify a delicate description of the caliph as an ignoramus, disguised as praise of his disposition: al-Muqtadir, while pious and full of good intentions, lacked experience and 'had not read the lives of famous people (*al-siyar*) or the chronicles (*al-akhbār*)'. Al-Ṣūlī attributes this assessment to Naṣr, safely dead at the time of writing, who 'would hint at this without expressing it in words'.[54] Al-Ṣūlī claims to have been the frequent recipient of Naṣr's confidence – indeed, as has been seen in Chapter Two, Naṣr's frustration with al-Muqtadir is made much clearer and detailed later in the *Awrāq*, when al-Ṣūlī returns on the subject of al-Rāḍī's education.

In the internal economy of the *Awrāq*, being in Naṣr's confidence reinforces the credibility of al-Ṣūlī's testimony in the eyes of his intended reader. On his part, the observant reader will notice how al-Ṣūlī measures out Naṣr's confidences carefully: when he relates Naṣr's scathing comments later in the book, al-Ṣūlī provides the key to interpreting the earlier benevolent assessment. The initial benevolent assessment, then, is not transmitted uncritically in the first place, but simply used judiciously.

Influence

The events discussed in Chapter Two offer a further example of access that is more remarkable because it implies al-Ṣūlī's reach outside the court. As we have seen, al-Ṣūlī relates that, after trying to interest the caliphal household of the improvements in the princes' education, he had been rudely rebuffed by the *qahramāna* Zaydān, who had sent a verbal message through a fellow-courtier:

> In the eyes of the Lady [Shaghab] and those who serve her, the virtues this man [promotes] are shortcomings. Tell him from me: 'Hey, you [*yā hādhā*], we don't want our children to become men of letters or scholars. Look at their father: he's not learned but there's nothing wrong with him! See that you act on this.'[55]

In the meantime, Ibn Abī l-Sāj (d. 315/928), the governor of Azerbayjān, Armenia and Arrān, was in Wāsiṭ, preparing to attack the Qarāmiṭa rebels. Al-Ṣūlī had addressed an epistle (*risāla ṭawīla*) to him, suggesting that he wait. He received a reply hand-delivered by one of Ibn Abī l-Sāj's secretaries, an Ibn Harāsha. Al-Ṣūlī does not describe the substance of the reply but mentions that, in the conclusion, the governor commiserated with al-Ṣūlī for his treatment, quoting Zaydān's words *verbatim*. Al-Ṣūlī, concerned that this had become a widespread rumour and that he may be blamed for originating it, confided in the chamberlain Naṣr. The latter reassured him: some eunuchs in the palace service were informer for Ibn Abī l-Sāj, and this is how he must have been informed.

Al-Ṣūlī's reasons for relating this episode – which can be dated to 315/927 – in the chronicle for the year 322/934–5, have been discussed in Chapter Two. It remains to investigate how it came to be that al-Ṣūlī was offering advice to a provincial governor and military leader, and why the governor's entourage should be interested in the details of al-Ṣūlī's life at court. Again, the curious reader will find an answer by going back to the chronicles of earlier years.

Ibn Abī l-Sāj takes up much space in the chronicle of 315/926–7. Al-Ṣūlī explains that ʿAlī b. ʿĪsā, newly reinstated vizier to replace ʿUbaydallāh al-Kalwadhhānī, disagreed with the latter's decision to summon Ibn Abī l-Sāj from the east for the purpose of fighting the Qarāmiṭa, who were at that point occupying Basra. In particular, nobody wanted Ibn Abī l-Sāj's troops to enter Baghdad, so he was rerouted to Wāsiṭ, where his men wreaked great havoc without his intervening to stop them, to the worry of his supporters. Al-Ṣūlī then explains that his acquaintance with Ibn Abī l-Sāj went back a few years, when, between 307/919 and 310/922, the latter had been imprisoned in Baghdad. After being moved from the Palace, where he was in the care of Zaydān, to another residence, Ibn Abī l-Sāj had summoned al-Ṣūlī and asked him to supply him with scholarly books (*kutub al-ʿulūm*). Al-Ṣūlī had found him an intelligent man, 'who knew what was due to him and what he owed', a generous and courteous friend, and paid him frequent visits until he was released from imprisonment and left Baghdad. Al-Ṣūlī now returns to the present of the year 315 and describes the contents of his twenty-page letter, where he encourages Ibn Abī l-Sāj to bide his time and not rush towards Basra. As in other occasions, his argument is based on precedent: he mentions 'the eastern Arabia (*al-Baḥrayn*) affair', i.e. the repression of Kharijite rebel Abū Fudayk (d. 73/693) at the hands of a large Umayyad army. In the end, concludes al-Ṣūlī, God decreed that things should go otherwise: Ibn Abī l-Sāj was forced to fight near Kufa, where he was captured and then killed. However, the Qarmaṭī army had been greatly weakened by the battle and was defeated shortly afterwards, before reaching Bagdhad.[56]

It is worth going back to the cluster of accounts on the princes' education discussed in Chapter Two, and add to its complexity. The cluster is found in the chronicle for the year 322/934 and is introduced as a flashback to explain an allusion al-Ṣūlī makes in a poem. It refers to events spanning three years, from al-Ṣūlī's appointment as a tutor in 312 to his dismissal in 315, but mainly connected to this later time. In the flashback, al-Ṣūlī mentions the letter to Ibn Abī l-Sāj. At this, point, the narrative goes back to the year 322, but the reader may pause and look up two places in the book: in the year 312, she will find mention of al-Ṣūlī's appointment to tutor the princes; in the year 315, she will find the contents of al-Ṣūlī's letter to Ibn Abī l-Sāj. Within the letter, there is a reference to events of the first century of Islam which may be assumed to be common knowledge, but al-Ṣūlī also explains his connection to Ibn Abī l-Sāj referring to his imprisonment in Baghdad between 307 and 310.

We have seen a similar web of cross-references in Chapter Three, where a poetic dispute between al-Rāḍī and Ibn al-Munajjim unveils a political and religious conflict spanning several generations. In that case, the connective tissue keeping together the story across time is poetry. Here, the central element is al-Ṣūlī's personal contact with, and attempted influence on, prominent people.

Of course, none of the examples we have seen so far is successful: the Palace does not pay for the princes' training in religious sciences; Ibn Abī l-Sāj does go into battle with the Qarāmiṭa; and al-Rāḍī does go to Mosul. Still, it is important, from a strategic point of view, to include al-Ṣūlī's advice, because it had been right in all three cases.

The vain memorialist

Sourdel's assessment at the beginning of this chapter is as cutting as it is vague: what is this 'sense of history' which al-Ṣūlī sorely lacks? This expression seems to condense different kinds of criticism levelled at al-Ṣūlī's work: formally and stylistically, poetry is too prominent; content-wise, too much attention is devoted to insignificant events of al-Ṣūlī's personal life and the confined world of the court; as for understanding, his petty troubles and short-term objectives cloud his reading of the past. This last point is especially ambiguous because it implies that al-Ṣūlī is at the same time naïve – not able to interpret events in a mature way – and cunning enough to manipulate his account of the past to use it for self-promotion.

Some of this criticism cannot be supported or refuted, as it concerns al-Ṣūlī's intentions. However, the cases discussed in this volume have hopefully provided enough evidence to argue against al-Ṣūlī's supposed lack of historical sense, and to draft a working definition of what his specific brand of historical sense is.

- Firstly, al-Ṣūlī's *perspective* is his own physical standpoint, i.e. for most of the chronicle, Baghdad. This is manifested in two ways: on the one hand, with his attention to the plight of the population; on the other, he relates events when news of their happening reaches the capital. When al-Ṣūlī leaves the capital, as during the expedition to Mosul, or after the death of al-Rāḍī, the narrative follows him, although even then Baghdad remains important.
- Secondly, while Miskawayh's main *focus* is the administration, al-Ṣūlī's is the caliph. As a consequence, the latter's actions are seen as most influential in shaping future events. This explains, as has been seen above, why Miskawayh sees the appointment of the first *amīr al-umarāʾ* as highly significant, because it marks the end of vizieral authority, al-Ṣūlī attributes more importance to the caliph's decisions and movements. In fact, al-Ṣūlī explicitly ties Baghdad to the caliph in this respect when he attributes al-Muttaqī's deposition to his decision to leave the capital.
- Thirdly, the distinguishing features of al-Ṣūlī's *style* point to an obsessive attention to detail and exactness: he only relates word-by-word dialogue when he is an involved or uninvolved participant; he aids the narrative with written or easy to memorize documents (notes, poetry, letters); and he often provides assessments of his sources' character.
- Finally, al-Ṣūlī's *interpretation* is based on precedent: many of his arguments cite similar events of the distant past, or trace reasons for the present situation back to previous decisions or episodes. In this sense, al-Ṣūlī maintains and promotes the memory of the caliphs and of the caliphate.

Conclusion

> *The relation to a normative self-image of the group engenders a clear system of values and differentiations in importance which structure the cultural supply of knowledge and the symbols.*[1]
>
> Jan Assmann

Going back to Muḥammad Kurd ʿAlī's remarks, quoted at the very the beginning of the Introduction, we may find that this volume has illustrated all of Kurd ʿAlī's points: al-Ṣūlī's status as a unique representative of the culture of his time, his standing at court, and his way of recording and disseminating 'the useful lessons that came his way'. Memory has been implicit in much that has been said in this volume, and indeed, it is consistent with al-Ṣūlī's scholarly reputation from early on: ʿArīb, as has been seen in Chapter Four, talks of al-Ṣūlī's 'knowledge of the accounts [of the Abbasids] and his memory (*ḥifẓuhu*) of what happened in their times'.[2] This last phrase connects with Assmann's description of communicative memory in relation to cultural memory: it may be argued that the clusters of accounts from the *Awrāq* which have been discussed in this volume, those in Chapters Three and Five in particular, capture this transition from communicative memory to cultural memory. One practical example, discussed in Chapter Five, is the appointment of Ibn Rāʾiq as *amīr al-umarāʾ* and the different ways in which al-Ṣūlī and Miskawayh relate it: for the latter, it is a fixed point; for the former, it is part of a process – it has no particular symbolic value, but this does not mean that it has no importance when read in context.

As was stated in the Introduction, and as should be abundantly clear by now, this book is not a life-and-times monograph, nor is it a life-and-works one. It is, rather, an attempt to illustrate how exploring the life, times and works of a complex individual can serve as a *fil rouge* to the investigation of contested concepts. We have elaborated on several reasons for al-Ṣūlī's validity as a case study: he is one of the few authors known to us who personally witnessed and recorded events at the Abbasid court; his view and use of the past to interpret contemporary events shed light on the culture of his time; his literary style illustrates key features of pre-modern Arabic narrative texts, such as the interplay of prose and poetry, which tend to be underrated in modern historical analyses; and, crucially, his account of himself and his times can be cross-checked with those of other sources. Chapter One and Two have hopefully illustrated the importance of this last point: acknowledging the distance between al-Ṣūlī's account of himself in the *Awrāq* and his portrayal in biographical collections highlights, on the one hand, the creative power of biographers who, far from being acritical compilers, produce curated profiles that fit the requirements of their work. On the other hand, it validates al-Ṣūlī's autobiographical remarks as original and individual.

In Chapter Five, we have seen that these autobiographical remarks affect al-Ṣūlī's historical accounts on two levels: isolated from the context, they form a personal history which is parallel to the political one; in context, they frame and punctuate the main narrative, serving as one of the tools that bind it into a tightly woven texture. If this binding function is ignored, Hilāl al-Ṣābi''s criticism becomes valid: al-Ṣūlī's work is filled with unnecessary stuffing and silly poetry.[3] Indeed, poetry is undoubtedly the second of these binding tools, intertwined with the first. In Chapter Four we have observed its function as a spinal cord for the *Awrāq* as a whole; in Chapters Two, Three, and Five we have seen examples of its use in the historical narrative, both within *akhbār* and as independent units.

What can an investigation on al-Ṣūlī tell us, then, in more general terms, on the interpretation of classical Arabic narrative material? Mostly, it poses problems and raises questions. First, it highlights shortcomings in modern analytical tools: while the literary analysis of historical narratives has been a staple of Arabic studies since the late twentieth century, its results are not always taken into account. After all, for instance, why should it matter, in the greater scheme of things, that the life and reputation of al-Ṣūlī differ so wildly? This book argues that it does indeed matter, because it informs our reading of the *Awrāq* and determines how seriously we take al-Ṣūlī as a mature historian: the memoir of a chess-player does not carry the same weight as the first-person account of a scholar.[4]

Investigating al-Ṣūlī also forces us to problematize our use of categories. Terminology such as 'biographical dictionary' and 'autobiography' have long been contested, and genre subdivisions (it may be argued, the concept of genre as a whole) are usually recognised as exogenous, but they are still often employed casually. The consequences are, again, in our reading: separating one section of the *Awrāq* from the rest leads us to overlook elements which do not belong to a narrow definition of genre or discipline – typically, disregarding narrative prose in the accounts of poets, or poetry in the accounts of caliphs. This is precisely where exploring an author's milieu and ways of disseminating his scholarship is of great help: al-Ṣūlī's references to his notebooks reveal a jagged landscape of intersecting disciplines and personal networks which can be related to the structure of his cultural production.[5]

Finally, the way in which al-Ṣūlī records the recent past, and makes sense of it by setting it against precedents and principles, provides a glimpse into the process through which personal experience – al-Ṣūlī's communicative memory, in Assmann's framework – becomes the memory of the caliphate.

Notes

Introduction

1 Muḥammad Kurd ʿAlī, *Kunūz al-ajdād fī siyar baʿḍ al-aʿlām* (Damascus: al-Majmaʿ al-ʿIlmī al-ʿArabī bi-Dimashq, 1950), 143.

2 On Muḥammad Kurd ʿAlī (1876–1953) see Charles Pellat, 'Kurd ʿAlī', in *EI2*.

3 Recent examples are Antoine Borrut, *Entre mémoire et pouvoir: l'espace syrien sous les derniers Omeyyades et les premiers Abbassides (v. 72–193/692–809)*, (Leiden: Brill, 2011); and Nadia Maria El-Cheikh, *Women, Islam, and Abbasid Identity* (Cambridge, MA: Harvard University Press, 2015). For a general discussion, see Michael Cooperson, 'The Abbasid "Golden Age": an Excavation,' *Al-ʿUṣūr al-Wusṭā* 25 (2017).

4 I borrow the expression from Sonja Brentjes, 'The Prison of Categories – "Decline" and its Company,' in *Islamic Philosophy, Science, Culture, and Religion: Studies in Honor of Dimitri Gutas*, eds Felicitas Opwis and David Reisman (Leiden: Brill, 2021). For a typical mid-twentieth century approach, see Charles Pellat, 'Was al-Masʿūdī a Historian or an *adīb*?' *Journal of the Pakistan Historical Society* 9 (1961).

5 Aḥmad Jamāl al-ʿUmarī, *Abū Bakr al-Ṣūli: al-ʿālim, al-adīb, al-nadīm* (Cairo: al-Hayʾa al-Miṣriyya al-ʿĀmma lil-Kitāb, 1973); Aḥmad Jamāl al-ʿUmarī, *Abū Bakr al-Ṣūli (255–336 H): ḥayātuhu wa-adabuhu, dīwānuhu* (Cairo: Dār al-Maʿārif, 1984). I have not been able to consult this second edition.

6 For example, Abū Tammām, *Sharḥ al-Ṣūlī li-dīwān Abī Tammām*, ed. Khalaf Rashīd Nuʿmān, 3 vols (Baghdad: Wizārat al-Aʿlām, 1977). One of the earliest studies on al-Ṣūlī's literary criticism is Ṣubḥī Nāṣir Ḥusayn, *Abū Bakr al-Ṣūlī nāqidan* (Baghdad: Dār al-Jāḥiẓ lil-Ṭibāʿa wa-l-Nashr, 1975).

7 Abū Bakr al-Ṣūlī, *Akhbār Abī Tammām*, eds Khalīl Maḥmūd ʿAsākir, Muḥammad ʿAbduh ʿAzzām and Naẓīr al-Islām al-Hindī (Cairo: Lajnat al-Taʾlīf wa-l-Tarjama wa-l-Nashr, 1937); Abū Bakr al-Ṣūlī, *The Life and Times of Abū Tammām*, ed. and trans. Beatrice Gruendler (New York: New York University Press, 2015).

8 Ḥammādī Ṣammūd, *Balāghat al-intiṣār fī l-naqd al-ʿarabī al-qadīm: risālat Abī Bakr al-Ṣūlī ilā Muzāḥim b. Fātik unmūdhijan* (Tunis: Dār al-Maʿrifa lil-Nashr, 2006); Issam Benchellel, 'Naqd al-naqd wa-tajliyātuhu ʿinda Abī Bakr al-Ṣūlī,' *Al-Judhūr* 55

(2019); al-Ḥusayn Mubārak Akhalīfa, *al-Khabar al-adabī ʿinda Abī Bakr al-Ṣūlī: muqāraba sardiyya tawāṣuliyya* (Amman: Dār al-Muʿtazz, 2017); Beatrice Gruendler, 'Meeting the Patron: an *akhbār* Type and its Implications for *muḥdath* Poetry,' in *Ideas, Images, and Methods of Portrayal: Insights into Classical Arabic Literature and Islam*, ed. Sebastian Günther (Wiesbaden: Harrassowitz, 2005); Beatrice Gruendler, 'Verse and Taxes: the Function of Poetry in selected literary *akhbār* of the third/ninth Century,' in *On Fiction and adab in medieval Arabic Literature*, ed. Philip F. Kennedy (Wiesbaden: Harrassowitz, 2005). In Chapter Four, I argue that a clear distinction between the literary and historical parts of the *Awrāq* is artificial. Therefore, the very notion of literary *akhbār* is fuzzy.

9 Abū Bakr al-Ṣūlī, *Akhbār al-shuʿarāʾ al-muḥdathīn*, ed. J. Heyworth Dunne (Beirut: Dār al-Masīra, 1934); Abū Bakr al-Ṣūlī, *Akhbār al-Rāḍī bi-llāh wa l-Muttaqī li-llāh, aw, Tārīkh al-dawla al-ʿabbāsiyya min sanat 322 ilā sanat 333 hijriyya min Kitāb al-Awrāq*, ed. J. Heyworth Dunne (Beirut: Dār al-Masīra, 1935); Abū Bakr al-Ṣūlī, *Ashʿār awlād al-khulafāʾ*, ed. J. Heyworth Dunne (Beirut: Dār al-Masīra, 1936) (henceforth, *ASM*, *ARM*, and *AAK* respectively). In a series of four articles, Ibrāhīm al-Samārrāʾī suggested specific corrections to these volumes (Ibrāhīm al-Sāmarrāʾī, 'Qirāʾāt fī l-kutub: 'al-Warāq' lil-Ṣūlī,' *Majallat al-ʿArab* 6 (1391/1971)).

10 Abū Bakr al-Ṣūlī, *Ak̲h̲bār al-Rāḍī bi-llāh wa'l-Muttaḳī li-llāh (Histoire de la dynastie abbaside de 322 à 333/934 à 944)*, 2 vols (Algier: Institut d'Études Orientales, 1946); Abū Bakr al-Ṣūlī, *Kitāb al-Awrāq. Kniga Listov*, ed. and trans. Anas B. Khalidov (St Petersburg: Tsentr Peterburgoskoe Vostokovedenie, 1998).

11 Abū Bakr al-Ṣūlī, *Qiṭʿa nādira min Kitāb al-awrāq*, ed. Hilāl Nājī (Baghdad: Dār al-Shuʾūn al-Thaqāfiyya al-ʿĀmma, 1990); Abū Bakr al-Ṣūlī, *Mā lam yunshar min Awrāq al-Ṣūlī: akhbār al-sanawāt 295–315*, ed. Hilāl Nājī (Beirut: ʿĀlam al-Kutub, 2000). References to this work are to this edition; the same unique manuscript has also been published in the edition of K.R. Nuʿmān, Baghdad, 1999, which I have not consulted.

12 Abū ʿAlī Aḥmad b. Muḥammad Miskawayh, *Tajārib al-umam: The Eclipse of the Abbasid Caliphate*, ed. H.F. Amedroz, trans. D.S. Margoliouth (Oxford 1920); ʿArīb b. Saʿd al-Qurṭubī, *Ṣilat tārīkh al-Ṭabarī: Tabarî Continuatus*, ed. M.J. De Goeje (Leiden: Brill, 1897).

13 One exception is Maaike van Berkel et al., *Crisis and Continuity at the Abbasid Court: Formal and Informal Politics in the Caliphate of al-Muqtadir (295–320/908–32)* (Leiden: Brill, 2013). As for works on administration and chancery, see for example Paul L. Heck, *The Construction of Knowledge in Islamic Civilization: Qudāma b. Jaʿfar and his Kitāb al-Kharāj wa-ṣināʿat al-kitāba* (Leiden: Brill, 2002), 65–72.

14 Andrew Bennett, *The Author* (London: Routledge, 2005), 73–83.

15 See for example the discussion in Lale Behzadi and Jaakko Hämeen-Anttila, eds. *Concepts of Authorship in Pre-Modern Arabic Texts* (Bamberg: University of Bamberg Press, 2015), and especially Behzadi's 'Introduction' (pp. 9–22). An example relevant to the subject of this volume is Julia Bray, 'Ibn al-Muʿtazz and Politics: The Question of the *Fuṣūl Qiṣār*,' *Oriens* 38 (2010).

16 Throughout this volume, I use court as a shorthand term for any situation in which a ruler or person in authority is surrounded by an entourage. My points of reference are Nadia Maria El Cheikh, 'The Court of al-Muqtadir: its Space and its Occupants,' in *Abbasid Studies II: Occasional Paper of the School of ʿAbbasid Studies, Leuven 28 June–1 July, 2004*, ed. John Nawas (Leuven: Peeters, 2010); and Nadia Maria El Cheikh, 'Court and Courtiers: a Preliminary Investigation of Abbasid Terminology,' in *Court Cultures in the Muslim World: Seventh to Nineteenth Centuries*, eds Albrecht Fuess and Jan-Peter Hartung (New York: Routledge, 2011). This is a much looser concept than that described, for instance, by Naaman (Erez Naaman, *Literature and the Islamic Court: Cultural Life under al-Ṣāḥib Ibn ʿAbbād* (London: Routledge, 2016), Chapter 2 especially). As a consequence, I use 'courtier' to describe a wider and more varied group. The most recent comprehensive (and, unlike Naaman's, comparative) discussion of the concept is provided in Christian Mauder, *In the Sultan's Salon: Learning, Religion, and Rulership at the Mamluk Court of Qanisawh al-Ghawri (r. 1501–1516)*, (Leiden: Brill, 2021), 15–28 and Chapter One in general.

17 Jan Assmann, 'Collective Memory and Cultural Identity,' *New German Critique* 65 (1995): 127.

18 Assmann, 'Collective Memory,' 129.

19 See, for instance, Beatrice Gruendler, *The Rise of the Arabic Book* (Cambridge, MA: Harvard University Press, 2020), 23–4.

1 Life and Afterlife

1 Fritz Krenkow, 'The Tarikh-Baghdad (Vol. XXVII) of the Khatib Abu Bakr Ahmad b. ʿAli b. Thabit al-Baghdadi: Short Account of the Biographies,' *Journal of the Royal Asiatic Society* (1912): 33.

2 The seminal work on this topic is Hilary Kilpatrick, 'Context and the Enhancement of the Meaning of *Akhbār* in the *Kitāb al-Aghānī*,' *Arabica* 38 (1991). The concept is given context in Stefan Leder and Hilary Kilpatrick, 'Classical Arabic Prose Literature: a Researcher's Sketch Map,' *Journal of Arabic Literature* 23 (1992). Other works will be cited in the course of this chapter.

3 Wadād al-Qāḍī, 'Biographical Dictionaries: Inner Structure and Cultural Significance,' in *The Book in the Islamic World: the Written Word and Communication in the Middle East*, ed. George N. Atiyeh (Albany: State University of New York Press for the Library of Congress, 1995), 94.

4 Wadād al-Qāḍī, 'Biographical Dictionaries as the Scholars' Alternative History of the Muslim Community,' in *Organizing Knowledge: Encyclopædic Activities in the Pre-Eighteenth Century Islamic World*, ed. Gerhard Endress and Abdou Filali-Ansary (Leiden: Brill, 2006); Claude Gilliot, 'Prosopography in Islam: an Essay of Classification,' *Medieval Prosopography* 23 (2002). Young clarifies this classification thus: 'Biography seeks to understand the individual and those features of character which make him or her unique; prosopography seeks to record a group of individuals having certain features in common, and these individuals are viewed in relationship to the prevailing characteristics of the group' (M.J.L. Young, 'Arabic Biographical Writing,' in *Religion, Learning and Science in the ʿAbbasid Period*, ed. M.J.L. Young (Cambridge: Cambridge University Press, 1990), 170). Maribel Fierro has discussed biographical writing in similar terms, asking why scholars belonging to some legal *madhhab*s in the Islamic West did not collect records of their lives (see for example Maribel Fierro, 'Why and How Do Religious Scholars Write about Themselves? The Case of the Islamic West in the Fourth/Tenth Century,' *Mélanges de L'Université Saint-Joseph* 58 (2005)).

5 Manuela Marín, ed., *Arab-Islamic Medieval Culture: Special Issue of Medieval Prosopography, 23 (2002)* (Kalamazoo: Medieval Institute Publications, Western Michigan University, 2002). For instance, Arie Schippers's contribution in this volume relies on poetry, and Jouan A. Souto's is based on epigraphic sources.

6 The same can be said for 'encyclopaedia'. See for example James Weaver, 'What Wasn't an Encyclopaedia in the Fourth Islamic Century? *Asiatische Studien – Études Asiatiques* 71 (2017). We shall return on the concept of 'encyclopaedism' in Chapter Four.

7 al-Qāḍī, 'Biographical Dictionaries,' 96.

8 Muḥammad b. Isḥāq Ibn al-Nadīm, *Kitāb al-Fihrist*, ed. A.F. Sayyid (London: al-Furqan Islamic Heritage Foundation, 2009), I/1, 3.

9 The latter view was first expressed by Otto Loth, 'Die Ursprung und Bedeutung der Tabaqat,' *Zeitschrift der Deutschen Morgenländischen Gesellschaft* 23 (1869); the former was adopted by Wilhelm Heffening, 'Ṭabaḳāt,' in *Encyclopaedia of Islam, First Edition (1913–1936)* (Leiden: Brill), decades later. In general, scholarship regarding biography as a direct filiation of *ḥadīth* studies has focused on biographies of religious practitioners, while leaving out, or putting down as 'later development,' collections on other professional categories (e.g. poets and grammarians). Studies considering biography writing as a typically Arab pre-Islamic, tribal interest in genealogy, have concentrated on exactly the latter

collections. The different arguments are summarized in Paul Auchterlonie, 'Historians and the Arabic Biographical Dictionary: Some New Approaches', in *Islamic Reflections, Arabic Musings: Studies in Honour of Professor Alan Jones*, eds Robert G. Hoyland and Philip F. Kennedy (Warminster: Gibb Memorial Trust, 2004).

10 Michael Cooperson, *Classical Arabic Biography: the Heirs of the Prophets* (Cambridge: Cambridge University Press, 2000), 6.

11 Kilpatrick and Leder place works of the *ṭabaqāt* type within the broad category of the compilations, stating that 'from the point of view of style there is no sharp distinction between specialized books and works of belles-lettres', and that 'a particularly close connection exists between those compilations which have an historical or a literary orientation, since they often include the same texts' (Leder and Kilpatrick, 'Classical Arabic Prose Literature', 17–18). I use 'profile' as a general term including both distinct entries in biographical collections and less formally arranged units, as defined in Hilary Kilpatrick, 'Abū-l-Faraj's Profiles of Poets: a 4th/10th Century Essay at the History and Sociology of Arabic Literature', *Arabica* 44 (1997). More recently, Julia Bray has argued that 'life-writing' should replace 'literature' as a catchall term 'in most contexts, because of the many components and features shared by storytelling, history and biography, all of which are largely constructed from anecdotes or purported reports attributed to historical actors or eyewitnesses, which were collected and circulated, orally and in writing, by named scholars, with pedigrees of transmission to situate them on the map of learning' (Julia Bray, 'Codes of Emotion in Ninth- and Tenth-Century Baghdad: Slave Concubines in Literature and Life-Writing', *Cultural History* 8 (2019): 184).

12 See, for example: Franz Rosenthal, *A History of Muslim Historiography*, 2nd ed. (Leiden: E.J. Brill, 1968), 93–8, 99-106, 72; Tarif Khalidi, *Arabic Historical Thought in the Classical Period* (Cambridge: Cambridge University Press, 1994), 46–8, 204–10; R. Stephen Humphreys, 'Taʾrīkh. II. Historical Writing. 1. In the Arab World,' in *EI2*, 271–80.

13 Indeed, for some aspects, it is the only way, as Roy Mottahedeh's oft-quoted remark aptly summarizes: 'Ulemalogy [sic] is a noble science – at least we have to think so, because it is almost all the Islamic social history we will ever have for this period' (Roy Mottahedeh, review of *The Patricians of Nishapur: a Study in Medieval Islamic Social History*, R.W. Bulliet, *Journal of the American Oriental Society* 95 (1975)). See also al-Rāfiʿī's summary quoted in al-Qāḍī, 'Scholars' Alternative,' 23.

14 Auchterlonie, 'New Approaches' provides a summary of the work carried out in this field up to the early 2000s.

15 One of the most notable examples is the above-mentioned Kilpatrick, 'Context,' which looks at the role of 'units of information' (i.e. *akhbār*) within such a large work as the *Kitāb al-Aghānī*, which encompasses several genres. Most recently, see Antonella Ghersetti, 'Classes of Grammarians East and West: *Ṭabaqāt al-naḥwiyyīn wa-l-lughawiyyīn of al-Zubaydī and Marātib al-naḥwiyyīn* of Abū l-Ṭayyib al-Lughawī,' *Journal of Abbasid Studies* 7 (2020).

16 The seminal work in this field is Fedwa Malti-Douglas, 'Controversy and its Effects on the Biographical Tradition of al-Khatib al-Baghdadi,' *Studia Islamica* 46 (1977). Even Auchterlonie, who considers this kind of investigation 'not strictly relevant to historians,' acknowledges, somewhat grudgingly, that 'they cannot afford to ignore any serious study of a such significant source for their own researches' (Auchterlonie, 'New Approaches,' 200).

17 Malti-Douglas, already in 1980, talks of 'the pitfalls inherent in the attempt to distinguish between purely literary or purely historical effect. A change in one aspect of the text most often represents a change in the other. This is because the Medieval Arabic biographical notice functions as a semiotic system, that is a system of signs. To be more precise, the biographical notices themselves should be understood as *parole*, while their *langue*, or system, would be the ensemble of semiotic codes which logically precede their composition' (Fedwa Malti-Douglas, 'Dreams, the Blind, and the Semiotics of the Biographical Notice,' *Studia Islamica* (1980): 140).

18 I am borrowing the terms 'frames' and 'fillings' from Julia Bray. See, in particular, Julia Bray, 'Literary Approaches to Medieval and Early Modern Arabic Biography,' *Journal of the Royal Asiatic Society* 20 (2010): 3–5.

19 I use *nisba* in a loose sense, as illustrated in Hayyim J. Cohen, 'The Economic Background and the Secular Occupations of Muslim Jurisprudents and Traditionists in the Classical Period of Islam (until the middle of the eleventh century),' *Journal of the Economic and Social History of the Orient* 13 (1970).

20 Kilpatrick, 'Profiles of Poets,' 100. In a later article, Kilpatrick differentiates between biographical dictionaries, which 'tend to present their subjects according to a fixed scheme,' and life writing contained in other types of works. Still, her argument about the fluctuating importance of chronological order often applies to profiles within biographical collections (Hilary Kilpatrick, 'Time and Death in Compiled *adab* "Biographies",' *al-Qanṭara* 25 (2004)).

21 Throughout this volume, I use different translations of *kātib/kuttāb* (secretary, clerk, bureaucrat) or leave it in transliteration, depending on context, to highlight the different ranks and specializations this term can describe.

22 The term *nadīm*, al-Ṣūlī's preferred synonym *jalīs*, and their English translation are discussed in Chapter Two.

23 *Kullu mā fī hadhihi l-khizāna samāʿī*. The concept of *samāʿ* will be discussed in Chapter Three; see also Letizia Osti, 'Notes on a Private Library in fourth/tenth-century Baghdad,' *Journal of Arabic and Islamic Studies* 12 (2012): 216–17.

24 Al-Ṣūlī's full bibliography will be looked at in Chapter Four. In this first version I translate book titles as much as possible to provide a general idea. Later, I will mostly transliterate the original Arabic in order to highlight specific elements and variations.

25 Yāqūt b. ʿAbdallāh al-Ḥamawī, *Muʿjam al-udabāʾ: Irshād al-arīb ilā maʿrifat al-adīb (irshād al-alibbāʾ fī maʿrifat al-udabāʾ)*, ed. Iḥsān ʿAbbās, 7 vols (Beirut: Dār al-Gharb al-Islāmī, 1993), 6, 2677–8.

26 Abū ʿUbayd Allāh Muḥammad b. ʿImrān b. Mūsā al-Marzubānī, *Muʿjam al-shuʿarāʾ*, ed. ʿAbd al-Sattār Aḥmad Farrāj (Cairo: Dār Iḥyāʾ al-Kutub al-ʿArabiyya/Muṣṭafā al-Bābī al-Ḥalabī wa-Awlāduhu, 1960), 431–2.

27 Abū ʿUbayd Allāh Muḥammad b. ʿImrān b. Mūsā al-Marzubānī, *Die Gelehrtenbiographien des Abū ʿUbaidallāh al-Marzubānī in der Rezension des Ḥāfiẓ al-Yaġmūrī (Nūr al-Qabas al-Muqtaṣar min al-Muqtabas fī Akhbār al-Nuḥat wa-l-Udabāʾ wa-l-Shuʿarāʾ wa-l-ʿUlamāʾ)*, ed. Rudolph Sellheim (Wiesbaden: Franz Steiner Verlag, 1964), 346.

28 Ibn al-Nadīm, *Fihrist*, I/2, 464–5 and 480.

29 al-Khaṭīb al-Baghdādī, *Taʾrīkh Baghdād*, ed. Muṣṭafā ʿAbd al-Qādir ʿAṭā, 21 vols (Beirut: Dār al-Kutub al-ʿIlmiyya, 1997), 4, 198–202.

30 ʿAbd al-Karīm b. Muḥammad b. Manṣūr al-Tamīmī al-Samʿānī, *al-Ansāb*, 13 vols (Hayderabad: Dāʾirat al-Maʿārif al-ʿUthmāniyya, 1952–82), 8, 348–50.

31 Abū l-Barakāt ʿAbd al-Raḥmān b. Muḥammad Ibn al-Anbārī, *Nuzhat al-alibbāʾ fī akhbār al-udabāʾ*, ed. Ibrāhīm al-Sāmarrāʾī (al-Zarqāʾ: Maktabat al-Manār, 1959), 204–6.

32 Abū l-Faraj ʿAbd al-Raḥmān b. ʿAlī Ibn al-Jawzī, *al-Muntaẓam fī tāʾrīkh al-mulūk wa-l-umam*, eds Muḥammad ʿAbd al-Qādir ʿAṭā and Muṣṭafā ʿAbd al-Qādir ʿAṭā, 19 vols (Beirut: Dār al-Kutub al-ʿIlmiyya, 1992–3), 14, 68–70. Al-Ṣūlī's biography appears in the section on 336/947–8, the year after his death: as the editor explains (p. 56, n. 4), the entry was taken out and then reinserted in the extant copy of the work.

33 Yāqūt, *Irshād*, 6, 2677–8.

34 ʿAlī b. Muḥammad ʿIzz al-Dīn Ibn al-Athīr, *al-Kāmil fī l-taʾrīkh*, ed. ʿUmar Tadmurī, 10 vols (Beirut: Dār al-Kitāb al-ʿArabī, 1997), 7, 174.

35 ʿAlī b. Muḥammad ʿIzz al-Dīn Ibn al-Athīr, *al-Lubāb fī tahdhīb al-Ansāb*, ed. ʿAbd al-Laṭīf Ḥasan ʿAbd al-Raḥmān, 2 vols (Beirut: Dār al-Kutub al-ʿIlmiyya, 2000), 1, 56–7.

36 Aḥmad b. Muḥammad Ibn Khallikān, *Wafayāt al-a ʿyān*, ed. Iḥsān ʿAbbās, 8 vols (Beirut: Dār al-Thaqāfa, 1968–72), 4, 356–61; Aḥmad b. Muḥammad Ibn Khallikān, *Kitāb Wafayāt al-a ʿyān: Ibn Khallikān's Biographical Dictionary*, trans. B. Mac Guckin De Slane, 4 vols (Paris: Oriental Translation Fund, 1843–71), 3, 68–73.

37 Ismāʿīl b. ʿAlī Abū l-Fidāʾ, *al-Mukhtaṣar fī akhbār al-bashar*, 4 vols (Cairo: al-Maṭbaʿa al-Ḥusayniyya al-Miṣriyya, s.d.), 2, 96.

38 Muḥammad b. Aḥmad b. ʿUthmān al-Dhahabī, *Tadhkirat al-ḥuffāẓ*, ed. Zakarīyā ʿUmayrāt (Beirut: Dār al-Kutub al-ʿIlmiyya, 1998), 3, 46.

39 Muḥammad b. Aḥmad b. ʿUthmān al-Dhahabī, *Ta ʾrīkh al-islām*, ed. ʿUmar Tadmurī (Beirut: Dār al-Kitāb al-ʿArabī, 1987–95), 25, 130–1.

40 Ṣalāḥ al-Dīn Khalīl b. Aybak al-Ṣafadī, *Kitāb al-Wāfī bi-l-wafayāt. Das biographische Lexikon des Ṣalāḥaddīn Ḫalīl ibn Aibak aṣ-Ṣafadī*, eds Helmut Ritter, Sven Dedering, et al., 32 vols (Leipzig; Wiesbaden; Beirut: Deutsche Morgenländische Geselleschaft, 1931–2013), 5, 190–2 (vol. 5 1970).

41 al-Yāfiʿī, *Mir ʾāt al-jinān wa- ʿibrat al-yaqẓān*, ed. Khalīl al-Manṣūr, 4 vols (Beirut: Dār al-Kutub al-ʿIlmiyya, 1997), 4, 240–4.

42 Ismāʿīl b. ʿUmar Ibn Kathīr, *al-Bidāya wa-l-nihāya*, ed. ʿAlī Shīrī (Beirut: Dār Iḥyāʾ al-Turāth al-ʿArabī, 1988), 11, 247–8.

43 Abū l-Maḥāsin Yūsuf Ibn Taghrībirdī, *al-Nujūm al-zāhira fī mulūk Miṣr wa-l-Qāhira* (Cairo: Dār al-Kutub al-Miṣrīya, 1929), 3, 296.

44 ʿAbd al-Hạyy b. Aḥmad Ibn al-ʿImād, *Shadharāt al-dhahab fī akhbār man dhahab*, eds ʿAbd al-Qādir Arnāʾūt and Maḥmūd Arnāʾūt, 11 vols (Damascus and Beirut: Dār Ibn Kathīr, 1986), 4, 192–6.

45 Ibn al-Nadīm, *Fihrist,* I/1, 3. On the terms *mu ʾallif* and *muṣannif*, in the *Fihrist* in particular, see Gruendler, *Arabic Book*, 52–3.

46 Ibn al-Nadīm, *Fihrist,* I/1, 5. The contents are also described, with slight changes, at the beginning of the chapter, I/2, 277; each heading is further repeated at the beginning of its section.

47 See Letizia Osti, 'Abbasid Rulers and their Standing as Authors', in *Rulers as Authors in the Islamic World: Knowledge, Authority and Legitimacy*, eds Maribel Fierro, Sonja Brentjes and Tilman Seidensticker (forthcoming).

48 al-Khaṭīb al-Baghdādī, *Ta ʾrīkh Baghdād,* 1, 227.

49 Ibn al-Anbārī, *Nuzhat al-alibbā ʾ*, 17.

50 Just after the above introduction, the *Nuzha* begins with the founder of Arabic grammar after ʿAlī, Abū l-Aswad al-Duʾalī (probably d. 69/688–9). And although the book includes individuals who are not necessarily known as primarily grammarians, it only records their educational pedigree in grammar. For instance, it only cites al-Mubarrad and Thaʿlab as the teachers of Ibn al-Muʿtazz (Ibn al-Anbārī, *Nuzhat al-alibbā ʾ*, 177).

51 Yāqūt, *Irshād,* 1, 7. Yāqūt's interests and selection criteria are discussed in Julia Bray, 'Yāqūt's Interviewing Technique: "Sniffy"', in *Texts, Documents and Artefacts: Islamic Studies in Honour of D.S. Richard*, ed. Chase F. Robinson (Leiden: Brill, 2003).

52 He cites Abū Bakr Muḥammad b. ʿAbd al-Malik al-Taʾrīkhī's (d. 330/942) *Taʾrīkh al-naḥwiyyīn*; Ibn Durustawayh (d. 347/958); al-Marzubānī's *al-Muqtabas*, which he describes as 'the *musnad* of grammarians'; al-Sīrāfī's (d. 368/978) *Ṭabaqāt al-naḥwiyyīn al-baṣriyyīn*; al-Zubaydī's (d. 379/989) *Ṭabaqāt al-naḥwiyyīn wa-l-lughawiyyīn*; al-Tanūkhī al-Maʿarrī's (d. 442/1050–1) *Taʾrīkh al-ʿulamāʾ al-naḥwiyyīn*; al-Mujāshiʿī (d. 479/1086–7); and Ibn al-Anbārī.

53 Yāqūt, *Irshād,* 1, 8.

54 For instance, in his profile of Ibn Bassām (d. 302/914), Yāqūt specifies that he will deal here with the prose production and refers to the other collection for Ibn Bassām's poetry (Yāqūt, *Irshād,* 4, 1860).

55 James E. Montgomery, 'Ẓarīf', in *EI2* (2001). As far as I'm aware, the only systematic treatment of *ẓarf* that also tackles its evolution is in two books by al-Bashīr al-Majdūb, *al-Ẓarf wa-l-ẓurafāʾ bi-l-Ḥijāz fī l-ʿaṣr al-umawī*, (Tunis: Dār al-Turkī lil-Nashr, 1988); al-Bashīr al-Majdūb, *al-Ẓarf bi-l-ʿIrāq fī l-ʿaṣr al-ʿabbāsī* (Tunis: Muʿassasāt ʿAbd al-Karīm b. ʿAbdallāh, 1992). See especially the introductory essay to the second volume, pp. 5–11.

56 Abū l-Ṭayyib Muḥammad b. Yaḥyā al-Washshāʾ, *Kitāb al-Muwashshā*, ed. Rudolf E. Brünnow (Leiden: Brill, 1886). On the ethics and morals of *ẓurafāʾ*, see Zoltan Szombathy, 'On Wit and Elegance: the Arabic Concept of Zarf', in *Authority, Privacy and Public Order in Islam*, ed. Barbara Michalak-Pikulska and Andrzej Pikulski (Leuven: Peeters, 2006). Szombathy argues that al-Washshāʾ's description of *ẓarf* is an idealized, Beduin version of an urban phenomenon.

57 See for example Wim Raven, 'Ibn Dāwūd al-Iṣbahānī and his Kitāb al-Zahra' (PhD Leiden, 1989), 27–8: 'When the adjective *ẓarīf* . . . in a biographical lexicon is applied to a man of letters, it virtually means nothing. It has become a cliché. [. . .] Sometimes, they are only used for the sake of rhyme.'

58 For the fifth individual, 'refined' is not qualified by another noun. More details on this group are given in Chapter Three below. The term *ẓarīf* occurs another handful of times in the *Fihrist*, but without this clear implication of a group affiliation.

59 These are mentioned in a separate list in al-Sayyid's index (Ibn al-Nadīm, *Fihrist,* II/2, 933).

60 Stefan Leder, 'al-Ṣūlī', in *EI2* quotes al-Ṭabarī on his ancestor 'Ṣūl the Turk', and describes the close bonds between the family and the ʿAbbasids since their accession to the caliphate.

61 He supposedly fought on the side of the Umayyad general Yazīd b. Muhallab Ibn Abī Ṣufra, who was also killed at ʿAqr in 102/720, defeated by Maslama b. ʿAbd al-Malik. 'His supporters fled to Sind [. . .], only to be caught and killed or sent to Syria for execution' (Patricia Crone, 'Muhallabids', in *EI2*). However, see Canard's reconstruction in al-Ṣūlī, *Histoire*, 1, 26; and al-ʿUmarī, *Abū Bakr al-Ṣūli*, 68–74.

62 'In the Arabic language there are a number of terms the meaning of which is imprecise . . . The word *murūʾa* is one of these' (*EI2*, 'murūʾa').

63 al-Washshāʾ, *Muwashshā*, 53. Only eight qualities are listed instead of the announced ten.

64 For a discussion of this point see Letizia Osti, 'A Grammarian's Life in his own Voice: Autobiographical Fragments in Arabic Biographical Literature', in *ʿAbbasid Studies IV. Occasional Papers of the School of ʿAbbasid Studies, Leuven, July 5–July 9, 2010*, ed. Monique Bernards (Warminster: Gibb Memorial Trust, 2013).

65 By 'research students' I mean mature students who went on to have a professional scholarly career, as opposed to, for instance, pupils from within the caliphal family. See Letizia Osti, 'The Practical Matters of Culture in Pre-Madrasa Baghdad,' *Oriens* 38 (2010): 155–7.

66 In this context, I understand *juzʾ* as 'pamphlet', but the word does not appear in other sources (Ibn Khallikān uses *khabar*). *Al-khāṣṣa wa-l-ʿāmma* are technical terms used in opposition with each other. See the distinction in Sabari, with also a third element, *al-nās* (Simha Sabari, *Mouvements populaires à Bagdad à l'époque ʿabbasside ixe-xie siècles* (Paris: Maisonneuve, 1981), 17–22). In the *Fihrist*, the expression probably indicates *sunnī* and *shīʿī*. Shawkat M. Toorawa, *Ibn Abī Ṭāhir Ṭayfūr and Arabic Writerly Culture: a Ninth Century Bookman in Baghdad* (London: RoutledgeCurzon, 2005), 53.

67 Kilpatrick, 'Context,' 352.

68 'This interaction depends on them sharing a prominent feature, a linguistic marker [. . .], a pattern of narrators [. . .], motifs important to the action [. . .], parallel series of episodes [. . .] or a combination of these. It is possible, too, that elsewhere other shared features function as pointers to interaction' (Kilpatrick, 'Context,' 365–6).

69 Malti-Douglas, 'Controversy,' 130.

70 To be sure, it is known that the *Irshād* as we have it today lacks some of the original biographies and includes instead extraneous material (see ʿAbbās's introduction to his edition, Yāqūt, *Irshād*, 1, أ-و). However, it would be surprising for an individual with al-Ṣūlī's profile not to be included in this collection from the start. It seems reasonable to assume that this is Yāqūt's portrayal of al-Ṣūlī's life, or at least a consciously put together version of it.

71 This episode is briefly discussed in Toorawa, *Writerly Culture*, 23–4.

72 al-Buḥturī (d. 284/897), *Dīwān*, 1998 (poem 766, line 4). The passage, until the end of the first variation, is also reported from *Taʾrīkh Baghdād* in *Akhbār al-Buḥturī*, 178.

73 See also Toorawa, *Writerly Culture*, 24.

74 These are lines n. 1, 3, 12 and 9 respectively.

75 Ibn Khallikān does not take into consideration individuals for whom he cannot find a date of death. He seems to stick to this principle throughout the book. See, for example, in the entry on al-Akhfash al-Aṣghar (Ibn Khallikān, *Wafayāt*, 3, 301–3; Ibn Khallikān, *Biographical Dictionary*, 2, 244–6), his reference to al-Akhfash al-Akbar: after giving some biographical information on him, the author goes on to explain: 'As I was unable to discover the date of his death, I could not devote a special article to him in this work.'

76 For an analysis of this account and its transmission into European sources, see Letizia Osti, 'The Grain on the Chessboard: Travels and Meanings,' in *Le Répertoire narratif arabe médiéval: transmission et ouverture. Actes du colloque international qui s'est tenu à l'Université de Liège du 15 au 17 septembre 2005*, eds Frédéric Bauden, Aboubakr Chraïbi, and Antonella Ghersetti (Genève: Droz, 2008).

77 Muḥammad b. Mūsā b. Shākir (d. 259/863) and his two brothers are credited with being the first in the Muslim world to have calculated the circumference of the earth (Ibn Khallikān, *Wafayāt*, 5, 161–3).

78 Ibn Khallikān, *Wafayāt*, 4, 359.

79 The first version known to me is in *Kitāb al-Shaṭranj. Book on Chess. Selected Texts from al-ʿAdlī, Abū Bakr al-Ṣūlī and others. Reproduced from MS 560 Lala Ismail Collection, Süleymaniyye Library, Istanbul*, ed. Fuat Sezgin (Frankfurt am Main: Institut für die Geschichte der Arabisch-Islamischen Wissenschaften, 1986), 6–7. This is the facsimile of an anonymous manuscript which Sezgin dates between late tenth and early twelfth century.

80 Not much more is known of this chess player. See H.J.R. Murray, *A History of Chess*, reprinted 1962, (Oxford: Clarendon Press, 1913), 199.

81 Abū-l-Ḥasan ʿAlī b. al-Ḥusayn al-Masʿūdī, *Murūj al-dhahab wa-maʿādhin al-jawhar*, eds C. Barbier de Meynard and A. Pavet de Courteille. Revue et corrigé par Charles Pellat, 7 vols (Beirut: Publications de l'Université Libanaise, 1965–79), §3470–1. This is a pun with al-Māwardī's name, as *māward* means rosewater.

82 Al-Ṣafadī's profile includes the variation on al-Buḥturī's line with part of the attached narrative; one short poem on al-Ṣūlī's poetic skills; al-Ṣūlī's match against al-Māwardī; and his bibliophilia.

83 Giovanni Canova, 'Una Pagina di *al-Kanz al-madfūn* sugli uomini più illustri,' in *Ultra Mare: Mélanges de langue arabe et d'islamologie offerts à Aubert Martin*, ed. Frédéric Bauden (Leuven: Peeters, 2004).

84 Richard Eales, *Chess: the History of a Game* (London: Batsford, 1985), 19–38.
85 al-Ṣūlī, *Histoire,* 1, 42.
86 Canard mentions a couple of occasions where al-Ṣūlī refers to episodes earlier in his book, but which we do not have among what is left to us. Canard suggests that there could be lacunae in the manuscript, or that other versions of the book could have existed. On the other hand, these facts could have been mentioned in parts of the book which have not come down to us. Although these parts deal with earlier times, it is possible that al-Ṣūlī went ahead of time in mentioning something which happened later, as he does on several occasions which Canard himself records (al-Ṣūlī, *Histoire,* 1, 44–6).
87 However, elsewhere in his work al-Ṣūlī mentions that in his youth he frequented the house of ʿAbdallāh b. al-Ḥusayn al-Quṭrabbulī 'to meet the chess players' (Abū Bakr al-Ṣūlī, *Akhbār al-Buḥturī*, ed. Ṣāliḥ al-Ashtar (Damascus: Matbūʿāt al-Majmaʿ al-ʿIlmī al-ʿArabī, 1958), 51). Even here, he does not elaborate.

2 In his own Words

1 Franz Rosenthal, 'Die arabische Autobiographie,' in *Studia Arabica I*, eds Franz Rosenthal, Gustav von Grünebaum, and W.J. Fischel (Rome: Pontificium Institutum Biblicum, 1937), 40.
2 Dwight F. Reynolds, ed., *Interpreting the Self: Autobiography in the Arabic Literary Tradition* (Berkeley, Los Angeles, London: University of California Press, 2001), 9.
3 Hilary Kilpatrick, 'Autobiography and Classical Arabic Literature,' *Journal of Arabic Literature* 22 (1991). For a more detailed discussion of Kilpatrick's proposed framework, see Osti, 'A Grammarian's Life.'
4 Iḥsān ʿAbbās, *Fann al-sīra* (Beirut: Dār Bayrūt lil-Ṭibāʿa wa-l-Nashr, 1956), 114.
5 See for example the discussion in Arie Schippers, 'Autobiography in Medieval Arabic Literature,' in *Actas del XVI Congreso de la U.E.A.I.*, eds M.A. Manzano and C.V. de Benito (Salamanca: Universidad de Salamanca, 1995); Susanne Enderwitz, 'Gibt es eine arabische Autobiograpie?' in *Understanding Near Eastern Literatures*, ed. Verena Klemm and Beatrice Gruendler (Wiesbaden: Reichert, 2000); and Paul Lunde, 'The Quest for Arabic Autobiography,' *The Medieval History Journal* 18 (2015).
6 It is perhaps ironic that Rosenthal should express this view to comment on Jacob Burckhardt, the great historian of the European Renaissance, who saw individualism as a trait setting the Arab man apart from other Asians (Rosenthal, 'Die arabische Autobiographie,' 40).

7 'Autobiographical discourse is retrospective as the author surveys her/his past life from her/his present point of view and attempts to explain the development of her/his personality [. . .]. The focus on inner life distinguishes autobiography from the memoir, which emphasises the author's public role among well-known contemporaries.' Martin Löschnigg, 'Autobiography,' in *Routledge Encyclopedia of Narrative Theory*, eds David Herman, Manfred Jahn and Marie-Laure Ryan (London: Routledge, Taylor & Francis Group, 2010).
8 al-Ṣūlī, *ARM*, 219.
9 al-Ṣūlī, *Mā lam yunshar*, 144–5.
10 al-Ṣūlī, *ARM*, 5–6.
11 al-Ṣūlī, *ARM*, 23–31.
12 al-Ṣūlī, *ARM*, 31. This passage is discussed by Fakhr al-Dīn ʿĀmir, *Maṣādir al-turāth fī kutub al-tarājim al-adabīya* (Cairo: ʿĀlam al-Kutub, 2000), 225.
13 Of course, there are also many occasions where al-Ṣūlī is an uninvolved participant, i.e. he is simply an observer.
14 al-Ṣūlī, *Mā lam yunshar*, 24.
15 al-Ṣūlī, *ARM*, 69.
16 Al-Ṣūlī give this information in the chronicle of the year 322, that of al-Rāḍī's accession, but other sources put Mārdāwij's death in Ṣafar 223/January 335 (see C.E. Bosworth, 'Mardāwīdj̲,' in *EI2*). For a vivid description of Bajkam, see Adam Mez, *The Renaissance of Islam*, trans. S. Khuda Bukhsh and D.S. Margoliouth, repr. ed. (Patna: Jubilee Printing & Publishing House, 1937), 28–9.
17 On the advantages and disadvantages of quoting poems in full within *akhbār*, see Gruendler, 'Meeting the Patron,' 59–60.
18 It must be noted that, in general, the chronicle of this year, which is the first of al-Rāḍī's caliphate, is often interrupted by clusters such as this one, which provide context for a better understanding of events. A few pages after this passage, al-Ṣūlī introduces a flash-forward, relating how al-Rāḍī explained his dealings with Bajkam and Ibn Rāʾiq over the following years (al-Ṣūlī, *ARM*, 41–4. See also below, Chapter Five).
19 This may well be the most-quoted account from the *Awrāq* in modern scholarship. Two recent examples are Houari Touati, 'Pour une histoire de la lecture au Moyen Âge musulman: à propos des livres d'histoire,' *Studia Islamica* (2007): 20–2; and Nadia Maria El Cheikh, 'To be a Prince in the fourth/tenth century Abbasid Court,' in *Royal Courts in Dynastic States and Empires*, eds Jeroen Duindam, Tülay Artan, and Metin Kunt (Leiden: Brill, 2011).
20 The *qahramāna*, or harem stewardess, was an older member of the caliphal household who managed its external relations, including financial matters. See

Nadia Maria El Cheikh, 'The Qahramâna in the Abbasid Court: Position and Functions,' *Studia Islamica* (2003).

21 This letter dates the whole episode to the year 315, as shall be seen in Chapter Five.

22 al-Ṣūlī, *Histoire,* 1, 42. See also Chapter One above.

23 al-ʿUmarī, *Abū Bakr al-Ṣūli*, 135–203, attempts a reconstruction of al-Ṣūlī's *dīwān*.

24 al-Ṣūlī, *Histoire,* I, 29–37.

25 Letizia Osti, 'The Remuneration of a Court Companion in Theory and Practice: a Case Study,' *Journal of Abbasid Studies* 1 (2014).

26 al-Ṣūlī, *ARM*, 24.

27 al-Ṣūlī, *ARM*, 8.

28 Interestingly, as far as I could ascertain al-Ṣūlī never describes himself as *nadīm*, although, as has been seen in Chapter One, his biographers use the latter term exclusively. It is hard to establish whether these two words define different roles, or if using one or the other is simply a stylistic choice. They may appear as separate items in lists, but normative literature provides no obvious distinction between them. Ibn al-Nadīm, for instance, places al-Ṣūlī amongst *al-nudamāʾ wa-l-julasāʾ* in the *Fihrist* (see Chapter One above); the financial cuts introduced in 315/928 by the vizier ʿAlī b. ʿĪsā concerned, amongst others, *al-julasāʾ wa-l-nudamāʾ* (Berkel et al., *Crisis and Continuity*, 198). However, al-Thaʿlabī [pseudo al-Jāḥiẓ], *Kitāb al-Tāj fī akhlāq al-mulūk*, ed. Aḥmad Zakī Bāshā (Cairo: al-Maṭbaʿa al-Amīriyya, 1914) uses *nadīm/nudamāʾ* exclusively; Hilāl al-Ṣābiʾ, *Rusūm dār al-khilāfa*, ed. Mīkhāʾīl ʿAwwād (Baghdad: Maṭbaʿat al-ʿĀnī, 1964) uses both terms, but with no apparent distinction; in Maḥmūd b. al-Ḥusayn Kushājim, *Adab al-nadīm*, ed. ʿAbd al-Wāḥid Shaʿlān ([Cairo]1987), *jalīs* only appears in quotations from other sources; Joseph Sadan, 'Nadīm,' in *EI2* does not describe *jalīs* as a separate function.

29 al-Ṣūlī, *Mā lam yunshar,* 26.

30 al-Ṣūlī, *ARM*, 194 5.

31 al-Ṣūlī, *ARM*, 141.

32 al-Ṣūlī, *Mā lam yunshar,* 141 (year 312/924). It is worth noting that, in the case of al-Rāḍī and his brother, al-Ṣūlī does not speak of *tarbiya* but of *khidma*.

33 al-Ṣūlī, *ARM*, 266.

34 This is of course not unique. Bray, for example, argues that Yāqūt's accounts of personal interactions with his subjects reveal his own self-perception (Bray, 'Sniffy').

35 al-Ṣūlī, *ARM*, 25.

36 al-Ṣūlī, *Mā lam yunshar,* 31. This is not the only place where al-Ṣūlī praises Naṣr. See for example al-Ṣūlī, *Mā lam yunshar,* 58.

37 al-Ṣūlī, *ARM*, 149–50.
38 al-Ṣūlī, *Mā lam yunshar*, 127.
39 al-Ṣūlī, *ARM*, 193.
40 al-Ṣūlī, *ARM*, 280–2. See also below, Chapter Five.
41 al-Ṣūlī, *ARM*, 268.
42 al-Ṣūlī, *ARM*, 260.
43 al-Ṣūlī, *ARM*, 211. On this episode, see Osti, 'Remuneration', 97–8.
44 al-Ṣūlī, *Histoire*, 43. Al-Ṣūlī's point of view will be discussed further in Chapter Five.
45 al-Ṣūlī, *ARM*, 211. The importance of al-Ṣūlī's notebooks will be investigated in Chapter Three.

3 In his own Time

1 Jeroen Duindam, review of Maurice A. Pomerantz and Evelyn Birge Vitz, eds. *In the Presence of Power: Court and Performance in the Pre-modern Middle East*. New York: New York University Press, 2018, *The Medieval Review* (2018).
2 Although, on the dual prescriptive/descriptive function of manuals, see van Berkel's remarks in Berkel et al., *Crisis and Continuity*, 88; and Bruna Soravia, 'Les Manuels à l'usage des fonctionnaires de l'administration ('*Adab al-Kātib*') dans l'Islam classique', *Arabica* 52 (2005).
3 Charles Pellat, *Le milieu baṣrien et la formation de Ǧāḥiẓ* (Paris: Maisonneuve, 1953).
4 Of course, al-Jāḥiẓ himself – and his milieu – has received renewed attention, notably in James E. Montgomery's volume on the *Kitāb al-Ḥayawān* and his forthcoming one on al-Jāḥiẓ's other work (James E. Montgomery, *Al-Jāḥiẓ: in Praise of Books* (Edinburgh: Edinburgh University Press, 2013)).
5 Monique Bernards, 'Ibn Abī Isḥāq (d. *c*. 125/743) and his Scholarly Network', in *Islam at 250: Studies in Memory of G.H.A. Juynboll* (Leiden: Brill, 2020); Monique Bernards, 'Grammarians' Circles of Learning: a Social Network Analysis', in *'Abbasid studies II: Occasional papers of the School of 'Abbasid Studies. Leuven, 28 June–1 July 2004*, ed. John Nawas (Leuven: Peeters, 2010); Monique Bernards, 'Medieval Muslim Scholarship and Social Network Analysis: a Study of the Baṣra/Kūfa Dichotomy in Arabic Grammar', in *Ideas, Images, and Methods of Portrayal: Insights into Classical Arabic Literature and Islam*, ed. Sebastian Günther (Leiden: Brill, 2005).
6 Monji Kaabi, *Les Ṭāhirides au Ḫurāsān et en Iraq (iiième H/ixème j.c.)*, 2 vols (Paris: Université de Paris-Sorbonne, Faculté de Lettres et Sciences Humaines

(Thèse de Doctorat d'État), 1983); C.E. Bosworth, 'The Ṭāhirids and Arabic Culture,' *Journal of Semitic Studies* 14 (1969); C.E. Bosworth, 'The Ṭāhirids and Persian Literature,' *Iran: Journal of the British Institute of Persian Studies* 7 (1969).

7 Julia Bray, 'Place and Self-image: the Buhlūlids and Tanūḫids and their Family Traditions,' *Quaderni di Studi Arabi* 3 (2008).

8 This is too broad a field to provide a meaningful bibliography. The special issue of *Arabica* on Baghdad is a classic (*Baġdād, volume spécial, publié à l'occasion du mille deux centième anniversaire de la fondation (tirage à part d'Arabica)* (Leiden: Brill, 1962)). Recent additions of note are three collections of articles, on Baghdad as a cultural centre, on education, and on court culture (Jens J. Scheiner and Damien Janos, 'Baghdād: Political Metropolis and Intellectual Center,' in *The Place to Go: Contexts of Learning in Baghdād, 750–1000 C.E.*, eds Jens J. Scheiner and Damien Janos (Princeton, NJ: Darwin Press, 2014); Sebastian Günther, *Knowledge and Education in Classical Islam: Religious Learning between Continuity and Change*, 2 vols (Brill, 2020); Albrecht Fuess and Jan-Peter Hartung, *Court Cultures in the Muslim World: Seventh to Nineteenth Centuries* (London: Routledge, 2011).

9 Harald Bowen, *The Life and Times of ʿAlì ibn ʿIsà, 'The Good Vizier'* (Cambridge: Cambridge University Press, 1928); Louis Massignon, *La passion de Husayn ibn Mansûr Hallâj, martyr mystique de l'islam*, 4 vols (Paris: Gallimard, 1975; first ed. Geuthner 1914–22); Adam Mez, *Die Renaissance des Islams*, (Heidelberg: C. Winter, 1922), translated by Bukhsh and Margoliouth in 1937. More recent studies include: Roy Mottahedeh, *Loyalty and Leadership in an early Islamic Society*, 2nd ed. (London: I.B. Tauris, 2001); Joel L. Kraemer, *Humanism in the Renaissance of Islam: the Cultural Revival during the Buyid Age* (Leiden: Brill, 1986); Berkel et al., *Crisis and Continuity*.

10 Yāqūt, *Irshād,* 5, 2329–30. There is another episode, recorded by al-Tanūkhī, depicting a reception hosted by al-Ṣūlī, where he encourages his guests to eat stuffed entrails with an obscene comparison. Despite the editor's identification, however, this may be al-Ṣūlī's uncle Ibrāhīm b. al-ʿAbbās, who is attributed a work on cookery (al-Muḥassin b. ʿAlī al-Tanūkhī, *Nishwār al-muḥādara wa-akhbār al-mudhākara*, ed. ʿAbbūd al-Shālijī (Beirut: Dār Ṣādir, 1975), 2, 229. For Ibrāhīm's bibliography, see Ibn al-Nadīm, *Fihrist,* I/2, 378–9.

11 On al-Qaṭṭān, see also al-Khaṭīb al-Baghdādī (*Taʾrīkh Baghdād,* 5, 249–50), who calls him *ṣadūq, adīb shāʿir*. Although the published versions of Yāqūt and al-Khaṭīb provide slightly different names (Muḥammad b. Aḥmad and Aḥmad b. Muḥammad respectively), there is little doubt that they refer to the same individual.

12 Other locations were the mosque, the court, and the homes of rich employers. See Osti, 'Practical Matters'. On the *madrasa*, see Günther, 'Education, General (up to 1500),' in *EI3*.
13 See Christopher Melchert, 'Abū Dāwūd,' in *EI3*.
14 See Richard W. Bulliet, 'The Age Structure of Medieval Islamic Education,' *Studia Islamica* 57 (1983): students typically begun receiving *ḥadīth* between the ages of five and ten and continued for about seventeen years; they started transmitting between the ages of fifty and seventy and died between seventy and ninety; although a scholar may continue to receive transmissions into his middle age, these would not be passed on to the next generation, as they would make *isnāds* unnecessarily long.
15 In the *Awrāq*, al-Ṣūlī recalls being a youth in Basra in the year 275/888–9 (al-Ṣūlī, *ARM*, 216), and meeting Ibn Abī Ṭāhir Ṭayfūr there in 277/890–1 (al-Ṣūlī, *ASM*, 210). However, elsewhere he says that Baghdad is his birthplace (*mawlidī*) (al-Ṣūlī, *ARM*, 194).
16 al-Khaṭīb al-Baghdādī, *Ta'rīkh Baghdād*, 3, 380 and 3, 170 respectively.
17 For the meaning of 'research student' in this context, see Osti, 'Practical Matters'.
18 al-Khaṭīb al-Baghdādī, *Ta'rīkh Baghdād*, 5, 210.
19 al-Khaṭīb al-Baghdādī, *Ta'rīkh Baghdād*, 13, 195 (7173).
20 al-Khaṭīb al-Baghdādī, *Ta'rīkh Baghdād*, 13, 476–80 (7321). Al-Ṣūlī describes his personal connection with the poet and his son at the beginning of *Akhbār al-Buḥturī* (al-Ṣūlī, *Akhbār al-Buḥturī*, 49–54).
21 al-Khaṭīb al-Baghdādī, *Ta'rīkh Baghdād*, 14, 228 (7530).
22 al-Khaṭīb al-Baghdādī, *Ta'rīkh Baghdād*, 12, 294 (6739); see also Yāqūt, *Irshād*, 5, 2140, where he is called a companion of the prominent Kufan grammarian al-A'rābī.
23 al-Khaṭīb al-Baghdādī, *Ta'rīkh Baghdād*, 13, 210 (7181).
24 al-Khaṭīb al-Baghdādī, *Ta'rīkh Baghdād*, 13, 124 (7109). See also Yāqūt, *Irshād*, 6, 2709; al-Ṣūlī claims to have attended his lecture (*sami'a minhu*) in the year 290/902–3.
25 al-Khaṭīb al-Baghdādī, *Ta'rīkh Baghdād*, 14, 230 (7534). See also Yāqūt, *Irshād*, 6, 2825–6 and al-Marzubānī, *Shu'arā'*, 493.
26 al-Khaṭīb al-Baghdādī, *Ta'rīkh Baghdād*, 10, 340–2 (5479). See also Ibn al-Nadīm, *Fihrist*, I/1, 363.
27 al-Khaṭīb al-Baghdādī, *Ta'rīkh Baghdād*, 1, 336 (246).
28 al-Khaṭīb al-Baghdādī, *Ta'rīkh Baghdād*, 12, 63 (6454) See also Letizia Osti, 'Ibn Bassām: a Case Study on Poetry and Power,' *Middle Eastern Literatures* 10 (2007).
29 al-Khaṭīb al-Baghdādī, *Ta'rīkh Baghdād*, 3, 113 (1121).
30 al-Khaṭīb al-Baghdādī, *Ta'rīkh Baghdād*, 5, 42 (2398).

31 al-Khaṭīb al-Baghdādī, *Ta ʾrīkh Baghdād,* 8, 270 (4366).

32 Yāqūt, *Irshād,* 1, 82–3 and 428.

33 This does not include the cases where the information comes from a book, in which case it is simply introduced with *qāla al-Ṣūlī.*

34 al-Khaṭīb al-Baghdādī, *Ta ʾrīkh Baghdād,* 7, 296.

35 al-Khaṭīb al-Baghdādī, *Ta ʾrīkh Baghdād,* 3, 383; 12, 419; 14, 345.

36 al-Khaṭīb al-Baghdādī, *Ta ʾrīkh Baghdād,* 13, 479.

37 al-Khaṭīb al-Baghdādī, *Ta ʾrīkh Baghdād,* 11, 316.

38 al-Khaṭīb al-Baghdādī, *Ta ʾrīkh Baghdād,* 13, 200.

39 al-Khaṭīb al-Baghdādī, *Ta ʾrīkh Baghdād,* 2, 143–4. See also al-Tanūkhī, *Nishwār,* 1, 298–9.

40 al-Khaṭīb al-Baghdādī, *Ta ʾrīkh Baghdād,* 7, 296 (3805).

41 Leder, 'al-Ṣūlī', reads this passage as a suspicion, on the part of Ibn al-Nadīm, that al-Ṣūlī may have 'produced the poetry ascribed to Ibn Harma himself'. I follow Bayard Dodge's interpretation (Muḥammad b. Isḥāq Ibn al-Nadīm, *The Fihrist of al-Nadīm*, ed. and trans. Bayard Dodge, 2 vols (New York: Columbia University Press, 1970), 352), which is consistent with the fact that Ibn al-Nadīm lists among al-Ṣūlī's works *The Life and Times of Ibn Harma and a Selection of his Poetry* (Ibn al-Nadīm, *Fihrist,* I/2, 465). See also Chapter Four.

42 See Osti, 'A Grammarian's Life'. The story is found in other sources, but not all versions refer to a scholar with dyed hair.

43 The lover suffers all the adversities of his travels only for the sake of women, in the same way in which Tha ʿlab bears the burden of teaching only because of the rewards which will be granted to him in Heaven.

44 See Wim Raven, 'Ibn Dāwūd,' in *EI3* and Omar Bencheikh, 'Nifṭawayh,' in *EI2* respectively. Ibn Dāwūd's *ẓāhirī* milieu is discussed in Jean-Claude Vadet, *L'esprit courtois en Orient dans les cinq premier siècles de l'Hegire*, (Paris: Maisonneuve, 1968), 273–91. Nifṭawayh shared not only some of al-Ṣūlī's teachers but also some of his students, such as, for example, Ibn Ḥayawayh, who will be discussed later in this chapter (Yāqūt, *Irshād,* 1, 114).

45 For instance, al-Zubaydī compares Nifṭawayh with Ibn al-Anbārī, saying that the former 'would associate with people and frequent their *majālis*' and even had 'slave-girls, one of whom was a singer,' while the latter would not do so, and 'nobody ever ate anything which he had offered' (Abū Bakr Muḥammad b. al-Ḥasan al-Zubaydī, *Ṭabaqāt al-naḥwiyyīn wa-l-lughawiyyīn*, ed. Muḥammad Abū-l-Faḍl Ibrāhīm (Cairo: Dār al-Ma ʿārif, [1973]), 48, in Ibn al-Anbārī's profile. Nifṭaway's is on p. 52).

46 al-Washshā ʾ, *Muwashshā,* 72. The theme of this section of the book is whether sins committed out of romantic love should be punished. On Nifṭawayh's being a

ẓarīf, see Lois Anita Giffen, *Theory of Profane Love Among the Arabs* (New York: New York University Press, 1971), 71–2 and Raven, 'Ibn Dāwūd al-Iṣbahānī,' 30–2, although the only biographer who describes him so explicitly is al-Qifṭī (ʿAlī b. Yūsuf Ibn al-Qifṭī, *Inbāh al-Ruwāt ʿalā Anbāh al-Nuḥāt*, ed. Muḥammad Abū-l-Faḍl Ibrāhīm, 3 vols (Cairo 1950–5), 181).

47 On this particular aspect, see Susanne Enderwitz, 'Du *Fatā* au *Ẓarīf*, ou comment on se distingue?' *Arabica* 36 (1989).

48 Ibn al-Nadīm, *Fihrist*, I/1, 263 and II/1, 63 respectively. Nifṭawayh also appears in the *Awrāq*, where al-Ṣūlī gives a scathing critique of his competence as a poet and poetry expert (al-Ṣūlī, *Mā lam yunshar*, 151–2).

49 al-Ṣūlī, *ASM*, 4. This is the beginning of a *qaṣīda* composed by Abān al-Lāḥiqī (d. *c.* 200/815) in praise of the Barmakids; al-ʿUmarī, *Abū Bakr al-Ṣūli*, 121, notes that it is perhaps a fortunate coincidence that al-Ṣūlī included it in the *Awrāq*, as it describes his own role as *nadīm*.

50 al-Ṣūlī, *ARM*, 195–6.

51 al-Ṣūlī provides a complete list of names when he describes how he helped the caliph put together the group, which included eight people beside al-Ṣūlī himself. Two of these were dead by the time al-Rāḍī died. See Osti, 'Remuneration,' 97.

52 On these two families, see Jean-Claude Vadet, 'Ibn Ḥamdūn,' in *EI2* and J. Lennart Berggren, 'al-Munajjim, Banū,' in *EI3*.

53 The same point can be made, for instance, about al-Jahshiyārī (d. 331/942). The difference is that al-Jahshiyārī's *Wuzarāʾ* stopped in 296/908 (the extant part stops much earlier) and is therefore unlikely to have contained many first-hand accounts of his time as an employee of ʿAlī b. ʿĪsā and Ḥāmid b. al-ʿAbbās (see Maria Giovanna Stasolla, *Come legge la storia un letterato del X secolo: al-Jahshiyārī e i Barmecidi* (Rome: Aracne, 2007), 9–22). Beatrice Gruendler has discussed the structure and function of exchanges between poets and patrons in what she describes as 'literary *akhbār*'. See for instance Gruendler, 'Verse and Taxes'; Gruendler, 'Meeting the Patron'. The concept of literary *khabar* is briefly discussed in the Introduction above).

54 al-Ṣūlī, *ARM*, 137.

55 al-Ṣūlī, *ARM*, 149. The concrete consequences of the Munajjim's hostility were not confined to occasional rifts. For instance, for a time al-Ṣūlī was struck off the pension list of the vizier Ibn Muqla (d. 328/940) who, led by the Munajjim brothers, had misinterpreted some poetry addressed to him by al-Ṣūlī. The latter regained his station only after Ibn Muqla's deposition (al-Ṣūlī, *ARM*, 90–1).

56 For more details on these events, see Osti, 'Remuneration,' 99.

57 al-Ṣūlī, *ARM*, 59–60. This mechanism is described perfectly by Bray, 'Codes of Emotion,' 185: 'In stories, when a character quotes poetry, this establishes a direct

emotional link with us, the readers or listeners, at the same time as triggering emotional reactions from the other characters in the story, a further complicating of the art-life relationship.'

58 An effective survey of Ibn al-Muʿtazz's political role and thought is provided in Bray, 'Ibn al-Muʿtazz and Politics.'

59 al-Ṣūlī, *Mā lam yunshar,* 24.

60 Other sources for these events are: Abū Jaʿfar Muḥammad b. Jarīr al-Ṭabarī, *Taʾrīkh al-rusul wa-l-mulūk*, ed. M.J. De Goeje et al. (Leiden: E.J. Brill, 1879–1901), III, 2281–3; ʿArīb, *Ṣila,* 25-28; Miskawayh, *Tajārib,* 1, 5–8. Incidentally, another close connection of al-Ṣūlī, Wakīʿ, was a supporter of Ibn al-Muʿtazz and was arrested during the attempted coup (Miskawayh, *Tajārib,* 1, 8–9).

61 al-Ṣūlī, *Mā lam yunshar,* 37.

62 al-Ṣūlī, *Mā lam yunshar,* 41 The episode is also related in al-Muḥassin b. ʿAlī al-Tanūkhī, *al-Faraj baʿda l-shidda*, ed. ʿAbbūd al-Shālijī (Beirut, 1978), 4, 110–12. Contrary to most other citations of al-Ṣūlī, here al-Tanūkhī summarizes the background of the story and then introduces al-Ṣūlī's eyewitness account with 'al-Ṣūlī says, in his *Kitāb al-Wuzarā*ʾ' (the editor specifies that one of the manuscripts has *Kitāb al-Khulafā*ʾ, and this may indeed refer to the *Awrāq*).

63 al-Ṣūlī, *Mā lam yunshar,* 43. It is worth noting that, while al-Ṣūlī devotes a long section of the *Akhbār awlād al-khulafā*ʾ to Ibn al-Muʿtazz (pp. 107–296), he does not mention the manner of his death there (this is discussed by Kilpatrick, 'Time and Death').

64 On this use of notebooks, see Gruendler, *Arabic Book*, 82–9. Ibn al-Muʿtazz would look up the notebook to review al-Ṣūlī's transcriptions of his own poetry.

65 This episode is discussed at length in Sarah Bowen Savant, 'Naming Shuʿūbīs,' in *Essays in Islamic Philology, History, and Philosophy*, eds Korangy Alireza et al. (Berlin: De Gruyter, 2016). Savant demonstrates that it would be wrong to see Yaḥyā as a member of a supposed *shuʿūbī* movement, which al-Ṣūlī never mentions. On the complex interaction of family, loyalty and ethnic ties, see also the analysis of al-Jahshiyārī's portrayal of the Barmakids in Stasolla, *Barmecidi*, 153–61 especially.

66 al-Ṣūlī, *Mā lam yunshar,* 51.

67 ʿĀmir, *Maṣādir al-turāth*, 225–6, makes a symmetrical argument for other parts of the *Awrāq* which are structured as biographical profiles equipped with selections of poetry, but through this poetry convey political content.

68 al-Ṭabarī, *Taʾrīkh,* III, 1637–41; al-Ṣūlī, *Kniga Listov,* 305.

69 al-Ṣūlī, *AAK,* 107–296. There is also a separate edition of the *opera omnia* of Ibn al-Muʿtazz: ʿAbdallāh Ibn al-Muʿtazz, *Dīwān*, ed. Bernhard Lewin (Cairo: Maṭbaʿat al-Maʿārif, 1945–50).

70 For a discussion on ethonyms and identity in Abbasid Iraq see Michael Cooperson, '"Arabs" and "Iranians": the Uses of Ethnicity in the Early Abbasid Period,' in *Islamic Cultures, Islamic Contexts: Essays in Honor of Professor Patricia Crone*, eds Asad Q. Ahmed, et al. (Leiden: Brill, 2014) and the works cited therein.

71 For some examples, see Letizia Osti, 'The Wisdom of Youth: legitimising the Caliph al-Muqtadir,' *Al-Masāq* 19 (2007).

72 See for example al-Ṣūlī, *Mā lam yunshar*, 33. This use of poetry to convey political meaning in all parts of the *Awrāq* is also mentioned in ʿĀmir, *Maṣādir al-turāth*, 226. For a survey of places of teaching before the institution of the *madrasa*, see Munir-ud-Din Ahmed, *Muslim Education and the Scholars' Social Status up to the 5th Century Muslim Era (11th century Christian Era) in the Light of Taʾrīkh Baghdād* (Zurich: Verlag der Islam, 1968), 112–41.

73 Samer M. Ali, *Arabic Literary Salons in the Islamic Middle Ages: Poetry, Public Performance, and the Presentation of the Past* (Notre Dame, IN: University of Notre Dame Press, 2010). For a discussion and further examples, see Lale Behzadi, 'Muslimische Intellektuelle im Gespräch: Der arabische literarische Salon im 10. Jahrhundert,' in *Von Rom nach Bagdad: Bildung und Religion von der römischen Kaiserzeit bis zum klassischen Islam*, eds Peter Gemeinhardt and Sebastian Günther (Tübingen: Mohr Siebeck, 2013). Naaman, *Literature and the Islamic Court*, 80–92, also describes instances of poetic exchanges between courtiers. Mauder, *Sultan's Salon*, 63–72 provides a comprehensive list of types of *majlis* (in this last case, of course, we must allow the term to have evolved in the 500 years between the reign of al-Rāḍī and that of Qanishaw).

74 al-Ṣūlī, *ARM*, 47 and 55. Both these episodes are mentioned in Mez, *Renaissance*, 144.

75 Ali, *Literary Salons*, 174.

76 Toorawa, *Writerly Culture*, 21.

77 Incidentally, when the burglars entered, al-Ṣūlī was in the house but did not notice anything because he was hosting a *majlis* with traditionists and litterateurs (*aṣḥāb al-ḥadīth wa-ahl al-adab*; al-Ṣūlī, *ARM*, 210).

78 al-Ṣūlī, *ARM*, 211.

79 al-Ṣūlī, *ARM*, 280.

80 al-Tanūkhī, *Faraj*, 3, 262–7. However modest al-Ṣūlī's income may have been in his view, this story suggests that his inheritance was substantial enough to be fought over. See also Osti, 'Remuneration,' 101.

81 Incidentally, al-Ṣūlī's teaching duties were beneficial to all *julasāʾ* who, to accommodate his Friday absence, were given two days off a week (al-Ṣūlī, *ARM*, 194).

82 On these three brothers, see Jere L. Bacharach, 'al-Barīdī,' in *EI3* .

83 al-Ṣūlī, *ARM*, 215

84 On this point, see the argument in Sarah Bowen Savant, 'People versus Books' (forthcoming). Savant reframes the oral/written dichotomy into people/books one, stressing the importance of connections between persons through *isnād*s, which are often tied to religious studies too tightly: 'People citation through such transmissive chains is a general phenomenon. Historians and computer scientists have more often treated *isnād*s and even history itself, as arising from *ḥadīth*. In terms of method, this assumption limits the ability of an algorithm to find *isnād*s elsewhere. It also provides a limiting view of the origins and evolution of history writing'.

85 al-Khaṭīb al-Baghdādī, *Taʾrīkh Baghdād,* 3, 431. In Chapter One we have seen a summary of this *khabar* by Yāqūt, who does not provide a source. Al-Ṣūlī uses the technical term *samāʿ*, which implies personal contact with a teacher through audition (see, for example, Gregor Schoeler, *The Genesis of Literature in Islam: from the Aural to the Read*, trans. Shawkat M. Toorawa (Edinburgh: Edinburgh University Press, 2009), 24 and 36). For a general discussion, see Konrad Hirschler, *The Written Word in the Medieval Arabic Lands: a Social and Cultural History of Reading Practices* (Edinburgh: Edinburgh University Press, 2012), 11–17.

86 Muḥammad b. al-ʿAbbās b. Muḥammad (al-Khaṭīb al-Baghdādī, *Taʾrīkh Baghdād,* 3, 121–2). The other scholars in al-Khaṭīb's list are: Abū l-Ḥasan b. al-Jundī (d. 321/933, al-Khaṭīb al-Baghdādī, *Taʾrīkh Baghdād,* 3, 324); Abū Aḥmad Muḥammad b. [ʿAbdallāh b. Jāmiʿ] al-Dahhān (399/1009, al-Khaṭīb al-Baghdādī, *Taʾrīkh Baghdād,* 5, 471); ʿUbayd Allāh b. ʿUthmān b. Yaḥyā, Abū l-Qāsim al-Daqqāq (d. 388/998, al-Khaṭīb al-Baghdādī, *Taʾrīkh Baghdād,* 10, 375–6); Abū Aḥmad al-Faraḍī; Al-Ḥusayn b. al-Ḥasan al-Ghaḍārī (d. 414/1023; al-Khaṭīb al-Baghdādī, *Taʾrīkh Baghdād,* 8, 34 , where he is appears as al-Ghaḍāʾirī); ʿAlī b. al-Qāsim al-Najjād al-Baṣrī [Abū l-Ḥasan al-Shāhid]; al-Ḥusayn b. al-Ḥasan al-Jawālīqī (al-Khaṭīb al-Baghdādī, *Taʾrīkh Baghdād,* 8, 33–4); and ʿAbbās b. ʿUmar al-Kalwādhānī (414/1023, al-Khaṭīb al-Baghdādī, *Taʾrīkh Baghdād,* 12, 162).

87 Al-Azharī (Ubayd Allāh b. Abī l-Fatḥ) is given a glowing reference in his own profile, where al-Khaṭīb remarks that he had one of the largest collections of Traditions, both in books and via oral transmission (*kitābatan wa-samāʿan*; al-Khaṭīb al-Baghdādī, *Taʾrīkh Baghdād,* 10, 385). On one occasion, in citing him he specifies that al-Azharī transmitted an item to him from his book (*ḥaddathanī ... min kitābihi*; al-Khaṭīb al-Baghdādī, *Taʾrīkh Baghdād,* 5, 441). This al-Azharī

should not be confused with the famous lexicographer Abū Manṣūr (d. 370/980), who, incidentally, does not approve of reliance on books (see for instance Schoeler, *Genesis*, 117).

88 This process is described by Schoeler, *Genesis*, 46. The trusted colleague in question was Abū l-Ḥasan b. al-Razzāz (d. 409/1018; see al-Khaṭīb al-Baghdādī, *Taʾrīkh Baghdād,* 11, 330). For later, physical examples of *samāʿ* certificates, see Tilman Seidensticker, 'Audience Certificates in Arabic Manuscripts: the Genre and a Case Study', *Manuscript Cultures* 8 (2015).

89 al-Khaṭīb al-Baghdādī, *Taʾrīkh Baghdād,* 3, 121–2.

90 al-Khaṭīb al-Baghdādī, *Taʾrīkh Baghdād,* 4, 17.

91 The scholar in question, Ibn al-Bāghandī (d. 312/925) had an ambiguous reputation and was known to be a forger (al-Khaṭīb al-Baghdādī, *Taʾrīkh Baghdād,* 3, 209–13. Ibn Ḥayawayh is listed as having transmitted from him).

92 Toorawa, *Writerly Culture*, 22–4, discusses al-Ṣūlī's criticism of Ibn Abī Ṭāhir as in contradiction with his own library. My point here is that al-Ṣūlī's (and al-Azharī's) assessment was not concerned with the books themselves, but with how they were used and composed.

93 On ʿAlī b. Abī ʿAlī and his contributions to the *Taʾrīkh Baghdād*, see Bray, 'Place and Self-image'.

94 See Leder, 'al-Sarrādj,' in *EI2*. On al-Sarrāj's criticism of Ibn Dāwūd, see Vadet, *Esprit courtois*, 477–86.

95 Vadet, *Esprit courtois*, 417 (pp. 415–24 discuss Ibn Ḥayawayh's role as a source for the *Maṣāriʿ*).

96 ʿAlī b. Muḥammad al-Tanūkhī, d. 342/953.

97 al-Tanūkhī, *Faraj,* 3, 262.

98 Touati, 'Lecture', 32–9, discusses the dissemination of historical works specifically, collecting examples from the eighth to the thirtheenth century.

99 Variations of this wording are found, for instance in al-Tanūkhī, *Faraj,* 1, 168, 81 and 308; 3, 88 and 246; 5, 15. I am following Julia Bray's translation in al-Muḥassin b. ʿAlī al-Tanūkhī, *Stories of Piety and Prayer: Deliverance follows Adversity*, ed. and trans. Julia Bray (New York: New York University Press, 2019).

100 For instance, al-Tanūkhī, *Faraj,* 1, 308, 311 and 331. For *ijāza* in this context, see Schoeler, *Genesis*, 46.

101 al-Tanūkhī, *Faraj,* 2, 16 and 18; 3, 362. In the first of these instances, al-Tanūkhī adds *wa-naqaltuhu min khaṭṭihi.*

102 al-Tanūkhī, *Faraj,* 3, 150.

103 For example, al-Tanūkhī, *Nishwār,* 2, 240.

104 al-Tanūkhī, *Nishwār,* 2, 356, translated in al-Muḥassin b. ʿAlī al-Tanūkhī, *The Table-Talk of a Mesopotamian Judge: being the first Part of the Nishwār al-muḥāḍarah or Jāmiʿ al-tawārīkh*, trans. D.S. Margoliouth, 2 vols (London: The Royal Asiatic Society, 1921–2), 2, 293.

105 al-Tanūkhī, *Nishwār,* 1, 298–9, translated in *Table-Talk,* 2, 145. The same episode is narrated in al-Khaṭīb al-Baghdādī, *Taʾrīkh Baghdād,* 2, 143–4. It is passed on to al-Khaṭīb by ʿAlī b. Abī ʿAlī and does not contain this introductory paragraph.

106 I use 'finalized' in the sense illustrated by Schoeler, *Genesis*, 1.

107 This procedure is called *munāwala* and is attested since the second/eight century (Schoeler, *Genesis*, 73).

108 For instance, Abū l-Ṭayyib al-Lughawī (d. 351/962, see Thomas Bauer, 'Abū l-Ṭayyib al-Lughawī,' in *EI3*) was a student of al-Ṣūlī, but we only know this from some of his biographical profiles (e.g. al-Ṣafadī, *Wāfī,* 19, 271) and direct quotations in his work (*akhbaranā* followed by an *isnad*; ʿAbd al-Wāḥid b. ʿAlī Abū l-Ṭayyib al-Lughawī, *Marātib al-Naḥwiyyīn*, ed. Muḥammad Abū-l-Faḍl Ibrāhīm (Cairo: Maktabat Naḥḍat Miṣr, [1955]). On a much larger scale, more than 300 *akhbār* in the *Kitāb al-Aghānī* are related on the authority of al-Ṣūlī (al-ʿUmarī, *Abū Bakr al-Ṣūli*, 105). For the wider context, Johannes Pedersen, *The Arabic Book*, trans. Robert Hillenbrand (Princeton: Princeton University Press, 1984), 24–36, collects and discusses examples of book transmission across a few centuries. For a survey of information on written material in the Islamic West in the same period, see Maribel Fierro, 'Writing and Reading in early Ifrīqiya', in *Promissa nes aspera curans: Mélanges offerts à Madame le Professuer Marie-Thérèse Urvoy*, eds Georgio Rahal and Heinz-Otto Luthe (Toulouse: Les Presses Universitaires, Institute Catholique de Toulouse, 2017). Other studies focusing on the Mamluk period will be mentioned in Chapter Four.

109 See Schoeler, *Genesis*, 23.

110 In a recent series of blog posts, part of the KITAB project, Sarah Savant e Masoumeh Seydi give a convincing description of al-Ṭabarī's notebooks which may be thought of along the same lines (Sarah Bowen Savant and Masoumeh Seydi, 'Dispatches from al-Ṭabarī,' *KITAB-project.org*, 2021). For another comparison with the Mamluk period, see al-Nuwayrī's (d. 732/1332) working method as described by Elias Muhanna, who has at his disposal fair copies of other author's works produced by al-Nuwayrī himself (Elias Muhanna, *The World in a Book: al-Nuwayri and the Islamic Encyclopedic Tradition* (Princeton: Princeton University Press, 2018), 105–22).

4 In his own Books

1 Fred M. Donner, *Narratives of Islamic Origins: The Beginnings of Islamic Historical Writing* (Princeton: The Darwin Press, 1998), xii.

2 Nadia Al-Bagdadi, 'Registers of Arabic Literary History', *New Literary History* 39 (2008): 442.

3 This is published as an introduction to the *Akhbār Abī Tammam* (al-Ṣūlī, *Life and Times*, 3. I follow Gruendler's translation). On the significance of this work in the history of Arabic criticism, see Ṣammūd, *Balāghat al-intiṣār*.

4 In fact, many of Thaʿlab's biographical profiles contain a story where Thaʿlab jokes about his own ignorance on many subjects (see, for instance, al-Khaṭīb al-Baghdādī, *Taʾrīkh Baghdād*, 5, 209). This passage is discussed in Beatrice Gruendler, 'World Philology', in *Early Arabic Philologists: Poetry's Friends or Foes?* eds Sheldon Pollock, Benjamin A. Elman, and Ku-ming Kevin Chang (Harvard University Press, 2015), 105–7.

5 al-Ṣūlī, *Life and Times*, 3–4. I follow Gruendler's translation with slight adjustments.

6 Humphreys, 'Taʾrīkh'.

7 Rosenthal, *History*, 67–8.

8 On the Arabic prosimetron in general, see Wolfhart Heinrichs, 'Prosimetrical Genres in Classical Arabic Literature', in *Prosimetrum: Cross-Cultural Perspectives on Narrative in Prose and Verse*, eds Joseph Harris and Karl Reichl (Cambridge: D.S. Brewer, 1997). On poetry in historiographical prose, see Geert Jan Van Gelder, 'Poetry in Historiography: Some Observations', in *Problems in Arabic Literature*, ed. Miklós Maróth (Piliscsaba: The Avicenna Institute of Middle Eastern Studies, 2004). See especially pp. 3–4, where van Gelder reviews the general attitude of modern historians to poetry and advocates the study of 'the ways in which poems or fragments of verse are quoted in the historical narrative'. Suleiman Mourad has indeed shown a practical example of the consequences of ignoring poetry in such contexts (Suleiman Mourad, 'Poetry, History, and the Early Arab-Islamic Conquests of al-Shām (Greater Syria)', in *Poetry and History: the Value of Poetry in Reconstructing Arab History*, eds Ramzi Baalbaki, Saleh Said Agha, and Tarif Khalidi (Beirut: American University of Beirut Press, 2011)). On poetry in biographical profiles, see Osti, 'Ibn Bassām'. Gruendler, 'Verse and Taxes', as has been seen above, focuses on poetry in literary *akhbār*.

9 Ibn al-Jawzī, *Muntaẓam*, 12, 357.

10 Yāqūt, *Irshād*, 1, 28.

11 Dominique Sourdel, 'Fragments d'al-Ṣūlī sur l'histoire des vizirs ʿabbāsides,' *Bulletin d'Études Orientales* 15 (1957).

12 Al-Ṣūlī explains the contents of this book in his introduction to the *dīwān* of Abū Nuwās (Abū Nuwās, *Der Dīwān des Abū Nuwās*, eds Ewald Wagner and Gregor Schoeler, 5+2 vols (Wiesbaden: Franz Steiner Verlag, 1958–2006), 6, 24. See also Schoeler's summary in vol. 7, xi–xvi).

13 Ibn al-Nadīm, *Fihrist,* I/2, 464–5.

14 Ibn al-Nadīm, *Fihrist,* I/2, 480. An unpublished manuscript of this work is extant (BnF Arabe 6881). It is worth noting that, while it does detail opinions and episodes on chess involving many authorities in Islamic history, it does not mention the Indian origin story described in Chapter One.

15 To my knowledge, the most recent survey of al-Ṣūlī's work, extant or otherwise, is in Hilāl Nājī's introduction to his edition of the *Awrāq* (al-Ṣūlī, *Mā lam yunshar,* 6–11); Khalidov's introduction to his edition contains more detailed information on the extant manuscripts of the *Awrāq* (al-Ṣūlī, *Kniga Listov,* 7–20). Other manuscripts are listed by Carl Brockelmann, *Geschichte der arabischen Literatur* (Leiden: E.J. Brill, 1937–49), G/I, 149–50 and S/I 218–19, and Fuat Sezgin, *Geschichte des arabischen Schrifttums*, 17 vols (Leiden; Frankfurt: Brill (1–9); Institut für Geschichte der Arabisch-Islamischen Wissenschaften an der Johann Wolfgang Goethe-Universität, 1967–2016), 1, 330–1 and 9, 166–7. Al-ʿUmarī, *Abū Bakr al-Ṣūlī*, 262–306, provides a detailed survey of the titles he is aware of and discusses their content (divided into five genres) but does not refer to editions or manuscripts. I am aware of two more editions published since Nājī's survey: Abū Bakr al-Ṣūlī, *Faḍl al-shubbān ʿalā kathīr mimman taqaddama min dhawī l-asnān*, ed. Muṣṭafā ʿAlī Qarmad (al-Manṣūra: al-Maktaba al-ʿAṣriyya lil-Nashr wa-l-Tawzīʿ, 2016); Abū Bakr al-Ṣūlī, *Dīwān ʿUlayya bt. al-Mahdī bi-riwāyat Abī Bakr Muḥammad b. Yaḥyā al-Ṣūlī*, ed. Muḥammad Abū l-Majd ʿAlī Basyūnī (Cairo: Maktabat al-Ādāb, 2004).

16 al-Ṣūlī, *Mā lam yunshar,* 26. The dedication does in fact mention both al-Muqtadir and Ibn al-Furāt (al-Ṣūlī, *Faḍl al-shubbān*, 69–70).

17 al-Ṣūlī, *Mā lam yunshar,* 131.

18 For example, Iḥsān ʿAbbās states that the *Akhbār Abī Tammām* is more a biography than a book of literary criticism (*yuʿaddu fī kutub al-sīra akthar mimmā yuʿaddu fī kutub al-naqd*) (Iḥsān ʿAbbās, *Tāʾrīkh al-naqd al-adabī ʿinda l-ʿArab: naqd al-shiʿr min al-qarn al-thānī ḥattā l-qarn al-thāmin al-hijrī* (Amman: Dār al-Shurūq lil-Nashr wa-l-Tawzīʿ, 1933), 151).

19 Ibn al-Nadīm, *Fihrist,* I/2, 464–6.

20 Ibn al-Nadīm, *Fihrist,* I/2, 505. Al-Ṣūlī expands on the many false attributions in his introduction to the edition (Abū Nuwās, *Dīwān,* 6, 4–5). See also Ewald

Wagner, 'Warum haben Ḥamza al-Isbahānī und Abū Bakr aṣ-Ṣūlī mehrere Weingedichte aus ihren Rezensionen des Abū Nuwās-Dīwān ausgeschieden?' *Asiatische Studien – Études Asiatiques* 62 (2008). On his part, in the introduction to the *Akhbār Abī Tammām*, he boasts that his edition of Abū Nuwās's poetry has supplanted all earlier versions (al-Ṣūlī, *Life and Times*, 27).

21 Ibn al-Nadīm, *Fihrist*, I/2, 505.

22 Ibn al-Nadīm, *Fihrist*, I/2, 507.

23 Ibn al-Nadīm, *Fihrist*, I/2, 508.

24 Ibn al-Nadīm, *Fihrist*, I/2, 516.

25 Ibn al-Nadīm, *Fihrist*, I/2, 528; published in print as Abū Tammām, *Sharḥ al-Ṣūlī*.

26 Ibn al-Nadīm, *Fihrist*, I/2, 529. This is not extant, but there is an *akhbār* work that Sezgin describes as 'eine Ausführung zum *dīwān*' (Sezgin, *GAS*, 1, 331; al-Ṣūlī, *Akhbār al-Buḥturī*).

27 Ibn al-Nadīm, *Fihrist*, I/2, 530.

28 Ibn al-Nadīm, *Fihrist*, I/2, 531 On this poet, see al-Ṣafadī, *Wāfī*, 13, 278.

29 Ibn al-Nadīm, *Fihrist*, I/2, 531.

30 Ibn al-Nadīm, *Fihrist*, I/2, 540.

31 Ibn al-Nadīm, *Fihrist*, I/2, 503.

32 Ibn al-Nadīm, *Fihrist*, I/2, 541.

33 Speaking of the fourth/tenth century Samanid historian Abū ʿAlī al-Sallāmī, al-Thaʿālibī states that his poetry is, like al-Ṣūlī's, *fī ashʿār muʾallifī al-kutub* (Abū Manṣūr al-Thaʿālibī, *Yatīmat al-dahr fī maḥāsin ahl al-ʿaṣr*, ed. Mufīd Muḥammad Qamīḥa, 6 vols (Beirut: Dār al-Kutub al-ʿIlmiyya, 2000), 4, 108).

34 Abū Nuwās, *Dīwān*, 6, 18.

35 ʿArīb, *Ṣila*, 155. It should be noted that, despite this remark, ʿArīb seldom cites al-Ṣūlī as his source, and rarely preserves the poetry. This is discussed in Letizia Osti, 'The Author as Protagonist: Biographical Markers in Historical Narratives,' *Jerusalem Studies in Arabic and Islam* 45 (2018). Something similar may be observed with al-Ṭabarī's use of material by Ibn Abī Ṭāhir Ṭayfūr: as Savant remarks, 'Ibn Abī Ṭāhir's book may have been viewed as a "practical data carrier" that did not require citation' (Sarah Bowen Savant, 'Al-Ṭabarī's Unacknowledged Debt to Ibn Abī Ṭāhir Ṭayfūr,' (forthcoming), borrowing the expression 'practical data carrier' from Gruendler, *Arabic Book*, 23). The reader may be reminded of Frédéric Bauden's extensive work on how the Mamluk historian al-Maqrīzī (d. 845/1442) uses his sources (see, in particular, Frédéric Bauden, 'Maqriziana IX: Should al-Maqrīzī Be Thrown out with the Bath Water? The Question of his Plagiarism of al-Awḥadī's *Khiṭaṭ* and the Documentary Evidence,' *Mamlūk Studies Review* 14 (2010)). Of course, it would be naïve to draw precise parallels

or, worse, assume a teleological link, between writers who lived half a millennium apart.

36 Hilāl b. al-Muḥassin al-Ṣābi', *al-Wuzarā' aw tuḥfat al-umarā' fī ta'rīkh al-wuzarā'*, ed. 'Abd al-Sattār Aḥmad Farrāj ([Cairo]: Dār Iḥyā' al-Kutub al-'Arabiyya, 1958), 2. Other historians' criticism of al-Ṣūlī's work is discussed in more detail in Osti, 'Author as Protagonist,' 239–44.

37 Abū Nuwās, *Dīwān,* 6, 11–12.

38 al-Ṣūlī, *Life and Times,* 6.1.

39 al-Marzubānī, *Shu'arā'*, 431.

40 al-Ṣafadī, *Wāfī,* 3, 62.

41 al-Ṣūlī, *AAK,* 3.

42 al-Ṣūlī, *AAK,* 5. This point is discussed in 'Āmir, *Maṣādir al-turāth*, 221.

43 Indeed, it has been pointed out that in some cases, *akhbār* works become in fact complete *dīwān*s, so that one criterion takes precedence over the other ('Āmir, *Maṣādir al-turāth*, 213–18).

44 We know of one work which took inspiration precisely from this rationale: the Andalusi Ibn al-Ṣāffār (d. 352/963) composed, at the request of the Umayyad caliph al-Ḥakam II, a – now lost – *Kitāb fī Ash'ār al-khulafā' min Banī Umayya* (see Jorge Lirola Delgado, ed., *Enciclopedia de Al-Andalus: diccionario de autores y obras andalusíes* (Granada: El Legado Andalusí, 2002), 'Ibn al-Ṣaffār'. I am grateful to Maribel Fierro for this reference).

45 al-Ṣūlī, *ARM,* 154.

46 Kraemer, *Humanism*, 53.

47 This poem is discussed as an example of al-Ṣūlī's style in 'Āmir, *Maṣādir al-turāth*, 216.

48 Ibn al-Nadīm, *Fihrist,* I/2, 510, describes him as a *mawlā* of the Abbasids, although his loyalties changed over the years (see Taieb El Acheche, 'Sudayf b. Maymūn,' in *EI2*).

49 Ibn al-Nadīm, *Fihrist,* I/2, 465.

50 Ibn al-Nadīm, *Fihrist,* I/2, 400–1.

51 The context of this accusation is discussed in 'Āmir, *Maṣādir al-turāth*, 211–12. On the attitude of the *Fihrist* to intellectual property, see Dieter Sturm, 'Ibn al-Nadīm's Hinweise auf das Verhältnis zum geistigen Eigentum im Historikerkapitel des *Kitab al-Fihrist*,' *Hallesche Beiträge zur Orientalwissenschaft* 13–14 (1990). Zoltan Szombathy, 'The Concept of Intellectual Property in Mediaeval Muslim Literary Culture,' *Jerusalem Studies in Arabic and Islam* 45 (2018), provides similar examples of an author's handwriting being used as proof in disputes about intellectual property.

52 al-Ṣūlī, *Life and Times,* 6.2. Al-Ḥāmid is described as irascible and ill-natured (al-Zubaydī, *Ṭabaqāt,* 152–3).

53 'They found a portion of my notebooks (*qaṭīʿa min dafātirī*) and plundered it.'

54 See also Beatrice Gruendler's considerations on 'the separation between the book as personally transmitted content and as a mobile physical object and the commercial possibilities of the latter as a commodity' (Beatrice Gruendler, 'Aspects of Craft in the Arabic Book Revolution,' in *Globalization of Knowledge in the Post-Antique Mediterranean, 700–1500*, eds Sonja Brentjes and Jürgen Renn (London: Routledge, 2016)).

55 See the discussion and bibliography in Letizia Osti and James Weaver, 'Organizing the Fourth/Tenth Century: Knowledge, Information, Tools,' *Journal of Abbasid Studies* 7 (2020), especially pp. 104–7, where we compare the vague idea of encyclopaedism employed for the fourth/tenth century with the much better defined concept formulated by Elias Muhanna and others for the Mamluk period.

56 Hilary Kilpatrick, 'A Genre in Classical Arabic: the *Adab* Encyclopedia,' in *Union européenne des arabisants et islamisants, 10th Congress: Edinburgh 9–16 September 1980: Proceedings*, ed. Robert Hillenbrand (Edinburgh: [s.n.], 1982).

57 Gregor Schoeler, 'Writing for a Reading Public: the Case of al-Jāḥiẓ,' in *Al-Jāḥiẓ: a Muslim Humanist for our Time*, eds Arnim Heinemann et al. (Würzburg: Egon Verlag, 2009).

58 See Johannes Thomann, 'From Serial Access to Random Access: Tables of Contents, Chapter Headings and Hierarchical Text Structures in Fourth/Tenth-century Scientific Books,' *Journal of Abbasid Studies* 7 (2020).

59 Abū Bakr al-Ṣūlī, *Adab al-kuttāb*, ed. Aḥmad Ḥasan Basaj (Beirut: Dār al-Kutub al-ʿIlmiyya, 1994), 20–1. Al-ʿUmarī, *Abū Bakr al-Ṣūli*, 247–8, argues that the way al-Ṣūlī organizes the *Adab al-kuttāb* points to an innovative teaching technique, where 'each topic leads to the topic that follows it and is strongly tied to it.'

60 al-Ṣūlī, *ARM*, 40. See also Osti, 'Notes,' 220. See, for comparison, a discussion of the arrangement of books in the Ashrafiya library on the basis of its catalogue, in Konrad Hirschler, *Medieval Damascus: Plurality and Diversity in an Arabic Library: the Ashrafiya Library Catalogue* (Edinburgh: Edinburgh University Press, 2016), Chapter II. There is of course no equivalent source for al-Ṣūlī's period.

61 al-Ṣūlī, *Adab al-kuttāb,* 191. See also F.C. De Blois, 'Taʾrīkh. I.1.,' in *EI2*. Of course, we have seen in Chapter One that al-Ṣūlī himself is not exempt from accusations of sloppiness: al-Khaṭīb highlights his mistakes in transmission, and Abū l-Faraj al-Iṣfahānī 'raps al-Ṣūlī over the knuckles for attributing to Yaḥyā ibn Marwān a short poem addressed by Marwān al-Aṣghar ibn Abī l-Janūb to al-Muntaṣir:

"*Hādhā ghalaṭun qabīḥ*" (This is a horrible blunder) (XII, 97)' (Hilary Kilpatrick, *Making the Great Book of Songs: Compilation and the Author's Craft in Abū l-Faraj al-Iṣbahānī's Kitāb al-Aghānī* (London: RoutledgeCurzon, 2003), 60).

62 The Mamluk period has been especially well studied in this respect. Beside works by Konrad Hirschler and Frédéric Bauden cited elsewhere in this volume, see Konrad Hirschler, *A Monument to Medieval Syrian Book Culture: the Library of Ibn 'Abd al-Hadi* (Edinburgh: Edinburgh University Press, 2020). See also the interesting argument on the archival value of chronicles in Fozia Bora, *Writing History in the Medieval Islamic World: the Value of Chronicles as Archives* (London: Tauris, 2019).

5 Insight and Hindsight

1 Dominique Sourdel, *Le Vizirat ʿabbāside de 749 à 936*, 2 vols (Damascus: Institut Français de Damas, 1959–60), 10. This chapter contains material reworked from my 'Author as Protagonist'.

2 Lale Behzadi summarizes the situation as follows: 'It remains difficult sometimes to examine so-called historical texts by applying methods deriving from literary theory without raising suspicions. There seems to be no middle ground between either viewing a non-fictional text as an authentic historical source on the one hand, or as a historical source that has been manipulated for some reason, either by the author himself or by later readers on the other' (Lale Behzadi, 'Authorial Guidance: Abū Ḥayyān al-Tawḥīdī's Closing Remarks,' in *Concepts of Authorship in Pre-modern Arabic Texts*, eds Lale Behzadi and Jakko Hämeen-Anttilla (Bamberg: University of Bamberg Press, 2015), 218–19). Studies on al-Ṣūlī's older – and much more prominent – contemporary al-Ṭabarī illustrate Behzadi's point (see for example the conflicting approaches in Tayeb El-Hibri, *Reinterpreting Islamic Historiography: Hārūn al-Rashīd and the Narrative of the ʿAbbāsid Caliphate* (Cambridge: Cambridge University Press, 1999) and Boaz Shoshan, *Poetics of Islamic Historiography: Deconstructing Ṭabarī's History* (Leiden: Brill, 2004). Some historians' reviews of the latter volume are indicative).

3 ʿArīb, *Ṣila*, 155. This passage is found in the account of the year 318/930; al-Ṣūlī discusses his relationship with one of the Abbasid princes, Hārūn b. al-Muqtadir, and quotes a poem he had dedicated to him.

4 al-Masʿūdī, *Murūj*, §11.

5 Hugh N. Kennedy, *The Prophet and the Age of the Caliphates*, 2nd ed. (London: Longman, 2004), 365.

6 A clear and concise account of this decade is given by Heribert Busse, *Chalif und Grosskönig: die Buyiden im Iraq (945–1055)*, (Beirut: In Kommission bei F. Steiner, Wiesbaden, 1969), 17–25.

7 Miskawayh, *Tajārib*, 1, 331.

8 The *Ḥujarīs* were originally slave troops stationed by al-Muʿtaḍid in the Palace rooms (*ḥujar*) and later became part of the cavalry. On the composition of the caliphal army in the post-Samarra period, see Hugh N. Kennedy, *The Armies of the Caliphs: Military Society in the Early Islamic State*, (London: Routledge, 2001), 156–64.

9 Miskawayh, *Tajārib*, 1, 339. ʿAskar Mukram is in Khuzistān, north of Ahwāz.

10 Miskawayh, *Tajārib*, 1, 349.

11 Miskawayh, *Tajārib*, 1, 352.

12 al-Ṣūlī, *ARM*, 70–86.

13 The *Sājīs*, named after their leader, the military contractor Abū l-Sāj, remained independent until the latter was captured and executed by the Qarāmiṭa in 266/879. They were then incorporated into the caliphal army (see Kennedy, *Armies*, 160–2).

14 al-Ṣūlī, *ARM*, 76.

15 al-Ṣūlī, *ARM*, 76.

16 al-Ṣūlī, *ARM*, 85.

17 al-Ṣūlī, *ARM*, 86.

18 On these events, see Kennedy, *Armies*, 159. The *Sājīs* were similarly neutered, with the consequence that al-Rāḍī was forced to depend on others for protection.

19 Konrad Hirschler, *Medieval Arabic Historiography: Authors as Actors* (London: Routledge, 2006), 122.

20 On the theory of emplotment, see Hayden White, 'Historical Emplotment and the Problem of Truth,' in *The History and Narrative Reader*, ed. Geoffrey Roberts (London: Routledge, 2001).

21 Hirschler, *Medieval Arabic Historiography: Authors as Actors*, 3.

22 Michael G. Carter, 'The Kātib in Fact and Fiction,' *Abr-Nahrain* 11 (1971).

23 A similar general point is made by Akhalīfa, *al-Khabar al-adabī* 9–10. This difference in focus is also remarked upon by Chris Wickham, 'Administrators' Time: the Social Memory of the Early Medieval State, East and West,' in *Islamic Cultures, Islamic Contexts: Essays in Honor of Professor Patricia Crone*, eds Behnam Sadeghi et al. (Leiden: Brill, 2015), 441: '[al-Ṣūlī] also wrote an account of the caliph al-Rāḍī and his immediate successor [. . .] which fronts the caliph in a way that is directly opposed to the administrative patterns that we have so far seen [in al-Tanūkhī's *Nishwār*] (and will see again in Miskawayh). Al-Ṣūlī was not

only a *kātib*, and did not only have an administrative mind-set, although he could show it if the genre required.'

24 al-Ṣūlī, *ARM,* 75.

25 al-Ṣūlī, *ARM,* 106.

26 al-Ṣūlī, *ARM,* 107.

27 Al-Kūfī had arrived in Baghdad as a representative of Abū ʿAbdallāh al-Barīdī and, according to Miskawayh, had actively conspired to replace al-Nawbakhṭī (Miskawayh, *Tajārib,* 1, 415).

28 A.B. Khalidov, 'The Cultural Program of Abbasid Court Life in Samarra (III/IX c.) after al-Ṣūlī's *Awraq*,' *Occasional Papers of the School of Abbasid Studies* 4 (1992 (publ. 1994)): 15.

29 Jocelyn Sharlet has reviewed and dissected motifs of communication and interaction between patron and poet in panegyrics. In the case discussed here, praise poetry is marginal but some of the themes, such as access, remain (Jocelyn Sharlet, *Patronage and Poetry in the Islamic World: Social Mobility and Status in the Medieval Middle East and Central Asia* (London: I.B. Tauris, 2011), 150–86).

30 As has been seen above, in 324 Nāṣir al-Dawla had sent one hundred *kurr* of flour to be distributed in Samarra and Baghdad amongst the Hashemites and the poor. 'People rejoiced, many merchant boats went down [the Tigris], and prices went back to normal' (al-Ṣūlī, *ARM,* 76).

31 al-Ṣūlī, *ARM,* 109.

32 al-Ṣūlī, *ARM,* 110.

33 al-Ṣūlī, *ARM,* 115.

34 al-Ṣūlī, *ARM,* 124–8.

35 al-Ṣūlī, *ARM,* 129–30.

36 For an analysis of the linguistic and pragmatic aspects of al-Ṣūlī's dialogue, see Letizia Osti, 'Al-Ṣūlī and the Caliph: Norms, Practices and Frames,' in *Il Dialogo nella cultura araba: strutture, funzioni, significati (VIII–XIII secolo),* Mirella Cassarino and Antonella Ghersetti (Soveria Mannelli: Il Rubbettino, 2015). See also, applied to a later period, Naaman, *Literature and the Islamic Court,* 60–6. For a general discussion of the etiquette of conversation at court, see Nadia Maria El Cheikh, 'Conversation as Performance: *Adab al-Muḥādatha* at the Abbasid Court,' in *In the Presence of Power: Court and Performance in the pre-modern Middle East,* Maurice A. Pomerantz and Evelyin Birge Vitz (New York: New York University Press, 2017).

37 Miskawayh, *Tajārib,* 1, 405–9.

38 al-Ṣūlī, *ARM,* 131. On the Abbasid general Abū Dulaf (d. 225–8/840–3) and the Ṣaffārid ʿAmr b. al-Layth (d. 289/902), see Jamel Eddin Bencheikh, 'al-Ḳāsim b. ʿĪsā,' in *EI2* and Robert J. Haug, 'ʿAmr b. al-Layth,' in *EI3* respectively.

39 al-Ṣūlī, *ARM*, 157 and 163–4 (against Ibn Rāʾiq); 160–2 and 168–70 (on the trip to Mosul).

40 See for example al-Ṣūlī, *ARM*, 129: al-Rāḍī's secretary ʿAlī b. Khalaf b. Ṭayyāb, left in Baghdad during the caliph's absence, tries, with little success, to collect the *kharāj* tax.

41 al-Ṣūlī, *ARM*, 119–22. On the role of the *ʿayyār* in these events, see D.G. Tor, *Violent Order: Religious Warfare, Chivalry, and the ʿayyār Phenomenon in the Medieval Islamic World* (Würzburg: Ergon, 2007), 266–7.

42 al-Ṣūlī, *ARM*, 108.

43 al-Ṣūlī, *ARM*, 129.

44 al-Ṣūlī, *ARM*, 131–2.

45 al-Ṣūlī, *ARM*, 224–5.

46 al-Ṣūlī, *ARM*, 281.

47 Another piece of context given here is a description of the caliph's relations with Muḥammad b. Ṭughj al-Ikhshīd (d. 334/946), the governor of Egypt (al-Ṣūlī, *ARM*, 44–5).

48 al-Ṣūlī, *ARM*, 41–2.

49 al-Ṣūlī, *ARM*, 43.

50 See Chapter One for the story of al-Ṣūlī's arrival at court as a chess player. As has been seen in Chapter Two, in the *Awrāq*, al-Ṣūlī mentions al-Muktafī's benevolence towards him (al-Ṣūlī, *ARM*, 69). The conversation on the caliph's deathbed is described in al-Ṣūlī, *Mā lam yunshar*, 21. Interactions with this caliph are also mentioned elsewhere (al-Ṣūlī, *Akhbār al-Buḥturī*, 179; al-Masʿūdī, *Murūj*, § 3387–9).

51 Al-Ṣūlī's access to al-Muʿtaḍid and al-Muqtadir is discussed in Osti, 'Remuneration'. Instances when al-Ṣūlī persuades al-Rāḍī are described in Osti, 'Norms'.

52 al-Ṣūlī, *ARM*, 121.

53 al-Ṣūlī, *ARM*, 130–1.

54 al-Ṣūlī, *Mā lam yunshar*, 31.

55 al-Ṣūlī, *ARM*, 26.

56 al-Ṣūlī, *Mā lam yunshar*, 157.

Conclusion

1 Assmann, 'Collective Memory', 131.

2 ʿArīb, *Ṣila*, 155.

3 See Chapter Four and Osti, 'Author as Protagonist,' 243–4.

4 See Chris Wickham's discussion of the pitfalls of positivist approaches on the one hand and textual ones on the other (James Fentress and Chris Wickham, *Social Memory* (Oxford: Blackwell, 1992), 144–5). This volume has attempted to avoid both.

5 Julia Bray's discussion of Ibn al-Muʿtazz's political thought is relevant here. Bray argues that decontextualising Ibn al-Muʿtazz's work from his political and intellectual environment may be 'a reaction to the forced parallels often drawn in conventional life-and-times approaches,' but that such an approach is not necessarily always distorting (Bray, 'Ibn al-Muʿtazz and Politics,' 109).

Bibliography

Abbreviations

AAK: *Akhbār awlād al-khulafāʾ*

ARM: *Akhbār al-Rāḍī wa-l-Muttaqī*

ASM: *Akhbār al-shuʿarāʾ al-muḥdathīn*

EI2: Bearman, Peri J., et. al., eds. *Encyclopaedia of Islam, New Edition*. Leiden: Brill, 1960–2009.

EI3: Fleet, Kate, et. al, eds. *Encyclopaedia of Islam THREE*. Leiden: Brill, 2007–.

Primary sources

Abū l-Fidāʾ, Ismāʿīl b. ʿAlī. *Al-Mukhtaṣar fī akhbār al-bashar*. 4 vols. Cairo: al-Maṭbaʿa al-Ḥusayniyya al-Miṣriyya, s.d.

Abū Nuwās. *Der Dīwān des Abū Nuwās*. Edited by Ewald Wagner and Gregor Schoeler. 5+2 vols. Wiesbaden: Franz Steiner Verlag, 1958–2006.

Abū Tammām. *Sharḥ al-Ṣūlī li-dīwān Abī Tammām*. Edited by Khalaf Rashīd Nuʿmān. 3 vols. Baghdad: Wizārat al-Aʿlām, 1977.

Abū l-Ṭayyib al-Lughawī, ʿAbd al-Wāḥid b. ʿAlī. *Marātib al-Naḥwiyyīn*. Edited by Muḥammad Abū-l-Faḍl Ibrāhīm. Cairo: Maktabat Naḥḍat Miṣr, [1955].

ʿArīb b. Saʿd al-Qurṭubī. *Ṣilat tārīkh al-Ṭabarī: Tabarî Continuatus*. Edited by M.J. De Goeje. Leiden: Brill, 1897.

al-Dhahabī, Muḥammad b. Aḥmad b. ʿUthmān. *Taʾrīkh al-islām*. Edited by ʿUmar Tadmurī. Beirut: Dār al-Kitāb al-ʿArabī, 1987–95.

al-Dhahabī, Muḥammad b. Aḥmad b. ʿUthmān. *Tadhkirat al-ḥuffāẓ*. Edited by Zakarīyā ʿUmayrāt. Beirut: Dār al-Kutub al-ʿIlmiyya, 1998.

Ibn al-Anbārī, Abū l-Barakāt ʿAbd al-Raḥmān b. Muḥammad. *Nuzhat al-alibbāʾ fī akhbār al-udabāʾ*. Edited by Ibrāhīm al-Sāmarrāʾī. Al-Zarqāʾ: Maktabat al-Manār, 1959.

Ibn al-Athīr, ʿAlī b. Muḥammad ʿIzz al-Dīn. *Al-Kāmil fī l-taʾrīkh*. Edited by ʿUmar Tadmurī. 10 vols. Beirut: Dār al-Kitāb al-ʿArabī, 1997.

Ibn al-Athīr, ʿAlī b. Muḥammad ʿIzz al-Dīn. *Al-Lubāb fī tahdhīb al-Ansāb*. Edited by ʿAbd al-Laṭīf Ḥasan ʿAbd al-Raḥmān. 2 vols. Beirut: Dār al-Kutub al-ʿIlmiyya, 2000.

Ibn al-ʿImād, ʿAbd al-Ḥayy b. Aḥmad. *Shadharāt al-dhahab fī akhbār man dhahab*. Edited by ʿAbd al-Qādir Arnāʾūt and Maḥmūd Arnāʾūt. 11 vols. Damascus and Beirut: Dār Ibn Kathīr, 1986.

Ibn al-Jawzī, Abū l-Faraj ʿAbd al-Raḥmān b. ʿAlī. *Al-Muntaẓam fī tāʾrīkh al-mulūk wa-l-umam*. Edited by Muḥammad ʿAbd al-Qādir ʿAṭā and Muṣṭafā ʿAbd al-Qādir ʿAṭā. 19 vols. Beirut: Dār al-Kutub al-ʿIlmiyya, 1992–3.

Ibn Kathīr, Ismāʿīl b. ʿUmar. *Al-Bidāya wa-l-nihāya*. Edited by ʿAlī Shīrī. Beirut: Dār Iḥyāʾ al-Turāth al-ʿArabī, 1988.

Ibn Khallikān, Aḥmad b. Muḥammad. *Kitāb Wafayāt al-aʿyān: Ibn Khallikān's Biographical Dictionary*. Translated by B. Mac Guckin De Slane. 4 vols. Paris: Oriental Translation Fund, 1843–71.

Ibn Khallikān, Aḥmad b. Muḥammad. *Wafayāt al-aʿyān*. Edited by Iḥsān ʿAbbās. 8 vols. Beirut: Dār al-Thaqāfa, 1968–72.

Ibn al-Muʿtazz, ʿAbdallāh. *Dīwān*. Edited by Bernhard Lewin. Cairo: Maṭbaʿat al-Maʿārif, 1945–50.

Ibn al-Nadīm, Muḥammad b. Isḥāq. *The Fihrist of al-Nadīm*. Edited and translated by Bayard Dodge. 2 vols. New York: Columbia University Press, 1970.

Ibn al-Nadīm, Muḥammad b. Isḥāq. *Kitāb al-Fihrist*. Edited by A.F. Sayyid. London: al-Furqan Islamic Heritage Foundation, 2009.

Ibn al-Qifṭī, ʿAlī b. Yūsuf. *Inbāh al-ruwāt ʿalā anbāh al-nuḥāt*. Edited by Muḥammad Abū-l-Faḍl Ibrāhīm. 3 vols. Cairo, 1950–5.

Ibn Taghrībirdī, Abū l-Maḥāsin Yūsuf. *Al-Nujūm al-zāhira fī mulūk Miṣr wa-l-Qāhira*. Cairo: Dār al-Kutub al-Miṣrīya, 1929.

al-Thaʿlabī [pseudo-al-Jāḥiẓ]. *Kitāb al-Tāj fī akhlāq al-mulūk*]. Edited by Aḥmad Zakī Bāshā. Cairo: al-Maṭbaʿa al-Amīriyya, 1914.

al-Khaṭīb al-Baghdādī. *Taʾrīkh Baghdād*. Edited by Muṣṭafā ʿAbd al-Qādir ʿAṭā. 21 vols. Beirut: Dār al-Kutub al-ʿIlmiyya, 1997.

Kitāb al-Shaṭranj. Book on Chess. Selected Texts from al-ʿAdlī, Abū Bakr al-Ṣūlī and Others. Reproduced from MS 560 Lala Ismail Collection, Süleymaniyye Library, Istanbul. Edited by Fuat Sezgin. Frankfurt am Main: Institut für die Geschichte der Arabisch-Islamischen Wissenschaften, 1986.

Kushājim, Maḥmūd b. al-Ḥusayn. *Adab al-nadīm*. Edited by ʿAbd al-Wāḥid Shaʿlān. [Cairo], 1987.

al-Marzubānī, Abū ʿUbayd Allāh Muḥammad b. ʿImrān b. Mūsā. *Muʿjam al-shuʿarāʾ*. Edited by ʿAbd al-Sattār Aḥmad Farrāj. Cairo: Dār Iḥyāʾ al-Kutub al-ʿArabiyya/Muṣṭafā al-Bābī al-Ḥalabī wa-Awlāduhu, 1960.

al-Marzubānī, Abū ʿUbayd Allāh Muḥammad b. ʿImrān b. Mūsā. *Die Gelehrtenbiographien des Abū ʿUbaidallāh al-Marzubānī in der Rezension des Ḥāfiẓ al-Yaġmūrī (Nūr al-Qabas al-Muqtaṣar min al-Muqtabas fī Akhbār al-Nuḥat wa-l-Udabāʾ wa-l-Shuʿarāʾ wa-l-ʿUlamāʾ).* Edited by Rudolph Sellheim. Wiesbaden: Franz Steiner Verlag, 1964.

al-Masʿūdī, Abū-l-Ḥasan ʿAlī b. al-Ḥusayn. *Murūj al-dhahab wa-maʿādhin al-jawhar.* Edited by C. Barbier de Meynard et A. Pavet de Courteille. Revue et corrigé par Charles Pellat. 7 vols. Beirut: Publications de l'Université Libanaise, 1965–79.

Miskawayh, Abū ʿAlī Aḥmad b. Muḥammad. *Tajārib al-umam: The Eclipse of the Abbasid Caliphate.* Edited by H.F. Amedroz. Translated by D.S. Margoliouth. Oxford: Blackwell, 1920.

al-Ṣābiʾ, Hilāl b. al-Muḥassin. *Rusūm dār al-khilāfa.* Edited by Mīkhāʾīl ʿAwwād. Baghdad: Maṭbaʿat al-ʿĀnī, 1964.

al-Ṣābiʾ, Hilāl b. al-Muḥassin. *Al-Wuzarāʾ aw tuḥfat al-umarāʾ fī taʾrīkh al-wuzarāʾ.* Edited by ʿAbd al-Sattār Aḥmad Farrāj. [Cairo]: Dār Iḥyāʾ al-Kutub al-ʿArabiyya, 1958.

al-Ṣafadī, Ṣalāḥ al-Dīn Khalīl b. Aybak. *Kitāb al-Wāfī bi-l-wafayāt. Das biographische Lexikon des Ṣalāḥaddīn Ḫalīl ibn Aibak aṣ-Ṣafadī.* Edited by Helmut Ritter, et al. 32 vols. Leipzig; Wiesbaden; Beirut: Deutsche Morgenländische Geselleschaft, 1931–2013.

al-Samʿānī, ʿAbd al-Karīm b. Muḥammad b. Manṣūr al-Tamīmī. *Al-Ansāb.* 13 vols. Hayderabad: Dāʾirat al-Maʿārif al-ʿUthmāniyya, 1952–82.

al-Ṣūlī, Abū Bakr. *Juzʾ fī l-Shiṭranj.* MS Paris, Bibliothèque nationale de France, arabe 6881.

al-Ṣūlī, Abū Bakr. *Akhbār al-shuʿarāʾ al-muḥdathīn.* Edited by J. Heyworth Dunne. Beirut: Dār al-Masīra, 1934.

al-Ṣūlī, Abū Bakr. *Akhbār al-Rāḍī bi-llāh wa l-Muttaqī li-llāh, aw, Tārīkh al-dawla al-ʿabbāsiyya min sanat 322 ilā sanat 333 hijriyya min Kitāb al-Awrāq.* Edited by J. Heyworth Dunne. Beirut: Dār al-Masīra, 1935.

al-Ṣūlī, Abū Bakr. *Ashʿār awlād al-khulafāʾ.* Edited by J. Heyworth Dunne. Beirut: Dār al-Masīra, 1936.

al-Ṣūlī, Abū Bakr. *Akhbār Abī Tammām.* Edited by Khalīl Maḥmūd ʿAsākir, *et al.* Cairo: Lajnat al-Taʾlīf wa-l-Tarjama wa-l-Nashr, 1937.

al-Ṣūlī, Abū Bakr. *Akhbār al-Rāḍī bi-llāh wa'l-Muttaḳī li-llāh (Histoire de la dynastie abbaside de 322 à 333/934 à 944).* 2 vols. Algier: Institut d'Études Orientales, 1946.

al-Ṣūlī, Abū Bakr. *Akhbār al-Buḥturī.* Edited by Ṣāliḥ al-Ashtar. Damascus: Matbūʿāt al-Majmaʿ al-ʿIlmī al-ʿArabī, 1958.

al-Ṣūlī, Abū Bakr. *Qiṭʿa nādira min Kitāb al-awrāq*. Edited by Hilāl Nājī. Baghdad: Dār al-Shuʾūn al-Thaqāfiyya al-ʿĀmma, 1990.

al-Ṣūlī, Abū Bakr. *Adab al-kuttāb*. Edited by Aḥmad Ḥasan Basaj. Beirut: Dār al-Kutub al-ʿIlmiyya, 1994.

al-Ṣūlī, Abū Bakr. *Kitāb al-Awrāq. Kniga Listov*. Edited and translated by Anas B. Khalidov. St Petersburg: Tsentr Peterburgoskoe Vostokovedenie, 1998.

al-Ṣūlī, Abū Bakr. *Mā lam yunshar min awrāq al-Ṣūlī: akhbār al-sanawāt 295–315*. Edited by Hilāl Nājī. Beirut: ʿĀlam al-Kutub, 2000.

al-Ṣūlī, Abū Bakr. *Dīwān ʿUlayya bt. al-Mahdī bi-riwāyat Abī Bakr Muḥammad b. Yaḥyā al-Ṣūlī*. Edited by Muḥammad Abū l-Majd ʿAlī Basyūnī. Cairo: Maktabat al-Ādāb, 2004.

al-Ṣūlī, Abū Bakr. *The Life and Times of Abū Tammām*. Edited and translated by Beatrice Gruendler. New York: New York University Press, 2015.

al-Ṣūlī, Abū Bakr. *Faḍl al-shubbān ʿalā kathīr mimman taqaddama min dhawī l-asnān*. Edited by Muṣṭafā ʿAlī Qarmad. Al-Manṣūra: al-Maktaba al-ʿAṣriyya lil-Nashr wa-l-Tawzīʿ, 2016.

al-Ṭabarī, Abū Jaʿfar Muḥammad b. Jarīr. *Taʾrīkh al-rusul wa-l-mulūk*. Edited by M.J. De Goeje et al. Leiden: E.J. Brill, 1879–1901.

al-Tanūkhī, al-Muhạssin b. ʿAlī. *The Table-Talk of a Mesopotamian Judge: being the first Part of the Nishwār al-muḥāḍarah or Jāmiʿ al-tawārīkh*. Translated by D.S. Margoliouth. 2 vols. London: The Royal Asiatic Society, 1921–2.

al-Tanūkhī, al-Muhạssin b. ʿAlī. *Nishwār al-muḥāḍara wa-akhbār al-mudhākara*. Edited by ʿAbbūd al-Shālijī. Beirut: Dār Ṣādir, 1975.

al-Tanūkhī, al-Muhạssin b. ʿAlī. *Al-Faraj baʿda l-shidda*. Edited by ʿAbbūd al-Shālijī. Beirut: Dār Ṣādir, 1978.

al-Tanūkhī, al-Muhạssin b. ʿAlī. *Stories of Piety and Prayer: Deliverance follows Adversity*. Edited and translated by Julia Bray. New York: New York University Press, 2019.

al Thaʿālibī, Abū Manṣūr. *Yatīmat al-dahr fī maḥāsin ahl al-ʿaṣr*. Edited by Mufīd Muḥammad Qamīḥa. 6 vols. Beirut: Dār al-Kutub al-ʿIlmiyya, 2000.

al-Washshāʾ, Abū l-Ṭayyib Muḥammad b. Yaḥyā. *Kitāb al-Muwashshā*. Edited by Rudolf E. Brünnow. Leiden: Brill, 1886.

al-Yāfiʿī. *Mirʾāt al-jinān wa-ʿibrat al-yaqẓān*. Edited by Khalīl al-Manṣūr. 4 vols. Beirut: Dār al-Kutub al-ʿIlmiyya, 1997.

Yāqūt b. ʿAbdallāh al-Ḥamawī. *Muʿjam al-udabāʾ: Irshād al-arīb ilā maʿrifat al-adīb (irshād al-alibbāʾ fī maʿrifat al-udabāʾ)*. Edited by Iḥsān ʿAbbās. 7 vols. Beirut: Dār al-Gharb al-Islāmī, 1993.

al-Zubaydī, Abū Bakr Muḥammad b. al-Ḥasan. *Ṭabaqāt al-naḥwiyyīn wa-l-lughawiyyīn*. Edited by Muḥammad Abū-l-Faḍl Ibrāhīm. Cairo: Dār al-Maʿārif, [1973].

Secondary sources

ʿAbbās, Iḥsān. *Tāʾrīkh al-naqd al-adabī ʿinda l-ʿArab: naqd al-shiʿr min al-qarn al-thānī ḥattā l-qarn al-thāmin al-hijrī.* Amman: Dār al-Shurūq lil-Nashr wa-l-Tawzīʿ, 1933.

ʿAbbās, Iḥsān. *Fann al-sīra.* Beirut: Dār Bayrūt lil-Ṭibāʿa wa-l-Nashr, 1956.

Ahmed, Munir-ud-Din. *Muslim Education and the Scholars' Social Status up to the 5th Century Muslim Era (11th century Christian Era) in the Light of Taʾrīkh Baghdād.* Zurich: Verlag der Islam, 1968.

Akhalīfa, al-Ḥusayn Mubārak. *Al-Khabar al-adabī ʿinda Abī Bakr al-Ṣūlī: muqāraba sardiyya tawāṣuliyya.* Amman: Dār al-Muʿtazz, 2017.

Al-Bagdadi, Nadia. 'Registers of Arabic Literary History.' *New Literary History* 39 (2008): 437–61.

Ali, Samer M. *Arabic Literary Salons in the Islamic Middle Ages: Poetry, Public Performance, and the Presentation of the Past.* Notre Dame, IN: University of Notre Dame Press, 2010.

ʿĀmir, Fakhr al-Dīn. *Maṣādir al-turāth fī kutub al-tarājim al-adabīya.* Cairo: ʿĀlam al-Kutub, 2000.

Assmann, Jan. 'Collective Memory and Cultural Identity.' *New German Critique* 65 (1995): 125–33.

Auchterlonie, Paul. 'Historians and the Arabic Biographical Dictionary: Some New Approaches.' In *Islamic reflections, Arabic Musings: Studies in Honour of Professor Alan Jones*, edited by Robert G. Hoyland and Philip F. Kennedy, 186–200. Warminster: Gibb Memorial Trust, 2004.

Bacharach, Jere L. 'al-Barīdī.' In *EI3*.

Baġdād, volume spécial, publié à l'occasion du mille deux centième anniversaire de la fondation (tirage à part d'Arabica). Leiden: Brill, 1962.

Bauden, Frédéric. 'Maqriziana IX: Should al-Maqrīzī Be Thrown out with the Bath Water? The Question of his Plagiarism of al-Awḥadī's *Khiṭaṭ* and the Documentary Evidence.' *Mamlūk Studies Review* 14 (2010): 159–232.

Bauer, Thomas. 'Abū l-Ṭayyib al-Lughawī.' In *EI3*.

Behzadi, Lale. 'Muslimische Intellektuelle im Gespräch: Der arabische literarische Salon im 10. Jahrhundert.' In *Von Rom nach Bagdad: Bildung und Religion von der römischen Kaiserzeit bis zum klassischen Islam*, edited by Peter Gemeinhardt and Sebastian Günther, 291–320. Tübingen: Mohr Siebeck, 2013.

Behzadi, Lale. 'Authorial Guidance: Abū Ḥayyān al-Tawḥīdī's Closing Remarks.' In *Concepts of Authorship in Pre-modern Arabic Texts*, edited by Lale Behzadi and Jakko Hämeen-Anttilla, 215–34. Bamberg: University of Bamberg Press, 2015.

Behzadi, Lale and Jaakko Hämeen-Anttila, eds. *Concepts of Authorship in Pre-Modern Arabic Texts*. Bamberg: University of Bamberg Press, 2015.

Bencheikh, Jamel Eddin. 'al-Ḳāsim b. ʿĪsā.' In *EI2*.

Bencheikh, Omar. 'Nifṭawayh.' In *EI2*.

Benchellel, Issam. 'Naqd al-naqd wa-tajliyātuhu ʿinda Abī Bakr al-Ṣūlī.' *Al-Judhūr* 55 (2019): 49–81.

Bennett, Andrew. *The Author*. London: Routledge, 2005.

Berggren, J. Lennart. 'al-Munajjim, Banū.' In *EI3*.

Berkel, Maaike van, Nadia Maria El Cheikh, Hugh Kennedy, and Letizia Osti. *Crisis and Continuity at the Abbasid Court: Formal and Informal Politics in the Caliphate of al-Muqtadir (295–320/908–32)*. Leiden: Brill, 2013.

Bernards, Monique. 'Medieval Muslim Scholarship and Social Network Analysis: a Study of the Baṣra/Kūfa Dichotomy in Arabic Grammar.' In *Ideas, Images, and Methods of Portrayal: Insights into Classical Arabic Literature and Islam*, edited by Sebastian Günther, 129–40. Leiden: Brill, 2005.

Bernards, Monique. 'Grammarians' Circles of Learning: a Social Network Analysis.' In *ʿAbbasid studies II: Occasional papers of the School of ʿAbbasid Studies. Leuven, 28 June–1 July, 2004*, edited by John Nawas, 143–64. Leuven: Peeters, 2010.

Bernards, Monique. 'Ibn Abī Isḥāq (d. *c*. 125/743) and his Scholarly Network.' In *Islam at 250: Studies in Memory of G.H.A. Juynboll*, 9–31. Leiden: Brill, 2020.

Bora, Fozia. *Writing History in the Medieval Islamic World: the Value of Chronicles as Archives*. London: I.B. Tauris, 2019.

Borrut, Antoine. *Entre mémoire et pouvoir: l'espace syrien sous les derniers Omeyyades et les premiers Abbassides (v. 72–193/692–809)*. Leiden: Brill, 2011.

Bosworth, C.E. 'Mardāwīdj.' In *EI2*.

Bosworth, C.E. 'The Ṭāhirids and Arabic Culture.' *Journal of Semitic Studies* 14 (1969): 45–79.

Bosworth, C.E. 'The Ṭāhirids and Persian Literature.' *Iran: Journal of the British Institute of Persian Studies* 7 (1969): 103–6.

Bowen, Harald. *The Life and Times of ʿAlì ibn ʿIsà, 'The Good Vizier'*. Cambridge: Cambridge University Press, 1928.

Bray, Julia. 'Yāqūt's Interviewing Technique: "Sniffy".' In *Texts, Documents and Artefacts: Islamic Studies in Honour of D.S. Richard*, edited by Chase F. Robinson, 191–209. Leiden: Brill, 2003.

Bray, Julia. 'Place and Self-image: the Buhlūlids and Tanūḫids and their Family Traditions.' *Quaderni di Studi Arabi* 3 (2008): 39–66.

Bray, Julia. 'Ibn al-Muʿtazz and Politics: The Question of the *Fuṣūl Qiṣār*.' *Oriens* 38 (2010): 107–43.

Bray, Julia. 'Literary Approaches to Medieval and Early Modern Arabic Biography.' *Journal of the Royal Asiatic Society* 20 (2010): 237–53.

Bray, Julia. 'Codes of Emotion in Ninth- and Tenth-Century Baghdad: Slave Concubines in Literature and Life-Writing.' *Cultural History* 8 (2019): 184–201.

Brentjes, Sonja. 'The Prison of Categories – "Decline" and its Company.' In *Islamic Philosophy, Science, Culture, and Religion: Studies in Honor of Dimitri Gutas*, edited by Felicitas Opwis and David Reisman, 131–56. Leiden: Brill, 2021.

Brockelmann, Carl. *Geschichte der arabischen Literatur.* Leiden: E.J. Brill, 1937–1949.

Bulliet, Richard W. 'The Age Structure of Medieval Islamic Education.' *Studia Islamica* 57 (1983): 105–17.

Busse, Heribert. *Chalif und Grosskönig: die Buyiden im Iraq (945-1055).* Beirut: In Kommission bei F. Steiner, Wiesbaden, 1969.

Canova, Giovanni. 'Una Pagina di *al-Kanz al-madfūn* sugli uomini più illustri.' In *Ultra Mare: Mélanges de langue arabe et d'islamologie offerts à Aubert Martin*, edited by Frédéric Bauden, 93–107. Leuven: Peeters, 2004.

Carter, Michael G. 'The Kātib in Fact and Fiction.' *Abr-Nahrain* 11 (1971): 42–55.

Cohen, Hayyim J. 'The Economic Background and the Secular Occupations of Muslim Jurisprudents and Traditionists in the Classical Period of Islam (until the middle of the eleventh century).' *Journal of the Economic and Social History of the Orient* 13 (1970).

Cooperson, Michael. *Classical Arabic Biography: the Heirs of the Prophets.* Cambridge: Cambridge University Press, 2000.

Cooperson, Michael. '"Arabs" and "Iranians": the Uses of Ethnicity in the Early Abbasid Period.' In *Islamic Cultures, Islamic Contexts: Essays in Honor of Professor Patricia Crone*, edited by Asad Q. Ahmed, *et al.*, 364–87. Leiden: Brill, 2014.

Cooperson, Michael. 'The Abbasid "Golden Age": an Excavation.' *Al- ʿUṣūr al-Wusṭā* 25 (2017): 41–65.

Crone, Patricia. 'Muhallabids.' In *EI2.*

De Blois, F.C. 'Taʾrīkh. I.1.' In *EI2.*

Donner, Fred M. *Narratives of Islamic Origins: the Beginnings of Islamic Historical Writing.* Princeton: The Darwin Press, 1998.

Duindam, Jeroen. Review of Maurice A. Pomerantz and Evelyn Birge Vitz, eds. *In the Presence of Power: Court and Performance in the Pre-modern Middle East.* New York: New York University Press, 2018. *The Medieval Review* (2018).

Eales, Richard. *Chess: the History of a Game.* London: Batsford, 1985.

El-Cheikh, Nadia Maria. *Women, Islam, and Abbasid Identity.* Cambridge, MA: Harvard University Press, 2015.

El-Hibri, Tayeb. *Reinterpreting Islamic Historiography: Hārūn al-Rashīd and the Narrative of the ʿAbbāsid Caliphate.* Cambridge: Cambridge University Press, 1999.

El Acheche, Taieb. 'Sudayf b. Maymūn.' In *EI2*.

El Cheikh, Nadia Maria. 'The Qahramâna in the Abbasid Court: Position and Functions.' *Studia Islamica* (2003): 41–55.

El Cheikh, Nadia Maria. 'The Court of al-Muqtadir: its Space and its Occupants.' In *Abbasid Studies II: Occasional Paper of the School of ʿAbbasid Studies, Leuven 28 June–1 July, 2004*, edited by John Nawas, 318–36. Leuven: Peeters, 2010.

El Cheikh, Nadia Maria. 'Court and Courtiers: a Preliminary Investigation of Abbasid Terminology.' In *Court Cultures in the Muslim World: Seventh to Nineteenth Centuries*, edited by Albrecht Fuess and Jan-Peter Hartung, 80–90. New York: Routledge, 2011.

El Cheikh, Nadia Maria. 'To be a Prince in the fourth/tenth–century Abbasid Court.' In *Royal Courts in Dynastic States and Empires*, edited by Jeroen Duindam, et al., 199–216: Brill, 2011.

El Cheikh, Nadia Maria. 'Conversation as Performance: *Adab al-Muḥādatha* at the Abbasid Court.' In *In the Presence of Power: Court and Performance in the pre-modern Middle East*, edited by Maurice A. Pomerantz and Evelyin Birge Vitz, 84–99. New York: New York University Press, 2017.

Enderwitz, Susanne. 'Du *Fatā* au *Ẓarīf*, ou comment on se distingue?' *Arabica* 36 (1989): 125–42.

Enderwitz, Susanne. 'Gibt es eine arabische Autobiograpie?' In *Understanding Near Eastern Literatures*, edited by Verena Klemm and Beatrice Gruendler, 189–99. Wiesbaden: Reichert, 2000.

Fentress, James, and Chris Wickham. *Social Memory.* Oxford: Blackwell, 1992.

Fierro, Maribel. 'Why and How Do Religious Scholars Write about Themselves? The Case of the Islamic West in the Fourth/Tenth Century.' *Mélanges de L´Université Saint-Joseph* 58 (2005): 403–23.

Fierro, Maribel. 'Writing and Reading in early Ifrīqiya.' In *Promissa nes aspera curans: Mélanges offerts à Madame le Professuer Marie-Thérèse Urvoy*, edited by Georgio Rahal and Heinz-Otto Luthe, 373–93. Toulouse: Les Presses Universitaires, Institute Catholique de Toulouse, 2017.

Fuess, Albrecht and Jan-Peter Hartung. *Court Cultures in the Muslim World: Seventh to Nineteenth Centuries.* London: Routledge, 2011.

Ghersetti, Antonella. 'Classes of Grammarians East and West: *Ṭabaqāt al-naḥwiyyīn wa-l-lughawiyyīn of al-Zubaydī and Marātib al-naḥwiyyīn* of Abū l-Ṭayyib al-Lughawī.' *Journal of Abbasid Studies* 7 (2020): 145–81.

Giffen, Lois Anita. *Theory of Profane Love Among the Arabs.* New York: New York University Press, 1971.

Gilliot, Claude. 'Prosopography in Islam: An Essay of Classification. *Medieval Prosopography* 23 (2002): 19–54.

Gruendler, Beatrice. 'Meeting the Patron: an *akhbār* Type and its Implications for *muḥdath* Poetry.' In *Ideas, Images, and Methods of Portrayal: Insights into Classical Arabic Literature and Islam*, edited by Sebastian Günther, 59–88. Wiesbaden: Harrassowitz, 2005.

Gruendler, Beatrice. 'Verse and Taxes: the Function of Poetry in selected literary *akhbār* of the third/ninth Century.' In *On Fiction and adab in medieval Arabic Literature*, edited by Philip F. Kennedy, 85–124. Wiesbaden: Harrassowitz, 2005.

Gruendler, Beatrice. 'World Philology.' In *Early Arabic Philologists: Poetry's Friends or Foes?* edited by Sheldon Pollock, et al., 92–113. Cambridge, MA: Harvard University Press, 2015.

Gruendler, Beatrice. 'Aspects of Craft in the Arabic Book Revolution.' In *Globalization of Knowledge in the Post-Antique Mediterranean, 700–1500*, edited by Sonja Brentjes and Jürgen Renn, 31–66. London: Routledge, 2016.

Gruendler, Beatrice. *The Rise of the Arabic Book.* Cambridge: Harvard University Press, 2020.

Günther, Sebastian. 'Education, General (up to 1500).' In *EI3.*

Günther, Sebastian. *Knowledge and Education in Classical Islam: Religious Learning between Continuity and Change.* 2 vols. Leiden: Brill, 2020.

Haug, Robert J. ''Amr b. al-Layth.' In *EI3.*

Heck, Paul L. *The Construction of Knowledge in Islamic Civilization: Qudāma b. Jaʿfar and his Kitāb al-Kharāj wa-ṣināʿat al-kitāba.* Leiden: Brill, 2002.

Heffening, Wilhelm. 'Ṭabaḳāt.' In *Encyclopaedia of Islam, First Edition (1913–1936).* Leiden: Brill.

Heinrichs, Wolfhart. 'Prosimetrical Genres in Classical Arabic Literature.' In *Prosimetrum: Cross-Cultural Perspectives on Narrative in Prose and Verse*, edited by Joseph Harris and Karl Reichl, 249–71. Cambridge: D.S. Brewer, 1997.

Hirschler, Konrad. *Medieval Arabic Historiography: Authors as Actors.* London: Routledge, 2006.

Hirschler, Konrad. *The Written Word in the Medieval Arabic Lands: a Social and Cultural History of Reading Practices.* Edinburgh: Edinburgh University Press, 2012.

Hirschler, Konrad. *Medieval Damascus: Plurality and Diversity in an Arabic Library: the Ashrafiya Library Catalogue.* Edinburgh: Edinburgh University Press, 2016.

Hirschler, Konrad. *A Monument to Medieval Syrian Book Culture: the Library of Ibn 'Abd al-Hadi.* Edinburgh: Edinburgh University Press, 2020.

Humphreys, R. Stephen. 'Ta'rīkh. II. Historical Writing. 1. In the Arab World.' In *EI2.*

Ḥusayn, Ṣubḥī Nāṣir. *Abū Bakr al-Ṣūlī nāqidan.* Baghdad: Dār al-Jāḥiẓ lil-Ṭibāʿa wa-l-Nashr, 1975.

Kaabi, Monji. *Les Ṭāhirides au Ḫurāsān et en Iraq (iiième H/ixème j.c.).* 2 vols. Paris: Université de Paris-Sorbonne, Faculté de Lettres et Sciences Humaines (Thèse de Doctorat d'État), 1983.

Kennedy, Hugh N. *The Armies of the Caliphs: Military Society in the Early Islamic State.* London: Routledge, 2001.

Kennedy, Hugh N. *The Prophet and the Age of the Caliphates.* Second edition. London: Longman, 2004.

Khalidi, Tarif. *Arabic Historical Thought in the Classical Period.* Cambridge: Cambridge University Press, 1994.

Khalidov, A.B. 'The Cultural Program of Abbasid Court Life in Samarra (III/IX c.) after al-Ṣūlī's *Awraq*.' *Occasional Papers of the School of Abbasid Studies* 4 (1992 (publ. 1994)): 10–20.

Kilpatrick, Hilary. 'A Genre in Classical Arabic: the *Adab* Encyclopedia.' In *Union européenne des arabisants et islamisants, 10th Congress, Edinburgh 9–16 September 1980: proceedings*, edited by Robert Hillenbrand, 34–42. Edinburgh: [s.n.], 1982.

Kilpatrick, Hilary. 'Autobiography and Classical Arabic Literature.' *Journal of Arabic Literature* 22 (1991): 1–20.

Kilpatrick, Hilary. 'Context and the Enhancement of the Meaning of *Akhbār* in the *Kitāb al-Aghānī*.' *Arabica* 38 (1991): 351–68.

Kilpatrick, Hilary. 'Abū-l-Faraj's Profiles of Poets: a 4th/10th Century Essay at the History and Sociology of Arabic Literature.' *Arabica* 44 (1997): 94–128.

Kilpatrick, Hilary. *Making the Great Book of Songs: Compilation and the Author's Craft in Abū l-Faraj al-Iṣbahānī's Kitāb al-Aghānī.* London: RoutledgeCurzon, 2003.

Kilpatrick, Hilary. 'Time and Death in Compiled *adab* "Biographies".' *al-Qanṭara* 25 (2004): 387–412.

Kraemer, Joel L. *Humanism in the Renaissance of Islam: the Cultural Revival during the Buyid Age.* Leiden: Brill, 1986.

Krenkow, Fritz. 'The Tarikh-Baghdad (Vol. XXVII) of the Khatib Abu Bakr Ahmad b. ʿAli b. Thabit al-Baghdadi: Short Account of the Biographies.' *Journal of the Royal Asiatic Society* (1912): 31–79.

Kurd ʿAlī, Muḥammad. *Kunūz al-ajdād fī siyar baʿḍ al-aʿlām.* Damascus: al-Majmaʿ al-ʿIlmī al-ʿArabī bi-Dimashq, 1950.

Leder, Stefan. 'al-Sarrādj.' In *EI2*.

Leder, Stefan. 'al-Ṣūlī.' In *EI2*.

Leder, Stefan and Hilary Kilpatrick. 'Classical Arabic Prose Literature: a Researcher's Sketch Map.' *Journal of Arabic Literature* 23 (1992): 2–26.

Lirola Delgado, Jorge. *Enciclopedia de Al-Andalus: diccionario de autores y obras andalusíes.* Granada: El Legado Andalusí, 2002.

Löschnigg, Martin. 'Autobiography.' In *Routledge Encyclopedia of Narrative Theory*, edited by David Herman, et al. London: Routledge, Taylor & Francis Group, 2010.

Loth, Otto. 'Die Ursprung und Bedeutung der Tabaqat.' *Zeitschrift der Deutschen Morgenländischen Gesellschaft* 23 (1869): 593–614.

Lunde, Paul. 'The Quest for Arabic Autobiography.' *The Medieval History Journal* 18 (2015): 430–51.

al-Majdūb, al-Bashīr. *Al-Ẓarf wa-l-ẓurafāʾ bi-l-Ḥijāz fī l-ʿaṣr al-umawī.* Tunis: Dār al-Turkī lil-Nashr, 1988.

al-Majdūb, al-Bashīr. *Al-Ẓarf bi-l-ʿIrāq fī l-ʿaṣr al-ʿabbāsī.* Tunis: Muʾassasāt ʿAbd al-Karīm b. ʿAbdallāh, 1992.

Malti-Douglas, Fedwa. 'Controversy and its Effects on the Biographical Tradition of al-Khatib al-Baghdadi.' *Studia Islamica* 46 (1977): 115–31.

Malti-Douglas, Fedwa. 'Dreams, the Blind, and the Semiotics of the Biographical Notice.' *Studia Islamica* (1980): 137–62.

Marín, Manuela, ed. *Arab-Islamic Medieval Culture: Special Issue of Medieval Prosopography, 23 (2002).* Kalamazoo: Medieval Institute Publications, Western Michigan University, 2002.

Massignon, Louis. *La passion de Husayn ibn Mansûr Hallâj, martyr mystique de l'islam.* New edition. 4 vols. Paris: Gallimard, 1975.

Mauder, Christian. *In the Sultan's Salon: Learning, Religion, and Rulership at the Mamluk Court of Qanisawh al-Ghawri (r. 1501–1516).* Leiden: Brill, 2021.

Melchert, Christopher. 'Abū Dāwūd.' In *EI3*.

Mez, Adam. *The Renaissance of Islam.* Translated by S. Khuda Bukhsh and D.S. Margoliouth. Patna: Jubilee Printing & Publishing House, 1937.

Mez, Adam. *Die Renaissance des Islams.* Heidelberg: C. Winter, 1922.

Montgomery, James E. 'Ẓarīf.' In *EI2*, 2001.

Montgomery, James E. *Al-Jāḥiẓ: in Praise of Books.* Edinburgh: Edinburgh University Press, 2013.

Mottahedeh, Roy. Review of *The Patricians of Nishapur: a Study in Medieval Islamic Social History*, R.W. Bulliet. *Journal of the American Oriental Society* 95 (1975): 491–5.

Mottahedeh, Roy. *Loyalty and Leadership in an early Islamic Society.* London: I.B. Tauris, 2001.

Mourad, Suleiman. 'Poetry, History, and the Early Arab-Islamic Conquests of al-Shām (Greater Syria).' In *Poetry and History: the Value of Poetry in Reconstructing Arab History*, edited by Ramzi Baalbaki, et al., 175–93. Beirut: American University of Beirut Press, 2011.

Muhanna, Elias. *The World in a Book: al-Nuwayri and the Islamic Encyclopedic Tradition.* Princeton: Princeton University Press, 2018.

Murray, H.J.R. *A History of Chess.* Oxford: Clarendon Press, 1913.

Naaman, Erez. *Literature and the Islamic Court: Cultural Life under al-Ṣāḥib Ibn ʿAbbād.* London: Routledge, 2016.

Osti, Letizia. 'Ibn Bassām: a Case Study on Poetry and Power.' *Middle Eastern Literatures* 10 (2007): 1–14.

Osti, Letizia. 'The Wisdom of Youth: legitimising the Caliph al-Muqtadir.' *Al-Masāq* 19 (2007): 17–27.

Osti, Letizia. 'The Grain on the Chessboard: Travels and Meanings.' In *Le Répertoire narratif arabe médiéval: transmission et ouverture. Actes du colloque international qui s'est tenu à l'Université de Liège du 15 au 17 septembre 2005*, edited by Frédéric Bauden, et al., 231–52. Genève: Droz, 2008.

Osti, Letizia. 'The Practical Matters of Culture in Pre-Madrasa Baghdad.' *Oriens* 38 (2010): 145–64.

Osti, Letizia. 'Notes on a Private Library in fourth/tenth-century Baghdad.' *Journal of Arabic and Islamic Studies* 12 (2012): 215–23.

Osti, Letizia. 'A Grammarian's Life in his own Voice: Autobiographical Fragments in Arabic Biographical Literature.' In *ʿAbbasid Studies IV. Occasional Papers of the School of ʿAbbasid Studies, Leuven, July –July 9, 2010*, edited by Monique Bernards, 142–80. Warminster: Gibb Memorial Trust, 2013.

Osti, Letizia. 'The Remuneration of a Court Companion in Theory and Practice: a Case Study.' *Journal of Abbasid Studies* 1 (2014): 85–107.

Osti, Letizia. 'Al-Ṣūlī and the Caliph: Norms, Practices and Frames.' In *Il Dialogo nella cultura araba: strutture, funzioni, significati (VIII–XIII secolo)*, edited by Mirella Cassarino and Antonella Ghersetti, 167–80. Soveria Mannelli: Il Rubbettino, 2015.

Osti, Letizia. 'The Author as Protagonist: Biographical Markers in Historical Narratives.' *Jerusalem Studies in Arabic and Islam* 45 (2018): 239–75.

Osti, Letizia. 'Abbasid Rulers and their Standing as Authors.' In *Rulers as Authors in the Islamic World: Knowledge, Authority and Legitimacy*, edited by Maribel Fierro, et al., forthcoming.

Osti, Letizia and James Weaver. 'Organizing the Fourth/Tenth Century: Knowledge, Information, Tools.' *Journal of Abbasid Studies* 7 (2020): 103–20.

Pedersen, Johannes. *The Arabic Book.* Translated by Robert Hillenbrand. Princeton: Princeton University Press, 1984.

Pellat, Charles. 'Kurd ʿAlī.' In *EI2*.

Pellat, Charles. *Le milieu baṣrien et la formation de Ǧâḥiẓ.* Paris: Maisonneuve, 1953.

Pellat, Charles. 'Was al-Masʿūdī a Historian or an *adīb*?' *Journal of the Pakistan Historical Society* 9 (1961): 231–4.

al-Qāḍī, Wadād. 'Biographical Dictionaries: Inner Structure and Cultural Significance.' In *The Book in the Islamic World: the Written Word and Communication in the Middle East*, edited by George N. Atiyeh. Albany: State University of New York Press for the Library of Congress, 1995.

al-Qāḍī, Wadād. 'Biographical Dictionaries as the Scholars' Alternative History of the Muslim Community.' In *Organizing Knowledge: Encyclopædic Activities in the Pre-Eighteenth Century Islamic World*, edited by Gerhard Endress and Abdou Filali-Ansary, 23–75. Leiden: Brill, 2006.

Raven, Wim. 'Ibn Dāwūd.' In *EI3*.

Raven, Wim. 'Ibn Dāwūd al-Iṣbahānī and his *Kitāb al-Zahra*.' PhD, Leiden, 1989.

Reynolds, Dwight F., ed. *Interpreting the Self: Autobiography in the Arabic Literary Tradition*. Berkeley, Los Angeles, London: University of California Press, 2001.

Rosenthal, Franz. 'Die arabische Autobiographie.' In *Studia Arabica I*, edited by Franz Rosenthal, et al., 1–40. Rome: Pontificium Institutum Biblicum, 1937.

Rosenthal, Franz. *A History of Muslim Historiography.* Leiden: E.J. Brill, 1968.

Sabari, Simha. *Mouvements populaires à Bagdad à l'époque ʿabbasside ixe-xie siècles.* Paris: Maisonneuve, 1981.

Sadan, Joseph. 'Nadīm.' In *EI2*.

al-Sāmarrāʾī, Ibrāhīm. 'Qirāʾāt fī l-kutub: "al-Warāq" lil-Ṣūlī.' *Majallat al-ʿArab* 6 (1391/1971): 42–8; 107–15; 202–7; 83–6.

Ṣammūd, Ḥammādī. *Balāghat al-intiṣār fī l-naqd al-ʿarabī al-qadīm: risālat Abī Bakr al-Ṣūlī ilā Muzāḥim b. Fātik unmūdhijan.* Tunis: Dār al-Maʿrifa lil-Nashr, 2006.

Savant, Sarah Bowen. 'Al-Ṭabarī's Unacknowledged Debt to Ibn Abī Ṭāhir Ṭayfūr.' forthcoming.

Savant, Sarah Bowen. 'People versus Books.' forthcoming.

Savant, Sarah Bowen. 'Naming Shuʿūbīs.' In *Essays in Islamic Philology, History, and Philosophy*, edited by Korangy Alireza, et al., 166–84. Berlin: De Gruyter, 2016.

Savant, Sarah Bowen and Masoumeh Seydi, 'Dispatches from al-Ṭabarī,' *KITAB-project.org*, 2021.

Scheiner, Jens J. and Damien Janos. 'Baghdād: Political Metropolis and Intellectual Center.' In *The Place to Go: Contexts of Learning in Baghdād, 750–1000 C.E*, edited by Jens J. Scheiner and Damien Janos, 1–45. Princeton, NJ: Darwin Press, 2014.

Schippers, Arie. 'Autobiography in Medieval Arabic Literature.' In *Actas del XVI Congreso de la U.E.A.I.*, edited by M.A. Manzano and C.V. de Benito, 481–7. Salamanca: Universidad de Salamanca, 1995.

Schoeler, Gregor. *The Genesis of Literature in Islam: from the Aural to the Read.* Translated by Shawkat M. Toorawa. Edinburgh: Edinburgh University Press, 2009.

Schoeler, Gregor. 'Writing for a Reading Public: the Case of al-Jāḥiẓ.' In *Al-Jāḥiẓ: a Muslim Humanist for our Time*, edited by Arnim Heinemann, et al., 51–63. Würzburg: Egon Verlag, 2009.

Seidensticker, Tilman. 'Audience Certificates in Arabic Manuscripts: the Genre and a Case Study.' *Manuscript Cultures* 8 (2015): 75–92.

Sezgin, Fuat. *Geschichte des arabischen Schrifttums.* 17 vols. Leiden; Frankfurt: Brill (1–9); Institut für Geschichte der Arabisch-Islamischen Wissenschaften an der Johann Wolfgang Goethe-Universität, 1967–2016.

Sharlet, Jocelyn. *Patronage and Poetry in the Islamic World: Social Mobility and Status in the Medieval Middle East and Central Asia.* London: I.B. Tauris, 2011.

Shoshan, Boaz. *Poetics of Islamic Historiography: Deconstructing Ṭabarī's History.* Leiden: Brill, 2004.

Soravia, Bruna. 'Les Manuels à l'usage des fonctionnaires de l'administration ("*Adab al-Kātib*") dans l'Islam classique.' *Arabica* 52 (2005): 417–36.

Sourdel, Dominique. 'Fragments d'al-Ṣūlī sur l'histoire des vizirs ʿabbāsides.' *Bulletin d'Études Orientales* 15 (1957): 99–108.

Sourdel, Dominique. *Le Vizirat ʿabbāside de 749 à 936.* 2 vols. Damascus: Institut Français de Damas, 1959–60.

Stasolla, Maria Giovanna. *Come legge la storia un letterato del X secolo: al-Jahshiyārī e i Barmecidi.* Roma: Aracne, 2007.

Sturm, Dieter. 'Ibn al-Nadīm's Hinweise auf das Verhältnis zum geistigen Eigentum im Historikerkapitel des *Kitab al-Fihrist*.' *Hallesche Beiträge zur Orientalwissenschaft* 13–14 (1990): 65–70.

Szombathy, Zoltan. 'On Wit and Elegance: the Arabic Concept of Zarf.' In *Authority, Privacy and Public Order in Islam*, edited by Barbara Michalak-Pikulska and Andrzej Pikulski, 101–20. Leuven: Peeters, 2006.

Szombathy, Zoltan. 'The Concept of Intellectual Property in Mediaeval Muslim Literary Culture.' *Jerusalem Studies in Arabic and Islam* 45 (2018): 1–36.

Thomann, Johannes. 'From Serial Access to Random Access: Tables of Contents, Chapter Headings and Hierarchical Text Structures in Fourth/Tenth-century Scientific Books.' *Journal of Abbasid Studies* 7 (2020): 207–28.

Toorawa, Shawkat M. *Ibn Abī Ṭāhir Ṭayfūr and Arabic Writerly Culture: a Ninth Century Bookman in Baghdad.* London: Routledge Curzon, 2005.

Tor, D.G. *Violent Order: Religious Warfare, Chivalry, and the ʿayyār Phenomenon in the Medieval Islamic World.* Würzburg: Ergon, 2007.

Touati, Houari. 'Pour une histoire de la lecture au Moyen Âge musulman: à propos des livres d'histoire.' *Studia Islamica* (2007): 11–44.

al-ʿUmarī, Aḥmad Jamāl. *Abū Bakr al-Ṣūlī: al-ʿālim, al-adīb, al-nadīm.* Cairo: al-Hayʾa al-Miṣriyya al-ʿĀmma lil-Kitāb, 1973.

al-ʿUmarī, Aḥmad Jamāl. *Abū Bakr al-Ṣūli (255–336 H): ḥayātuhu wa-adabuhu, dīwānuhu.* Cairo: Dār al-Maʿārif, 1984.

Vadet, Jean-Claude. 'Ibn Ḥamdūn.' In *EI2*.

Vadet, Jean-Claude. *L'esprit courtois en Orient dans les cinq premier siècles de l'Hegire.* Paris: Maisonneuve, 1968.

Van Gelder, Geert Jan. 'Poetry in Historiography: Some Observations.' In *Problems in Arabic Literature*, edited by Miklós Maróth, 1–13. Piliscsaba: The Avicenna Institute of Middle Eastern Studies, 2004.

Wagner, Ewald. 'Warum haben Ḥamza al-Isbahānī und Abū Bakr aṣ-Ṣūlī mehrere Weingedichte aus ihren Rezensionen des Abū Nuwās-Dīwān ausgeschieden?' *Asiatische Studien – Études Asiatiques* 62 (2008): 1086–96.

Weaver, James. 'What Wasn't an Encyclopaedia in the Fourth Islamic Century?' *Asiatische Studien – Études Asiatiques* 71 (2017): 959–991.

White, Hayden. 'Historical Emplotment and the Problem of Truth.' In *The History and Narrative Reader*, edited by Geoffrey Roberts, 375–89. London: Routledge, 2001.

Wickham, Chris. 'Administrators' Time: the Social Memory of the Early Medieval State, East and West.' In *Islamic Cultures, Islamic Contexts: Essays in Honor of Professor Patricia Crone*, edited by Behnam Sadeghi, et al., 430–67. Leiden: Brill, 2015.

Young, M.J.L. 'Arabic Biographical Writing.' In *Religion, Learning and Science in the ʿAbbasid Period*, edited by M.J.L. Young, 168–87. Cambridge: Cambridge University Press, 1990.

Index

al-ʿAbbās b. al-Ḥasan, 68–70
ʿAbbās I., 40
Abū ʿAbdallāh, son of al-Muqtadir, 43
Abū l-ʿAynāʾ, 59, 86, 87
Abū Dāwūd al-Sijistānī, 59
Abū Hāshim al-Jubbāʾī, 88
Abū Khalīfa al-Jumaḥī, 28, 60
Abū Jaʿfar Muḥammad, b. ʿAbdallāh b. Ḥamdūn, 66, 68, 119
Abū Muḥammad ʿAbdallāh b. Ḥamdūn, 68, 69
Abū Mūsā al-Ḥāmid, 95
Abū Saʿīd al-Jannābī, 88
Abū Saʿīd al-Sukkarī, 62–3
Abū Tammām, 90
Aḥmad b. Būya, 100
Aḥmad b. Muḥammad b. Thawāba, 61
Aḥmad b. Yaḥyā al-Munajjim, 66–73, 123
akhbār, 40, 41
Akhbār Abī Tammām, 2–3, 9, 50–1, 54, 55, 58, 87, 90, 95
ʿAlī b. Hārūn al-Munajjim, 66–7
ʿAqr, battle of, 22
Arabic literature and historiography, 2
Assmann, J., 6–7, 125, 127
authorship, 3–4
autobiography, 39–42, 141n7
- components, 41
- definition, 42
- fragmented, 42, 44, 50–1
- introspection, 41–2
- motivations, 42–5
- personal information and opinions, 40
- starting date, 41

al-Azharī, Abū l-Qāsim, 76–7, 150–1n87

Bacchic behaviour, 73
Baghdad, 24–5, 46–7, 59, 95, 100, 108, 109–23, 112, 113–15, 122
Bajkam, 65–6, 67, 75, 108, 110, 113, 113–14, 114–15, 117, 118
al-Barīdī, Abū Yūsuf Yaʿqūb, 75
Basra, 25, 59, 74–6, 78, 88
Behzadi, L., 158
Bernards, M., 5, 56
bibliophilia, 4, 22, 25–6, 30, 35, 36
biography, 3–4, 132–3n9
- conceptualization, 9–12
- framework, 13–14
- origins, 11
- qualifications, 21
- *tarjamat al-nafs* ('self-entry'), 40
- using, 12–15

books, reliance on, 76–8, 81
Bosworth, C.E., 57
Bowen, H., 57
Bray, J., 57

caliphal access, 110–13
caliphal management, 118–20
Canard, M., 3, 37, 50, 53, 140n86
chancery, 38
chess, 23, 26, 33–5, 36, 37, 38, 87
collective memory, 6
communicative memory, 6–7, 127
Cooperson, M., 11
court activity, 22–3, 28–9, 50–1, 55
court culture, 57
court years, proximity connections, 65–7
courtiers, accounts of, 84–5
cultural environment, 48–9, 57–8
cultural memory, 6
cultural production, 127
culture, objectivized, 7

al-Dhahabī, 16, 17
Donner, F. M., 83
Duindam, J., 55

elegies, 93–4
encyclopaedism, 95–7

European interpretive categories, 1
events, main, 46, 46–7

first person narratives, 4
flashbacks, 46, 47–8, 70–1, 116–17, 122–3
fragmented autobiography, 42, 44, 50–1

Gilliot, C., 10, 12
Gruendler, B., 2

ḥadīth, 10, 18, 59, 145n14
Ḥamza al-Iṣfahānī, 90
al-Ḥasan b. ʿAbdallāh b. Ḥamdān, 103, 109–14, 120
al-Ḥasan b. Hārūn, 53
Heyworth-Dunne, J., 3
Hirschler, K., 106
historical data, 48–9
historical effect, 134n17
historical events, 42–3, 50
historical narrative, poetry in, 2

Ibn Abī l-Sāj, 48, 121–3
Ibn al-Anbārī, 30, 36, 64
Ibn al-Bāghandī, 151n91
Ibn Dāwūd, 64
Ibn Ḥamdān
  ʿAlī (Sayf al-Dawla), 109
  al-Ḥasan, 103, 109–14, 120
Ibn Ḥamdūn
  Abū Jaʿfar Muḥammad b. ʿAbdallāh, 66, 68, 119
  Abū Muḥammad ʿAbdallāh, 68, 69
Ibn Harma, 63
Ibn Ḥayawayh, 76–8
Ibn Khaldūn, 1
Ibn Khallikān, 25, 31–6, 36–7, 139n75
Ibn al-Jawzī, 30, 36, 86
Ibn al-Muʿtazz, 50, 61, 67, 69–72
Ibn al-Nadīm, 5, 10, 17, 21, 22, 23, 24, 58, 64, 87–9, 90–2, 94–5
Ibn Rāʾiq, 100, 101–6, 106, 108, 109, 114, 115, 119, 125
Ibn Shādhān, 76–7, 77–8
Ibrāhīm b. al-ʿAbbās al-Ṣūlī, 22, 61, 88
ideological meaning, 12
intellectual environment, 5
intertextuality, 11
introspection, 41–2
Isḥāq b. al-Muʿtamid, 66

jalīs, 50–1
junctions, 46
Jurjān, 22

Kaabi, M., 57
al-Kanz al- madfūn, 37
Kennedy, H., 100, 106
khabar, the, 9, 25–6, 40, 45–6
Khalidov, A.B., 3, 109
al-Khaṭīb al-Baghdādī, 9, 17–18, 22, 23, 24, 26, 26–31, 36–7, 58–61, 68, 76–7, 151n91
Kilpatrick, H., 11, 13, 25, 40, 95, 133n11
Kitāb al-ʿAbbās b. al-Aḥnaf, 87
Kitāb adab al-kuttāb, 87, 96
Kitāb akhbār Abī ʿAmr b. al-ʿAlāʾ, 87
Kitāb akhbār al-Jubbāʾī b. Abī Saʿīd, 87
Kitāb al-anwāʾ, 87
Kitab ashʿār Quraysh, 94
Kitāb al-Awrāq, 3, 37, 42–3, 80–1, 120–1, 125, 127
  accounts of courtiers, 84–5
  autobiographical remarks, 126
  career account, 45–50
  chronicles of al-Muqtadir, 92
  end, 74
  left unfinished, 91
  on life in Basra, 75–6
  organizational principles, 5
  poetry, 68–72, 90–4, 99–100, 109
  proximity connections, 64–5, 66–7
  al-Raḍī's years, 92–3
  settings, 72–4
  structure, 148n67
  style and structure, 92
Kitāb al-Fihrist (al-Nadīm), 5, 10, 17, 64, 85, 87–9
knowledge, classification of, 5
Krenkow, F., 9
Kurd Ali, M., 1, 3, 125

Leder, S., 11, 133n11
library, 75–6, 76–8, 95
life expectations, 45
lineage, 56–7
literary analysis, 126

literary criticism, 2–3
literary effect, 134n17
literary salon's, 73

Malti-Douglas, F., 25, 134n17
Mardāwīj b. Ziyār, 43–4, 46–7
al-Marzubānī, 22, 23, 58
al-Masʿūdī, 35, 100
Massignon, L., 57
mathematics, 33–4
memory, 6–7, 79, 125, 127
Mez, A., 57
Miskawayh, 100, 106–7, 110, 124
    account of the year 324/935–6, 101–2, 105–6
    expedition to Mosul account, 113
mnemonic skills, 23
Montgomery, J.E., 21
moral qualities, 23
Mosul, expedition to, 109–23
    arguments, 113–16
    caliphal management, 118–20
    framing arguments, 117
    interpretive key, 116–17
    personal level narrative, 117–18
    preparation, 116–17
    al-Rāḍīs education flashback, 116–17
Mottahedeh, R., 133n13
Muḥammad b. Dāwūd b. al-Jarrāh, 70–1, 72
Muḥammad b. Īnāl, 53
Muḥammad b. Yāqūt, 43, 47
Mujālasa, 73
al-Munajjim
    family tree, 68
    Abū Aḥmad Yaḥyā b. ʿAlī, 66–72, 93–4
    Abū l-Ḥasan Aḥmad b. Yaḥyā, 66–7, 71–2, 73, 123
    Abū l-Ḥasan ʿAlī b. Hārūn, 66–7, 72
    Abū Manṣūr, 66
    Abū l-Qāsim Yūsuf, 66
al-Muqtadir, caliph, 1, 43–4, 45, 48, 118
    character, 52
    coup against, 50, 67, 68–72, 88
murūʾa, 23
al-Muttaqī, caliph, 52–3, 65, 115

narrative interventions, 6
narrative techniques, 2–3
narratives, power of, 25–6
Naṣr al-Qushūrī, 52, 120–1, 121–2
notebooks, 73–4, 74–6, 80, 127, 152n110
Nuzhat al-alibbāʾ, 136n50

oral/written dichotomy, 150n84
orality, 6
organizational principles, 5, 90–2

Pellat, C., 56
perspective, 105, 106–8, 124
persuasion, 109–23
poetry, 18–19, 24, 26, 28–30, 37–8, 39, 47, 51, 54, 62, 66, 89, 99–100, 126, 127, 153n8
    effects of, 92–4
    elegies, 93–4
    in historical narrative, 2
    Kitāb al-Awrāq, 68–72, 90–4
    organization, 90
    performative aspect, 73
    and politics, 68–72, 149n72
    role, 90–2, 109–13
    role of, 49
    al-Ṣūlī's scholarship, 2
politics, and poetry, 68–72, 149n72
profiles, 39, 58–61
    constants, 24
    death, 24–5
    Ibn Khallikān's, 31–6, 36–7
    al-Khaṭīb's, 26–31, 36–7, 58–61
    names, 19–21
    power of, 25–6
    skills, 21
    structure, 13–14, 26–7, 31–2, 32–3, 36
    transmission work, 27
    Yāqūt's 14, 26
prosopographical obsession, 4
proximity, 5, 61, 61–5

al-Qāḍī, W., 10, 11, 12
quantitative history, 57

al-Rāḍī, caliph, 43, 46, 48, 50–1, 65–7, 73, 74, 79, 107
    education, 120–1, 122–3
    education flashback, 116–17
    expedition to Mosul, 109–23
    expedition to Mosul arguments, 113–16

fondness for, 52
management of, 118–20
poetry, 92–3
readership, 43
reliability, 30
religious scholarship, 51
research students, 24
resemblance, 5
Reynolds, D.F., 40
Risāla fī l-saʿāda, 87
Rosenthal, F., 39, 41, 42, 54, 85

Samarra, 109–13
Ali, S., 73
Savant, S.B., 150n84, 152n110
Schoeler, G., 74, 96
scholarly network, 24
self-promotion, 43–4
self-promotional insertions, 107–8, 112, 123–4
social network analysis, 5, 55–81
Basra, 74–6
and coup against al-Muqtadir, 68–72
court years, 65–7
library, 76–8
lineage, 56–7
proximity, 61, 61–5
settings, 72–4
al-Tanūkhī, 78–80
teachers and students, 58–61
texts, 80–1
textual and narrative clues, 56
social standing, 106–7
sources, 2–3, 4, 13
Sourdel, D., 99, 100
style, 44, 49, 54, 66, 103, 113, 124, 126
Sudayf b. Maymūn, 94
al-Ṣūlī, Abū Bakr, 1–2
account of the year 324/935–6, 103–6
attention to organization, 90–2
autobiographical arc, 53, 53–4
autobiographical motivations, 42–5
autobiographical remarks, 126
avarice, 58
bibliophilia, 75–6
biographical information, 4, 9–38
career, 45–50, 86
contempt for some of contemporary know-it-alls, 83–5
contribution, 2
and coup against al-Muqtadir, 68–72
court role, 50–1
court years, 65–7
credibility, 120–1
as a credible source, 49–50
death, 74
disappointment with life, 54
education, 58–61
encyclopaedism, 95–7
expedition to Mosul, 109–23
genres of production, 2
in his own books, 83–97
as an historian, 5–6
Ibn Khallikān's profile, 31–6, 36–7
image, 51
impartiality, 51–2
importance, 16
on the importance of specializing, 84–5
influence, 121–3
interpretation, 124
as judge of character, 51–3
al-Khaṭīb's profile, 26–31, 36–7, 58–61
library, 75–6, 76–8, 95
life in Basra, 74–6
literary criticism, 2–3
milieu, 80
mnemonic skills, 23
name, 19–21
narrative voice, 105
noble lineage, 22
notebooks, 73–4, 74–6, 80, 127
own account of life, 45–50
in own writings, 39–54
persona, 37–8, 53–4
perspective, 124
pervasiveness of, 15–19, 37–8
plagiarism accusation, 94–5
profile appearances, 88–9
profiles, 13, 15–19, 19–25, 39
qualifications, 21–3
reliability, 29–30

reliance on books, 76–8, 81
as a religious scholar, 16
religious studies, 17
reputation, 4
role, 4
roles, 46, 49
ruthlessness, 52
self-promotional insertions, 123–4
self-worth, 4, 54
skills, 21
social network, 5, 55–81
status, 125
teachers and students, 58–61, 86
teaching career, 43–4, 47–8, 49, 51, 52, 75
timeline, 8
use of his own poetry, 2
use of poetry, 89
validity as a case study, 125–7
value, 5–6, 100–8
versatility, 19–21
voice, 45–50
works, 87–9
Yāqūt's profile, 14, 26

Ṭabaqāt works, 11
Takrit, 111, 113
al-Tanūkhī, al-Muḥassin b. ʿAlī, 74, 78, 78–80, 81, 144n10, 148n62
Taʾrīkh Baghdād, 16, 17–18, 26, 26–31, 38, 68
library description, 76–7
proximity connections, 61–2
teachers and students, 58–61
teachers, 24, 58–61
terminology, 126–7
texts, social network analysis, 80–1
Thaʿlab, 62, 63–5, 153n4
Toorawa, S., 5, 56, 61
translations, 3
transmission work, 27
truth, 85

udabāʾ, 61
ʿUmar b. Muḥammad, 120
al-ʿUmarī, A.J., 2

Wafayāt al-aʿyān (Ibn Khallikān), 31–6
al-Washshāʾ, 21–2, 23
Wāsit, 48–9, 51, 65, 75, 95, 101–6, 117
White, H., 106

Yāqūt, 14, 16, 18–19, 25–6, 33, 35, 58, 61, 138n70
year 324/935–6, accounts of the, 101–6

ẓarīf, 21, 64
Zaydān, 121, 122

www.ingramcontent.com/pod-product-compliance
Lightning Source LLC
Chambersburg PA
CBHW052120300426
44116CB00010B/1746
* 9 7 8 0 7 5 5 6 4 7 8 1 1 *